GEORGE HEARST

GEORGE
HEARST

═══════════════

SILVER KING
OF THE GILDED AGE

MATTHEW BERNSTEIN

UNIVERSITY OF OKLAHOMA PRESS : NORMAN

Elements from chapter 11 were previously published in "Murder in the Black Hills," *Wild West* 31, no. 4 (December 2018), and appear here in revised and expanded form.

Parts of chapters 14 and 15 were previously published in "The Playwright Who Captured Geronimo," *Wild West* 32, no. 4 (December 2019), and appear here much revised.

Library of Congress Cataloging-in-Publication Data

Names: Bernstein, Matthew, 1981– author.
Title: George Hearst : silver king of the Gilded Age / Matthew Bernstein.
Description: Norman : University of Oklahoma Press, [2021] |
    Includes bibliographical references and index.
Identifiers: LCCN 2021010538 | ISBN 978-0-8061-6934-7 (hardcover) |
    ISBN 978-0-8061-6935-4 (paperback)
Subjects: LCSH: Hearst, George, 1820–1891. | Millionaires—West (U.S.)—Biography. |
    Politicians—California—Biography. | Silver mines and mining—West (U.S.)—
    History—19th century. | West (U.S.)—History—19th century. | LCGFT: Biographies.
Classification: LCC E664.H43 B47 2021 | DDC 328.73/092 [B]—dc23
LC record available at https://lccn.loc.gov/2021010538

To my nephew,
Max Gregory Stragnell

CONTENTS

Part III. The Art of the Possible

ACKNOWLEDGMENTS

This biography would never have existed had it not been for Gregory Urbach, whose encouragement kept me writing. Lita Fice also provided invaluable feedback, listening to chapter after chapter on our long drives. Chris Stewart accompanied me to some of Hearst's stomping grounds: Virginia City; Franklin County; Washington, D.C.; and Deadwood (twice). Anastasia Robinson helped me locate Hearst's tomb and showed me San Francisco. Thanks, everyone.

To the staff of the Huntington Research Library, who pointed me in the right direction, I am particularly grateful. At the Bancroft Library in Berkeley I was shown a treasure trove of indispensable materials. Debra Kaufman of the California Historical Society provided many Hearst family photographs. Furthermore, the boys at *Wild West* magazine, Gregory Lalire and David Lauterborn, offered valuable insight. That Charles E. Rankin, the veteran western historian, thought the project worthwhile helped tremendously.

Naturally, the previous biographers of the Hearst family laid the groundwork. The 1933 biography of George Hearst by Cora and Fremont Older gave me a place to start. The detailed research on the Hearst family completed by Judith Robinson became a terrific resource. Alexandra M. Nickliss's exploration of Phoebe's passion for education helped sharpen the focus of the political picture. Terrific biographies of William Randolph Hearst, penned by W. A. Swanberg, David Nasaw, and Kenneth Whyte, crackle with energy; along with providing significant details, they demonstrated masterful writing techniques. Austine McDonnell Hearst's *Horses of San Simeon* and Victoria Kastner's *Hearst Ranch: Family, Life, and Legacy* cast a bright light in dark places.

As much as this book is about nineteenth-century mining, politics, and capitalism, it tells the story of one man's adventures to the wild places of the Old West. In that respect, I'd like to thank my fellow adventurers—Natalie Bates, Caitlin Bates, Jim Sanchez, and Chris and Lita—for all the footloose times we've shared.

NOTE ON EDITORIAL PRINCIPLES

The material on which this biography is based was gathered primarily from the Huntington Research Library in San Marino, the Bancroft Library at the University of California–Berkeley, newspaper accounts, and autobiographies and biographies of the Hearst family. To preserve the flavor of their communication, misspellings made by George and Phoebe are kept as they were written, as is their unique punctuation. I have occasionally modified spelling and punctuation in newspaper accounts for clarity, but most accounts appear as they were first printed. The industrious work of the Hearst family biographers is justly credited in the notes.

PROLOGUE

A Sick Man in Mexico (1889)

When you get off the line of railroads in Mexico traveling is anything
but pleasant; but that wouldn't have disturbed me in the least
if I had not contracted the fever.
—George Hearst

As the four Americans entered the Mexican town of Parral in May of 1889, they prayed they would make it out alive. They were 200 miles from a train track, 420 miles from the U.S. border, and one of them was deathly ill.

The party consisted of Robert C. Chambers, the superintendent of Senator George Hearst's silver mines outside Salt Lake City; Addison E. Head, who had partnered with Hearst in several Arizona Territory mines and managed their cattle ranch in New Mexico Territory; and Jack Follansbee, a Harvard man who managed one hundred thousand acres of Hearst's million-acre cattle ranch in Babicora, Mexico. The fourth man was the one they had been charged to protect at all costs, the senator himself, who desperately needed a doctor.

Chambers, Head, and Follansbee knew Hearst as the boss. One of the brightest Silver Kings of the Gilded Age, Hearst was more than that. To some, he was a family man. Others saw him as a drinker and an embarrassment to his cultured wife. To many he was a friend and benefactor, openhanded to charities. To the orphaned girl who lived five years in the Hearst home, he was a surrogate father.

More than a few saw him as a scheming robber baron, motivated by greed. Many knew him as a political rival or ally and a close adviser to President Grover Cleveland. Still others saw him as an unlettered backwoodsmen, as much an oddity in the U.S. Senate as a Neanderthal in King Arthur's Court. To California's forty-niners, he was "Quartz George," traipsing through ravines and over mountains, searching for telltale signs of gold. To everyone, Hearst was a titan of industry, presiding over the greatest mining empire in the United States.

If Chambers, Head, and Follansbee didn't act fast, Hearst's next role would be that of a corpse. Two telegrams were hastily written. One was to a doctor 190 miles away. The other was to the senator's son, William Randolph Hearst, fifteen hundred miles away in San Francisco. While Hearst's friends awaited a response, Hearst hunkered down in the bunk of a miserable hotel. Shivering and sweating, Hearst reflected on his life as he felt it slipping away.

— PART I —
PRODIGAL SON

Each man delights in the work that suits him best.
—Homer

— 1 —

FRANKLIN COUNTY

(1820–1850)

I always had to have it my own way or not at all.
—George Hearst

In his memoirs, George Hearst related his family history. The family name was initially spelled Hyrst. Later it was changed to Hurst, then Hearse, and finally Hearst. The name is of Saxon origin, meaning "a wooded hillock." His great-grandfather John Hearst, or Hurst, sailed from Scotland to the British colonies of North America, landing in 1680. Before sailing from Scotland, the family had made the lowlands their home, though some had moved as far south as Salisbury in England. In the New World, John Hearst purchased ten acres and nine slaves.[1]

In 1766 Hearst descendants settled in Abbeville, South Carolina. By the time the Revolutionary War erupted nine years later, the Hearsts had become prosperous. In the family were two doctors, a state legislator, and several plantation owners. They were a religious, hardscrabble clan of Presbyterian Covenanters, strictly anti-Catholic, as at home wielding swords as plowshares. Near the end of the war, during 1782 and 1783, John and Joseph Hearst served in the revolutionary militia. After the war, a wave of westward immigration commenced, intensified by the Louisiana Purchase in 1803. The Hearst family was one of many who traveled through the Cumberland Gap to settle in Missouri Territory. The pioneers included George Hearst's grandfather George; his grandmother Jane Pressly Hearst; his father, William George Hearst, and his uncle Joseph Hearst. They settled in what soon became Meramec Township of Franklin County, not far from the present-day town of Sullivan, near the banks of the Meramec River. Named for Benjamin Franklin, Franklin County proved rich with mineral deposits and arable land. There, on a high ridge, the Hearsts farmed wheat and corn, bred horses and cattle, and traded with settlers in St. Louis, sixty miles northeast.[2]

William G. Hearst cut a striking figure. He had wealth, ambition, and a physical presence that few men could match. In 1817 William G. Hearst married Elizabeth Collins, whose heritage was Irish by way of Georgia. The daughter of neighboring farmer Jacob Collins, Elizabeth was blonde, a bit stout—George estimated she was 165 pounds when young—and taken with wearing "cashmere shawls and leghorn bonnets."[3] She was also very industrious, a master seamstress, and imbued with uncommon practical sense. In William, Elizabeth must have recognized a catch in more ways than one. George remembered his father as "a very muscular man, not very large, but strong. He probably weighed about 175 pounds. He was a farmer, but I don't think there was his equal in the country for lifting weights and suchlike."[4]

Shortly after the marriage, William and Elizabeth moved with their parents to Texas Territory, then under the Spanish flag. The plan was to expand their fortune in cattle, but disaster soon struck. Disease wiped out their livestock. Ultimately, the family returned to Missouri Territory and to the banks of the Meramec River. Upon their return, William bought from the government a tract of land. On September 3, 1820, "on the Miami, 40 miles from St. Louis," Elizabeth Collins Hearst gave birth to a blue-eyed son. They named him George, for his paternal grandfather. On August 20, 1821, two weeks before George's first birthday, as part of the Missouri Compromise, Missouri joined the United States of America as a slave state.[5]

In 1822 Grandpa George Hearst died. Baby George became *the* George Hearst.

Born on the frontier, George grew up living the idyllic American boyhood. The farmhouse his father had purchased was ideally suited to a young boy. George loved the hundred-year-old trees on the property, particularly an elm tree in whose branches he spent many Sunday afternoons napping. He loved the porch that surrounded the farmhouse, personally threading vines through the columns of the gallery. The property, which Hearst estimated at six hundred to eight hundred acres, growing with every year, included a well, a barn, an orchard, a wheat field, a cornfield, a beautiful front lawn, horses, cattle, sheep, geese, chickens, ducks, and a copper mine. The immense property held three separate farms. One hundred and fifty acres were under cultivation.[6]

Working the farm was difficult, but George appears to have felt pride in doing the work his ancestors had done, commenting that "ancestors on both sides were southern people." William and George were not alone in blistering their hands and cutting the wheat with sickles. During lean seasons, the Hearsts owned three or four slaves. When times were flush, they owned as many as nineteen slaves. One of these slaves was Tempey, who prepared their meals.[7]

Slavery in Franklin County differed from slavery in the Deep South. Rather than large plantations with more than one hundred slaves on each, Missouri was known for small farms and fewer slaves than other slaveholding states. The 1860 census shows that of the 4,340 slaveowners in the Show-Me State, 2,883 (66 percent) owned fewer than twenty slaves. The slaves were generally farmhands, working side by side with their masters. Oftentimes they were hired out to other farms. Women, such as Tempey, did domestic work inside the farmhouse. Black children performed the same chores as white children, gathering eggs and chopping wood.[8]

George recalled the farmhouse fondly. The barn was kept freshly painted, the blinds were a vibrant green, the well provided the coolest water in the world, and the fruit from the orchard was delicious. His lifelong love of horses was also born on the farm, for the place was so vast that walking from one end to the other could take most of an afternoon.[9]

Franklin County was also a boy's paradise (as long as he wasn't a slave). William Clark—famous for his explorations with Lewis Merriweather—was the governor of Missouri Territory when George was born, and like the governor, young George became enamored with exploration. Like another Missouri boy, Samuel Clemens—born in 1835 in Florida, Missouri, 120 miles north of Franklin County—George spent a significant portion of his boyhood exploring caves.

Much of the horizon of Missouri Territory, known as "the land of caves," was dominated by the Ozarks. Technically an enormous plateau, the Ozarks were the most expansive mountain range between the Appalachians and the Rocky Mountains. The Ozarks around Franklin County predominantly contained sandstone, dolomite, and lead. Because lead was a valuable commodity, the area became known as the "lead belt." Making mining particularly attractive were the caves that riddled the area. Aboveground, the Ozarks were largely covered with oak-hickory forests. Dogwoods and bluebells were in abundance. From the air came the screech of the hawk, the croak of the great blue heron, and the metallic chirp of the cardinal. Flowing through the Ozarks was the Meramec River—what Algonquian Indians called the Miaramigoua, meaning "ugly fish" or "cat fish"—containing rainbow trout, bass, and catfish.[10] Making the mountains their home were beavers, deer, and black bears. Red wolves also commonly prowled the Ozarks during the early nineteenth century. Almost extinct today, red wolves stalked Franklin County and the Hearst farm. "My early childhood was spent in a wild sort of way," George recalled.

> Of course, we lived in a wilderness, and our surroundings were of the roughest kind. The Indians were around in every direction, and every summer visited us. The wolves would come time and again and make away with our chickens, geese and sheep. When I was old enough to work they used to set me at penning up the ducks and chickens at night, and later on to put the sheep in the fold to keep them away from the wolves. The geese we used to raise principally for the feathers to make feather beds, and of course we had to utilize the wool from the sheep for our clothes. A little fellow like me always had lots to do.[11]

Other duties included gathering eggs. When he got old enough, he began chopping wood. "I was my mother's boy," George recollected. He also noted that his mother was "the best spinner in that section, and she could make cloth and cut it out with the best of them all." This was a necessary western skill in the days before the cotton gin. George also grew up loving and admiring his father, William. The big man was a terror to those who crossed him but was never strict with his family:

> I can recollect that anyone who did anything outrageous towards him, he would try to chase him out; those were rough days, remember. . . .
>
> He was a man of pretty good judgement and accumulated something. He always seemed to have plenty and was very kind to his neighbors, giving away a great deal. I remember that he was not very strict in the family; in fact I never got a licking from my mother or father at any time. I think it was his idea merely to set a good example. I was young when he died, but he seemed to have always taken to me kindly, and talked to me sensibly, telling me what was the best thing to do. Occasionally he would get mad, but as a rule he would not. I remember my mother once coming towards me with a little switch, but I do not think she meant to use it. My father took a great interest in public affairs, and he belonged to the militia, was first lieutenant, went to all parades, and in everything public evinced a public spirit.[12]

That William Hearst was prone to "giving away a good deal" signified the family's relative wealth. Though they fashioned their own featherbeds and sewed their own clothing—"beat[ing] the flax and cotton seed out on the hearth before the fire"—the Hearsts were the most affluent family in the area. Of the forty-one slaves owned in Franklin County, the Hearsts at times owned nearly half. In 1830 William Hearst purchased his brother Joseph Hearst's interest in the farm.[13]

But the Hearsts' financial comfort did not bring about permanent marital bliss. At one point, when William showed interest in another woman, Elizabeth refused to speak to him.[14] William's temper, even though never directed at his family, may also have been trying. Though he "in everything aimed to be loyal to his friends, [he] never forgot his enemies," George remembered, and "was somewhat inclined to fight." But altogether the family flourished. Two more children were born to William and Elizabeth. The first was Martha, born in 1823, remembered as "a large, fleshy and rosy-cheeked girl," whom George and others called Patsy. When she grew old enough, Martha took over management of the household affairs. The second was Jacob, called Jake, named after Elizabeth's father, Jacob Collins. George remembered his brother as a "cripple" and "a remarkably handsome child [who] much resembled my mother." It was reported that a disease had rendered Jacob helpless.[15]

Being affluent in Missouri was not the same as being affluent in Philadelphia, New York City, or Boston. A wealthy Bostonian might send his son to Harvard, but there were no universities in Missouri during the early nineteenth century. Washington University in St. Louis would not be founded until 1853. In fact, St. Louis wouldn't boast a population greater than fifteen thousand until George turned twenty.[16]

When George was eight years old, he spent "a part of three months" attending school. There were only a few other pupils, all of whom lived within a radius of three or four miles. George did not attend school every day, and the location fluctuated. Sometimes the classroom was in a log cabin. Other times it was in a neighbor's spare room. After this, George traveled to St. Louis, where he stayed with his aunt. It was from her that he learned to say his prayers. Another teacher, Dr. Silas Reed, was a family friend and neighbor. Reed loaned George books on geology and mineralogy, and encouraged his interest in mining. George's patchy education continued in his teens, when he studied at a schoolhouse for a fifteen-month stretch. At twenty he did another three months. "Two and a half years was all the time I ever spent in a schoolhouse," Hearst recalled. "I liked the school first-rate, and was very ambitious to learn everything, and it would worry me terribly if I could not succeed."[17]

George learned to read, write, and do arithmetic but learned to "do it in my own way." He had a propensity for litigation and could comprehend fine points of law, but spelling and capitalization bedeviled him. One teacher, Hugh C. Berry, recalled that if George was stumped by a problem, he would stay after hours until he had solved it. And George often found himself stumped: "At school I never accomplished anything that I did not have to work hard for, but after all I got along as well as anybody else. Some people could pick things up a good deal quicker than I could, and it was a very difficult matter to get me straight on figures." Berry also noted that George learned the rules of arithmetic but preferred finding answers according to his own notions of how problems should be solved: "I always had to have it my own way or not at all, and this has been my disposition all through life."[18]

The influence of his mother, Elizabeth Collins Hearst, also played a part in George's education. She was "quite a managing woman," George recalled. With his father, George drove pork to market, but it was Elizabeth who managed the farm. And it was Elizabeth who trained George to take over the chief responsibilities:

> What she said was to the point, and I never recollect her being wrong. She was . . . very conservative under all circumstances. I never saw her mad in all my life. She was very hard to excite on any subject, always cool and always gave good advice. I think I get most of my success from my mother, although my father was a very industrious man; yes, I believe I owe most of my success to her rather than to him.[19]

Elizabeth always had a bright outlook on life and generally took her children's side in any family squabbles. She was religious but did not let that stop her children from having a good time. "If she found any of us young people playing or fishing on Sunday she would say to us that that was not very nice, but she would never make much fuss over it." This philosophy nicely coincided with her husband's religious inclinations. William had been raised as a Presbyterian and was inclined in that direction, but as a whole he was not very religious. So George only sporadically attended church. But his days were soon filled with other pursuits.[20]

When George was fifteen, lead was discovered by French miners fifteen miles from the house. Before long George was entertaining himself by crawling into the mine, separating the lead from galena, limestone, and clay. He sold the nuggets he extracted, sometimes earning six bits a day. It was a beginning. But while his interest in mining was budding, Elizabeth was giving him more and more responsibilities at home. At sixteen years old, George took over managing "the laboring men." At sixteen or seventeen, he began staying on the property's lower farm.[21]

In 1838, when George was seventeen or eighteen, he attended a course at the Franklin County Mining School. The search for precious minerals became a passion to him. With boundless energy and exulting happiness, he traipsed about the Ozarks, barefoot with his pantaloons rolled up, cooling his blistered feet in hog wallows. Initially, he was mildly successful. The family copper mine, though not producing a notable amount, doubtless provided George with useful lessons. The lead mines the French had discovered also provided him with invaluable experience.[22]

George recalled, "My father knew these people very well and we used to make considerable money by driving pork to the miners and selling it to them." In this manner, George was exposed to Missouri French, or Paw Paw French, a rare French dialect. Missouri French stemmed from the town Old Mines, roughly forty miles southeast of the Hearst farm. Old Mines was largely settled by French miners, who over time created their own dialect—closer to Canadian French than Louisiana French but with a mixture of American Indian and African slave words, pronounced in gravelly, nasally French rather than sonorous Parisian French.[23]

> The Frenchmen used to mine in little shallow diggings and as soon as they got out a few hundred pounds of ore they would sell it, and I of course saw that there was money in it. I would always go with father when he drove the hogs there. . . . There were big merchants there that had every sort of nice French things. My people lived in log houses, and these French things were very extraordinary to us. We had tables and beds and chairs and that was about all, but these people had things which they had brought from France which were very beautiful I thought. . . . They were smelters, and bought from anybody, and I naturally saw that they had a good deal of money. I think that was what induced me to go into mining. Farming was such a slow way to make money. You could make a living at it and that was about all. I used to hear father say that if he saved a couple of hundred dollars a year he was doing well.
>
> The men down there were not very scientific, and I soon saw how things were done.[24]

In 1842 George began working in the mine. He didn't initially make a fortune, but he was learning the mechanics of the craft. He was also learning to "do it in my own way." Before long the local Indians began calling him Boy-That-Earth-Talks-To, and it seemed to George that they had taken a liking to him. He reflected that it may have been because they felt he understood them.[25]

As George grew from a boy to a young man, he became conspicuous for his speech and his appearance. His voice never fully deepened, and he spoke with a pronounced southern accent. St. Louis was only sixty miles northeast, but young George never picked up cosmopolitan speech or manners. Instead he developed simple tastes. He acquired a love of brandy and whiskey. For dinner he relished hog and hominy, or string beans with two strips of bacon, or fried chicken served with cornbread and coffee. Tempey was kept busy. By the time George had stopped growing, he was well over six feet tall—a blond-haired, blue-eyed giant.[26]

To help with George's education, he and his father began raising money to build a much-needed seminary. A family friend, W. V. N. Bay, whom Hearst met in the spring of 1837, noted that the fund had "reached twenty thousand dollars and would have soon reached fifty thousand dollars had not both George and his father learned that the money had been loaned out by the County Court to irresponsible parties upon insufficient security, and was entirely lost."[27]

Bay was a U.S. congressman representing Franklin County. A letter he wrote to political adversaries in 1849 sheds light on the racially charged environment in which George Hearst was raised: "I have no feeling or sympathy for Northern Abolitionists, or Northern Slave Agitators, and shall promptly resist, as far as in my power, all enactments upon the rights of the slave-holding States."[28]

In addition to his aunt in St. Louis and his parents and siblings, George also spent time with his cousins Joseph E. Clark and Jacob Clark (called J. C.); his maternal aunt Ann Collins Clark; and her husband, Austin Clark. In a letter, George affectionately referred to "little old dried up Uncle Austin."[29]

William G. Hearst was also close with his cousins in the Apperson family. Randolph Walker Apperson, born April 10, 1809, in Washington County, Virginia, had moved with his parents to Franklin County when he was twenty. Before becoming an elder at the Cumberland Presbyterian Church, Apperson clerked at a general store that William Hearst frequented and occasionally worked on the Hearst farmstead. Randolph Apperson married Drusilla Whitmire, whose family had settled near the Hearsts, north of where the Meramec River meets Saltpeter Cave (present-day Meramec Caverns), a rumored hideout of Jesse James.

On December 3, 1842, Drusilla Whitmire Apperson gave birth to her first child, a girl named Phoebe Elizabeth Apperson. "Phoebe" was for Drusilla's aunt. "Elizabeth" was for Elizabeth Collins Hearst, Drusilla's close friend and neighbor. Randolph and Drusilla's second child, Sarah Agnes, died in infancy. Their last child, born June 10, 1851, was named Elbert Clark Apperson. "Clark" was for their neighboring cousins. George and Phoebe were related through her aunt Phoebe Whitmire, who had married the Reverend Jacob Clark, son of Mary Hearst, whose grandparents had been South Carolina Hearsts: John and Elizabeth Knox Hearst. In her 1928 biography of Phoebe, Winifred Bonfils described George as "a cousin's cousin" to Phoebe.[30]

Fremont Older and Cora Older's biography of Hearst has it that George occasionally visited the Appersons and treated young Phoebe—whom he called Puss—to horseback rides. In his own memoirs, George Hearst states that as a young man he "knew of" but never met Phoebe. An account by Hearst's friend Clarence Greathouse affirms Hearst's statement. Perhaps the Olders created this fiction to obfuscate the fact that before Drusilla married Randolph Apperson, George had courted Drusilla.[31]

In November 1844, William G. Hearst suddenly died, thrusting twenty-four-year-old George into the role of patriarch. The most pressing issue George needed to tackle was his father's debts, to the tune of $10,000. In raising money for the seminary and other public projects, William had set as security the farmstead. Fortuitously, George had been studying business contracts that Bay had provided. He easily slipped into the role of man of the house—even though the house was in arrears. George was able to save the family farm by selling off two slaves: Allen, a twenty-eight-year-old, and Tempey. Allen fetched $500 while Tempey went for $200. George also rented out portions of the three farms. Allen remained on the Hearst farmstead. Part of the price negotiated for his sale was that Elizabeth Hearst could keep Allen for one year "without remuneration for the care and attention of Jacob." The following year, nineteen-year-old Jacob died, leaving George the only male Hearst left in Franklin County.[32]

Bay was impressed by George's skill, encouraging him to go into law. He saw in George "a keen perception . . . a searching and probing mind." George was interested in litigation, but his passions were taking him elsewhere. On August 9, 1847, he attended a Democratic Committee meeting in Union, Missouri, about twenty-five miles from the Hearst farmhouse. At twenty-six years old, George was looking to enter politics. But politics, for the time being, would play second fiddle to his first love: making money. He and a neighbor, P. Phillips, formed a partnership. Six months after the Democratic Committee meeting, Missouri's *Palmyra Weekly Whig* announced that Hearst, Phillips and Co. had struck copper fourteen miles south of Union. George also continued to work the lead mine fifteen miles from the farmhouse. He later estimated that between copper and lead, from 1842 to 1849, he made $4,000 to $5,000.[33]

During this time, George considered becoming a Mason. A friend was a master Mason, and he suggested that George join. Another friend, who belonged to the Odd Fellows, talked George out of it. He told George that he paid the Odd Fellows $3 a month, sometimes more, and though he personally was satisfied with the group, joining the Masons would be a tax on George for the rest of his life. George considered the matter and decided his friend was right. He would be his own man.[34]

By 1849 George's mother had remarried. Her new husband was Joseph Funk, a postmaster and a county judge at Traveler's Repose, present-day St. Clair, Missouri. Elizabeth had subsequently moved from the farmhouse into town. After the marriage, George bought from the newlyweds the rights to the farmhouse, making George and his sister, Martha, the sole heirs. George next began living with his prosperous friend James N. Inge, working at Inge's general store. One of the main topics of conversation was California gold.[35]

On January 24, 1848, James Marshall—a carpenter from New Jersey—had been building a sawmill on the South Fork of the American River when he discovered a golden nugget. The find initially went unnoticed by the warring United States and Mexico. Nine days later, on February 2, Mexico signed a peace treaty and California—considered a backwater—became a territory of the United States. Meanwhile, Marshall had alerted his employer, John Sutter, a native of Switzerland, whose plan of creating an agricultural empire did not include gold being found on his property. The two attempted to keep the discovery of gold a secret. Sutter asked his men to continue working on the mill and to dig for gold in their spare time, but word quickly spread to San Francisco.[36]

In January 1848, San Francisco (then called Yerba Buena) was more a village than a city, with a population of about eight hundred. One of its residents was Sam Brannan, a Mormon merchant who had initially come to San Francisco in July 1846, having sailed around Cape Horn from the East Coast with 237 other Mormons, who desired a safe haven from American religious persecution. In March and April, the *Californian* and the *California Star* reported that gold had been discovered, and in April Sam Brannan traveled from San Francisco to the American River. He returned with a bottle of gold dust and the seeds of a plan. On May 12, 1848, on a San Francisco street, Sam Brannan held high the bottle of gold dust, shouting, "Gold! Gold! Gold from the American River!"[37]

Two months later, San Francisco stood half-abandoned. The men who traveled to the American River knew little of mining, but they didn't need to know much. All they needed was a pan—oftentimes a frying pan—with which they could dredge the bottom of a creek bed. The lighter sand and gravel rose to the top, where it was "washed out." The heavier gold—flakes and nuggets—remained at the bottom and could be easily removed. In some cases, gold nuggets were discovered wedged between rocks. The ease with which men were pulling gold out of the river was convincing. Farmers, teachers, lawyers, rustlers, sailors—anyone could do it.[38] Walter Colton, the alcalde of Monterey, noted,

> The blacksmith dropped his hammer, the carpenter his plane, the mason his trowel, the farmer his sickle, the baker his loaf, and the tapster his bottle. All were off . . . some on carts, some on crutches, and one on a litter. Debtors ran, of course. I have only a community of women left, and a gang of prisoners, and here and there a soldier who will give his captain the slip at first chance. I don't blame the fellow a whit; seven dollars a month, while others are making two or three hundred a day![39]

An ex-rancher who was a neighbor to Sutter hired fifty Indians to help him wash gold out of the river. After five weeks they had pulled out river gold valued at $16,000. Though John Sutter was unable to deal with the sudden flood of trespassers on his land and eventually went bankrupt, Sam Brannan saw his plan come to fruition. Between May 1 and July 10, Brannan's store at Sutter's Fort grossed $36,000. Tents, picks, shovels, bowls, knives, buckets—Brannan sold everything he could, and for a premium. Rich men could afford to pay high prices.

In June 1848, California's military governor, Richard Barnes Mason, along with his chief of staff, William Tecumseh Sherman, left Monterey for the American River. On July 5 they reached the Mormon Island diggings, where they found two hundred men living in "boarding shanties." The men had been growing rich off their findings in dry riverbeds. Two men were reported to have discovered $17,000 worth of gold in short order. Another dry riverbed had yielded $12,000. Hundreds of other creeks and ravines were completely unexplored. Mason estimated that all told, four thousand men—half of them Indians—were making fortunes. He estimated that they were making $30,000 to $50,000 a day, "if not more."

"No capital is required to obtain this gold," Mason wrote, "as the laboring man wants nothing but his pick and shovel and tin pan with which to dig and wash the gravel, and many frequently pick gold out of the crevices of rocks with their butcher knives in pieces of from one to six ounces."[40]

Initially, it all seemed too good to be true. On October 26, 1848, the *Palmyra Weekly Whig* echoed the sentiments of many papers: the "gold" discovered in California was "arsenite of copper, containing a little nickel and zinc, and mixed with iron pyrites." In other words: fool's gold. But this conflicted with the letters Missourians were receiving from friends and families who had emigrated to California Territory. These said that fortunes were being made overnight.[41]

On December 5, 1848, President James K. Polk boomed the news during the second session of the Thirtieth Congress. "The accounts of the abundance of gold in that territory are of such extraordinary character as would scarcely command belief were they not corroborated by authentic reports of officers in the public service." Horace Greeley, editor in chief of the *New York Tribune*, who during the depression of the 1840s had popularized the phrase "Go west, young man," made a pronouncement just as significant: "Fortune lies . . . as plentiful as the mud in our streets." Caught up in the spirit of Manifest Destiny, thousands of Missourians began heading to California.[42]

Like most men who grew up mining, George thought he would have the advantage over the greenhorns who had begun flooding California, and the papers supported his belief. Once the gold rush was well under way, the *Palmyra Weekly Whig* airily noted that the California mines were "well stocked with lawyers, doctors and schoolmasters."[43]

"I think I was naturally a mineralogist," George later mused. "The knowledge seems to me instinctive." With his skills, why shouldn't he go to California and show those lawyers how real mining was done? He had almost convinced himself to leave Missouri behind when he visited Nannie's Iron Works, calling on the "old folks" there. In actuality, George was "quite sweet on his girl." George explained that he intended to set out for California, but the old man talked him out of it: "No, don't go. There is nothing there. This gold was discovered some seventy-five years ago, by the Jesuits." Next he pulled *Coast Range* from his bookshelf and read some of it to George, illustrating the point. George was dissuaded, believing that "this would blow out too."[44]

In 1850, having learned the ropes, George opened up his own general store in nearby Judith Springs, Missouri, on a public road called "the old Springfield."[45] It was there that the reports from the West became more and more persistent. The bonanza that had been struck in California was no fairy tale.

"Then the Gold fever broke out," Hearst recalled.[46]

—2—

THE GOLD RUSH

(1850–1859)

> I believe that the discovery of gold in California and the consequent increase
> of the circulating medium in the country had a much greater effect than
> anything else to develop the resources of the country.
> —George Hearst

Cutting his mother's apron strings proved difficult. Elizabeth Collins had lost one son; she did not want to lose another. But when Hearst explained that a Californian could make $40 or $50 a day, she saw reason. "I never thought I was a man until I was over 30 years old," Hearst later reflected. More than ever before, he was taking charge of his own destiny.[1]

Hearst also took charge of the trip. The party to California comprised about fifteen people, one-third of whom were women. Three of them were friends and family: Phillips, Joe Clark, and J. C. Clark. After selling the family copper mine for $1,900, Hearst personally outfitted Phillips and his cousins. Joe and J. C. would go ahead with the covered wagons, having a ten-day head start. Hearst and Phillips would travel on horseback, planning to "overtake the wagon somewhere about the Blues."[2]

When the Clarks set out, Hearst busied himself by putting his affairs in order. He put management of the farm in the hands of country doctor William N. Patton, whom Hearst trusted implicitly. Of Patton, Hearst later said, "I made Mr. Patton my agent; I had all confidence in him; I was raised with him; he was my family physician; he had set by me many a night; and when he was in my neighborhood he always made my home his home; and I did his when I was in the neighborhood. I believed he was an honest, sterling man."[3]

It's probable that Hearst also got roaring drunk. In rapidly growing St. Louis, which now boasted more than eighty thousand residents, he purchased a gallon of brandy for $16.[4] Naturally, he said his good-byes. According to the Olders, when Hearst visited the Appersons, seven-year-old Phoebe burst into tears. "Puss, don't cry like a papoose," he said. "I'll send you a nice present from California."[5]

Hearst and Phillips departed along the Oregon Trail on May 12, 1850. Traveling with them on horseback for the first two days were Hearst's mother and sister. Several times Hearst nearly lost his nerve. The thought of leaving Elizabeth and Martha behind, as well as his home, was terrible. "If it had not been for pride when my mother and sister left me I would not have thought of going. . . . I felt it in my bones." In fact, this would be the last time he saw Martha. Four years later, she would die.[6]

Hearst and Phillips took "the Ridge" on the way out of Missouri—rolling hills that parallel the south bank of the Missouri River—heading north by northwest. On the way to Independence, just east of Kansas City, they passed through Californiaville and Sedalia. They had not yet left Missouri, and already Hearst had journeyed farther than he had ever been in his life. By the time they reached the Big Blue River, more than fifty miles from Fort Kearny (in present-day Nebraska), they still hadn't caught up with the Clark brothers.[7]

Hearst and Phillips were eager to catch their party, but they were delayed at the river. A storm had swollen it, and several caravans had stopped along its banks. Hearst and Phillips halted as well, worried about losing more time but more concerned by the river. After days of futilely waiting for the river level to drop, Hearst and Phillips determined they would construct a makeshift raft. "We tied a lot of wagon beds together, put our bedding in them and finally had quite a respectable boat made," Hearst recalled. "Then the question was to get a rope across the raging torrent in order to pull the raft over. No one of the party could swim, and for even the bravest swimmer it looked like death to go into that raging flood."[8]

They cast about, not knowing what to do, until "a fat, red-haired, blue-eyed boy" offered to swim the river with the rope. The boy looked to Hearst muscular and courageous, and Hearst and Phillips decided to let him try. Once on the other side, the boy tied the rope, allowing Hearst and Phillips to safely cross. After fording the river, the Missouri boys threw up their hats and whooped for joy.

The story of the red-headed boy was one that Senator Hearst enjoyed retelling. While in Washington, D.C., eating walnuts and drinking wine at Chamberlin's with Colonel Tom Ochiltree of Texas, John Russell Young, and several others, Hearst recounted the story. "I never think of my early life but that I remember that red-haired boy, I have looked for him everywhere and I cannot find him. Had he not been there I probably would have gone back to Missouri, and my gratitude to him is beyond description. Why, gentlemen, if I could find that red-haired boy I would give him a million dollars."

Ever the joker, Ochiltree rose, tears in his eyes. "Senator, I was that red-haired boy."[9]

Having forded the Big Blue, Hearst and Phillips shortly reached Fort Kearny. Named for Brigadier General Stephen Watts Kearny, Fort Kearny was manned by the First U.S. Dragoons, whose purpose was to negotiate with the Comanche, Arapaho, Pawnee, Kaw, Sioux, and Cheyenne tribes. By the time Hearst and Phillips arrived, the fort was plagued by desertion, several soldiers having joined the exodus to the California goldfields.[10]

Hearst and Phillips stayed only one night at Fort Kearny. In the morning a tremendous storm overtook them. The rains played havoc with the supplies of other wagon parties, sending cattle in all directions and up into the hills. More ominously, at every mile they came across at least one grave.

A couple days later, outside Plumtree, amid grasses that were six feet tall, Hearst took a chill. He didn't need a doctor to diagnose him; he'd come down with cholera. Hearst swallowed some pills he had bought in St. Louis for such an event. Afterward, his bowels ran out like water. He looked at the grass and thought about lying down in it, but he knew Phillips would never leave him. Instead, Hearst helped himself to a bit of brandy. The liquor helped, and the following day he felt much better. But soon another storm was upon them; it wouldn't let up for three weeks. To Hearst, it seemed the more it rained, the more travelers came down with cholera and measles.[11]

Ahead of Hearst and Phillips had been a party from Indiana, a husband and wife and five sons. At Plum Creek, Hearst and Phillips saw husband and wife driving toward them with their team. The couple explained that they had buried all five of their sons and were heading back the way they had come. The only reason they had come out this way in the first place was to be with their boys. They stayed with Hearst and Phillips for some time, awash with grief.[12]

On June 9, 1850, the *Republican* published an account of the outbreak of cholera and measles, as well as the thunderstorm. The newspaperman reported that between June 1 and June 7, cholera broke out in every wagon train in Plum Creek valley. The *Palmyra Weekly Whig* later estimated that of 35,000 emigrants traveling through the Plum Creek valley on 7,500 wagons, 250 people had perished from the outbreak.[13]

Hearst and Phillips must have wondered how the Clarks and the rest of their party were faring up ahead. Four hundred miles later, following the North Platte, they reached Fort Laramie. Shortly beyond the fort, they finally overtook the wagon.

Fortune had smiled on the party. Every man and woman was alive. To celebrate their good health, they slaughtered and cooked a buffalo heifer. Hearst was also impressed by the "spanking team of oxen." But their good fortune did not last long. Hearst overheard the young fellow driving the team telling his partner that he was thirsty and asking if he could drive. Hearst knew extreme thirst to be the first sign of cholera. The next Sunday the young fellow died. One or two others died of measles, and another suffered paralysis. Hearst himself maintained good health for the next thousand miles. It wasn't until they were in the Humboldt Desert in Utah Territory, present-day Nevada—having traded the Oregon Trail for the popular California Trail—that Hearst was "nearly broken up by an attack of fever." The fevers gave him little peace.

Adding to Hearst's misery was the fact that he was almost broke. By the time they reached California, all he had left was a five-franc piece, having spent his last dollar on a hundred-pound sack of flour. The flour kept him from starving, and, ultimately, in October 1850, the party reached California. The first place they stopped was Hangtown, ten miles southeast of Sutter's Mill.[14] This was in the heart of the gold rush: El Dorado County. Finally, George Hearst had arrived.

The problem was, so had everybody else.

In 1847 the population of San Francisco had been less than eight hundred. By the time Hearst arrived in the fall of 1850, San Francisco had more than twenty-five thousand residents. Well over a hundred thousand argonauts were searching for gold in the riverbeds and mountains of California, which had been granted statehood the month before, on September 9, 1850. Any hopes of making an easy killing quickly evaporated.

Hearst wasn't about to give up, but he was weak from fever. He simply lacked the energy for pick and shovel. With Phillips and the Clark brothers, he traveled to Pleasant Valley, eight miles away, and convalesced. After about a week they moved on to Diamond Springs, ten miles to the west. A man pointed out to Hearst where several others were "washing gold out of the river." Though panning for gold still occurred in late 1850, many used the more sophisticated rocker, or cradle. A rocker was four to six feet long, wooden, with an open box and a series of cleats. After gold-bearing gravel was pressed into the opening, along with water, the cleats captured the heavier gold while the lighter gravel was drawn to the sieve-like bottom.[15]

Hearst determined they would go thirteen miles south and try their luck at washing out gold. The creek they reached was called Jackass Gulch, named when miners shot an unlucky jackass, mistaking it for a grizzly bear.[16]

For the next nine months, Hearst roamed the California streams and mountains, searching for gold. Pick, shovel, pan, and rocker were his best friends, but they were fickle. Every time he found a rich gulch, upward of forty men would descend on it—"in fact would swallow it up," Hearst remembered. Rules were quickly established so that all men would gain a share; and according to the widely adopted Missouri system, for making the original discovery, Hearst was entitled to double what the others made. But despite his background in Missouri mining, he did not prove successful. Though he mined enough gold to keep from starving, he was constantly impoverished. At one point, Hearst was so deep in debt that a local policeman caught him attempting to flee from El Dorado on a mule and confiscated the animal. Hearst rarely washed. In his memoirs he notes that when they came to water "after a dusty tramp," the "Chinamen" he was traveling with—whom Hearst admired for their industry and habits—"would run down, bare their breasts, and thoroughly wash themselves; which, I am free to confess, is far more than I often did."[17]

It wasn't a glamorous life. The *Anaconda Standard* categorized Hearst as "a prospector accustomed to mixing his own sour dough, frying his own bacon and splitting his pack with a burro as he tramped the hills of California." Another sad fact about California was a dearth of women. "The first five years in California a woman was a curiosity," Hearst observed. A Sonoran newspaper published in April 1850 bears the truth of this statement, noting that of the nearly six thousand emigrants it recorded in five towns, only one hundred had been women. Beyond prostitution, women cooked, ran laundries, and managed stores.[18]

Recalled Hearst: "As to the advantage of having a woman our [*sic*] West in those early days, of course, if she was a good woman, it was a good thing to have her . . . they could coin money keeping little eating houses there; for we had to pay a dollar for any kind of meal. There was no kind of little place that could not take in a couple of hundred dollars a day."[19]

Eventually, Hearst traipsed fifty miles north of Jackass Gulch to a ravine named Gold Flat, dappled by a pine forest. The ravine lay between two small boomtowns, Grass Valley and Nevada. Gold Flat was three miles north of Grass Valley, formerly dubbed Boston Ravine and Centerville before the new post office gave it its official name. The man who put Grass Valley on the map was George D. Roberts, a lumberman from Ohio.

In 1850 twenty-two-year-old Roberts, who would become a friend, partner, and sometimes adversary of Hearst, had discovered an outcropping of quartz with a vein of gold running through it. Roberts established the Ophir Hill Mine but grew frustrated with extracting the gold from the quartz, selling the mine for $350 to Woodbury, Park and Company, which quickly sold it at auction to the Empire Mine Company. By 1851, the newly christened Empire Mine had crushed $20,000 worth of gold from its quartz mill, sending Roberts into a fit and creating a rush to Grass Valley.

Closer than Grass Valley to Gold Flat was Nevada, where George Hearst spent much more time. The boomtown, established on the banks of Deer Creek, originally carried with it a number of monikers: Coyoteville, Caldwell's Upper Store, Deer Creek Dry Diggings. The one that stuck was Nevada, Spanish for "snow-covered." When Nevada was given statehood in 1864, the name of the town was changed to Nevada City to avoid confusion.

The *Nevada City Herald* tells a story of Hearst's grim early days in California:

Hearst . . . a plain, very plain sort of man . . . had been prospecting a long time with poor success and was getting hard up for money. His clothing was seedy and his stomach was empty. He went to one of the butcher shops that flourished here and, addressing the butcher, said: "I'm all-fired hungry and I want some meat. I need a pair of overalls, too, the worst way, as these are ready to drop off. I've got six bits in my pocket. I can't get trusted for the overalls. Now what shall I do—go without the meat or the overalls?"

The butcher told him to get the pants and he would trust him for the meat. Hearst did so and left the shop, feeling in much better spirits than when he entered.[20]

To Hearst, overalls were often a luxury. "Hearst used to mine around in Nevada in patched trousers," recalled the *Grass Valley Tidings*.[21]

Though broke, Hearst felt that Gold Flat held riches. Hearst and his fellow Missourians built a cabin on a small hill, protecting themselves from the elements and grizzly bears. They also made two discoveries on Gold Flat. One was a vein of quartz—near the Rivett and Skinner Mill—on which they established the Merrimac Mine, named for the Meramec River in Franklin County. They constructed a tunnel, 125 feet long, on a slight incline and from this tunnel were able to smash quartz, revealing gold. The other discovery was a ravine where lay patches of smooth rock. Near one such patch, they constructed a rudimentary mineshaft, a sixty-foot-deep hole buttressed by wooden planks, where they engaged in "dry digging."

The association of smooth rock with gold, and with quartz and gold, was not widely known in the early days of the gold rush. But they were learning. As river gold became scarcer and scarcer, miners realized that the source of the gold lay in the mountains, not in the rivers. While searching the mountains for veins of gold, miners looked for two clues that gold might be in the vicinity. One was smooth rocks or boulders in a dry ravine. The smooth rocks and boulders indicated that the ravine had once been a river, so gold might still be found in the dry riverbed. Such dry riverbeds were known as dry diggings. The second clue was quartz. During the volcanic creation of California's coastal mountains—the smashing of one tectonic plate into another—preexisting quartz liquefied, turning into streams and rivulets of quartz. These molten streams of quartz gathered up gold as they flowed. As they solidified, they became quartz veins with gold locked inside. With a smash of a pick or shovel, the quartz could be broken apart, revealing gold—bright yellow among the white quartz.

One day in the summer of 1851, Hearst was in the mineshaft in the Gold Flat ravine, harnessed to a windlass, when one of his companions, Bill, called down, "George, oh George."

"Well, what do you want?" Hearst hollered back.

"There's a man here who wants to see you," Bill replied

"Well, pull me up."

When Hearst reached the top, he unhitched himself, glanced at the stranger—a beardless man with the look of the city—and dusted off the brown Kentucky jeans tucked roughly into his boots.

Hearst did not know it at the time, but he had just met a lifelong friend.

"My name is Paul—Almarin B. Paul. At your leisure I want to have a talk with you on business. You are one of the owners of the Merrimac, are you not?"

"Yes," Hearst admitted, "with a lot of others."

"I want to talk to you about consolidating the Rivett & Skinner mill and the Merrimac mine."

"That takes a good deal of talk," Hearst said, "as there are others interested in the claim, and all have a say. Bill, we'll knock off; done enough work for one day."

"I think so," Bill agreed, "the way you kept pulling at that damned old windlass."

Hearst turned again to Paul. "Well, Mr. Paul, you had better stay all night if you want to talk to the boys about the Merrimac. Besides, it will be dark before you could get back to Nevada, and you might get lost in the woods going over and have to lay out all night, and you might run on a stray grizzly. There's our cabin over on the sidehill. We can take care of you, and the boys will be coming in soon."

Paul was glad for the invitation, and the trio walked to the cabin. Hearst washed up—possibly indicating how seriously he took the offer of consolidation—and gave Bill orders as to dinner. Then Hearst and Paul sat on a log to discuss the offer. The offer was what Paul called a "square deal": half the mine for half the mill. Before long, five others arrived at the cabin, all Missourians working dry diggings of their own.

Dinner was soon ready. A fire was built in the expansive fireplace, and news from the east was discussed. Eventually, Hearst brought the conversation back to business. "Well, boys, Mr. Paul is in for a trade for the Merrimac, and proposes to give us half the Rivett & Skinner mill for half the mine. Now what do you all say?"

Hearst was asked for his opinion, but he wanted the others to go first. When the opinions came, it was like an avalanche.

"We know nothing about working the rock if we have a mill."

"Who bosses the mine if we have only half?"

"How are we going to crush the rock without a mill, and not enough money to build one?"

"We don't know the fellows who own the other half."

"Now George, what have you got to say?" asked Bill.[22]

Deferring to Hearst had become second nature. William M. Stewart, whom Hearst was about to meet, summed it up best. At mining, Hearst displayed "the true instincts of a miner . . . [who] seemed to know at a glance whether geological formations were suitable for mines of the precious metals." Equally important was Hearst's abilities as a leader. Bill Stewart recalled that Hearst's "strong common sense inspired confidence and made him a leader of public opinion and of men. He also had a vein of humor which amused and fascinated the learned as well as the illiterate. He was at home in the company of men of all conditions." W. V. N. Bay echoed these sentiments: "Hearst was a young man of exuberant spirits . . . the life and soul of the company . . . [who] told a good anecdote."[23]

Hearst admitted that trading half the Merrimac Mine for half the Rivett and Skinner Mill was worth considering, for each side needed the other. It was at this point that Paul mentioned that he, too, was from Missouri. "It seemed to me I have seen you somewhere before," he said to Hearst. "Did you ever come up to St. Louis from New Madrid?"

"Why yes. Are you from St. Louis?"

Paul said he was, and the others were put at ease. Paul also sweetened the deal. It was still half the mill for half the mine, but the contract would state that George Hearst would run the mine. Everyone in the cabin agreed, and when Paul returned to Sacramento, Rivett agreed as well. The Rivett and Skinner Mill had twenty horsepower and could crush up to three tons of rock a day. Soon it was crushing Merrimac quartz.

With the help of Hearst and his team, the Rivett and Skinner Mill began crushing five tons of quartz a day. Each ton yielded $50 to $300 worth of gold. To increase production, they built four new mills out of the pines and oaks around them. The mills incorporated German shaking tables to separate the gold from other materials.[24]

It was at this point, in the autumn of 1851, that Hearst began living large. Partnering with Hamlet Davis, who would later become the first mayor of Nevada City, Hearst opened up a general store on the northeast corner of Pine and Broad Streets. Shortly afterward, Hearst and Davis converted the loft above the store into a theater, the Dramatic Hall, Nevada City's first theater. In the capacity of theater owner, Hearst met two men who would become great friends: Niles Searls and Bill Stewart. The first play on the boards was *Christopher Strap*. The theater also sported a second-story reading room, furnished with free newspapers courtesy of the Sacramento post office, which had no use for uncollected newspapers.[25]

Hearst had been in California for one year and already he owned a gold mine, a general store, and a theater. The world was ripe for the taking. By 1852 the Missourians of Gold Flat had purchased a neighboring mine, the Potosi, and formed the Merrimac and Potosi Gold Mining Company. Hearst, Paul, and Edward Downs were the owners. The stockholders were Hearst, Paul, Downs, Phillips, Joseph Clark, J. C. Clark, Jason Carr, P. G. Gibson, Andy Shoemaker, and J. W. Alexander. Throughout 1852, they averaged $100 in gold per each ton of ore, and they brought up tons of ore per day.[26]

"Good things cannot last forever," reflected Paul. Because of the expense of the stamps (used to crush the ore and extract the gold), which the hard quartz eventually wore down, they needed one ounce of gold per ton of quartz to keep the operation profitable. By the end of 1852, the Merrimac and Potosi were all but played out. After auctioning the mines off, Hearst and a few others had one last glittering surprise. As they tore down the sluices, they discovered $3,000 worth of gold.[27]

This money funded Hearst's next expansive scheme. Hearst believed that the four or five thousand Missourians he estimated to be in California were the sharpest, most experienced miners in the country, but he also knew that most of the people enriching themselves from the gold rush weren't the miners themselves. They were the men who sold goods to the miners, knowing they could charge exorbitant rates.[28]

The winter of 1851–1852 was an exceptionally hard one. Little mining could be done, and the merchants, who were running out of goods, were selling at huge markups. "Nothing could be purchased for less than a dollar a pound," Hearst lamented, "except beef which was 60 cents a pound." So that winter Hearst established a merchandising business in Sacramento, "Hearst & Company, Wholesale Merchants" at 92 K Street, where Hearst also kept his residence. Paul was Hearst's partner on the venture.[29]

Hearst and Paul were strange bedfellows as far as their politics were concerned. Hearst was a Democrat and Paul a Whig. But in other ways, they were brothers. Both were notable for their sense of humor. Hearst was generally easygoing, and later in life could riff with none other than Mark Twain to gales of laughter. Paul became the talk of Sacramento when, on a dare, he strolled down the city's main street wearing a beaver hat and dressed as a dude, becoming the first well-dressed man in Sacramento. Both Hearst and Paul were willing to take risks. Hearst had given up a comfortable life in Missouri when struck with gold fever. Likewise, Paul had first traded St. Louis for the copper mines of Lake Superior in 1845. Furthermore, both Hearst and Paul had ancestors who had fought against the British during the Revolutionary War. Hearst and Paul may have stuck together for these reasons.

Sacramento's K Street proved a popular street for future millionaires. It was there that Leland Stanford established his own small store at 58 K Street. Like Stanford, Hearst was interested in politics. Moving to Sacramento may have intensified his interest. On becoming a state, California had moved its capital from Monterey to San Jose and then Vallejo. After only a week in Vallejo, the capital moved to Sacramento on January 16, 1852. (The capital would move again to Vallejo for a month and then to Benicia for two weeks before permanently settling in Sacramento.) The first governor of California, Peter Burnett, had resigned amid ridicule, and the newly appointed governor, John McDougall, was even less experienced. Politics would have been on everyone's mind, and Hearst and Stanford were doubtless both thinking, *I could do a better job.*[30]

Unlike Stanford, who proved to be a successful businessman in Sacramento, Hearst was a disaster at merchandising. In a biographical sketch of Hearst's life, the *Los Angeles Times* commented, "The money that was so easily acquired in quartz-mining was sunk with equal facility—swept away by a single hapless venture in the general merchandising line in Sacramento."[31]

Paul summed it up in less sweeping terms: "I formed a co-partnership with George Hearst under the title of Hearst & Co. and we started business in Sacramento but the times had so changed and we soon found there was no success in merchandising and we discontinued."[32]

In early 1852, Hearst shuttered the store, returning to placer mining. To a newspaperman, Hearst related, "I had some hard times. I worked in the mines with a pick and a shovel, and lived on salt meat and hard crackers." In his memoirs, Hearst reflected, "So we went on until 1856, sometimes making a little and sometimes losing. I never succeeded much in placer mining."[33]

Hearst was mildly successful, however, in selling mines *before* they played out. More than anything, he sought quartz veins, so much so that fellow miners sometimes called him Quartz George. As Paul recalled, "Hearst . . . was always talking quartz, hunting quartz and studying quartz."[34]

In 1857, as he had in 1851, Hearst struck it rich with a quartz vein outside Nevada City. There, on the quartz vein, Hearst purchased the Lecompton Mine with his cousins Joe and J. C. Clark and his friend George D. Roberts. The mine was located three miles up the steep, narrow Deer Creek Trail.

It had been seven years since Roberts had sold, for $350, the Ophir Hill Mine—a mine that would bring in $130 million (in 1956 dollars) by the time it closed. But that setback hadn't chased him away from Grass Valley and Nevada City. Always looking for another score, Roberts had partnered with Hearst and the Clarks in the Lecompton Mine.

With the forest full of pine trees and Deer Creek teeming with great blue herons, brown trout, and rainbow trout, Hearst must have enjoyed the location of his newest mine. Perhaps the croaking of the great blue heron and the sight—and taste—of the rainbow trout reminded him of the Meramec River back in Missouri.

Hearst, the Clarks, and Roberts quickly set up a mill. They sold a half interest to two men, McLane and Givens. The mine yielded $60,000 in a two-year period. Once again, Hearst was a man on the make. Hearst was credited with helping contain a fire spreading in Nevada City in early 1858. While walking down the main thoroughfare, Hearst and a friend, E. G. Waite, saw that a fire was threatening the offices of the *Nevada Democrat*. One of the newspaper owners, Tallman H. Rolfe, in a letter to his brother Sam, described their actions: "We have again been visited by a disastrous fire which originated in a Chinese wash house on Broad Street. . . . Our office narrowly escaped and we are under obligations to E. G. Waite and George Hearst for timely assistance in putting wet blankets on the gable on the Broad Street side and keeping them wet."[35]

Hearst's rise in Nevada City illustrates how far he had come—from having six bits in his pockets and needing to buy meat on trust to saving a newspaper office from a fire and owning a paying quartz mine. Again, Hearst considered joining the Masons. The group was quite a draw. Many of the town elders, including Niles Searls, frequented Masonic Lodge No. 13, and there Hearst could be at the center of things. But Hearst ultimately decided against it. "I made up my mind that a good man was a good man anywhere, and that there was no occasion for joining any affiliation societies. I made up my mind to be independent, and decided not even to belong to a church." The $3 a month fee he'd been warned about by his Missouri friend may also have factored in.[36]

Unfortunately for Hearst, things in Missouri had deteriorated in his absence. In 1853 Hearst had been reported dead. As a result, for several months his friends and relatives in Missouri believed him a corpse. This may have emboldened the predatory lawyers who set about carving out chunks of the Hearst farmstead. In 1858 Hearst's stepfather, Joseph Funk, sent him word of the trouble, encouraging George to come home. But Hearst felt he was home:

Nevada City, March 19, 1858

Dear Father,

. . . You say you would like for me to come home: now, I would like to see you and mother and some of the people, and particularly that little old dried up Uncle Austin and Aunt Ann, much better than you suppose, but to come home without money is out of the question, but if I have any kind of luck I will come home soon and stop awhile, though I do not expect to make the state my home; I am satisfied that I could not stand that climate. . . . You say I must not get out of heart; that is the greatest trouble in this country, but I have got the nerve and can stand anything until death calls for me, and then I must weaken, and not until then. The only thing that gives me much trouble is my old mother. I would like to see her have all that life could desire, and be with me a part of the time, but if God has fixed and ordained otherwise, so it must be.

I will also send you a power of attorney with all the power I could have if I were there myself, which you can use to the best of your judgment. . . .

As regards anything you may do about those lands, it will be all right, but if you have to pay anything like what they are worth, let them go, for I am not stuck after any kind of lands in that part of the world, and I am tired of sending good money after bad. If I had let all [go at] the start and went at something that would have paid me a good living, I think it would have been [better] for me today; but if you should see a chance to save something, do, for it is more than I have been able to do, and furthermore, I do not think that God intended for me to have one cent of that property. I will likely send you some more money soon.

Yours,
George Hearst[37]

Liberated from responsibilities in Missouri, Hearst operated the Lecompton Mine for two years before hearing a rumor that would change his life and the fate of the country. Silver had been discovered in Utah Territory.

The Washoe excitement was about to begin.

— 3 —

THE WASHOE EXCITEMENT

(1859–1860)

We worked away till we got about 45 tons. Some people said it was no good,
and nobody believed it was silver.
—George Hearst

In 1859, Quartz George decided to try his luck in one of the most desolate places
on the planet. It had a number of different names. Some called it Washoe Territory, for the Indian tribes who lived nearby. Others called it Virginia, named for
a hard-drinking, grizzled prospector. Technically, it was part of Utah Territory,
held by the United States. Whatever the name, it was a semiarid sagebrush desert
where coyotes picked the bones of careless prospectors. Samuel Clemens, who
made his mark there as a newspaper writer, described it as a place "where even
the devil would be homesick."

The devil was on his way.

Hearst had been hearing rumors of wealth there for years. Since the spring
of 1852, about forty or fifty prospectors had been canvasing the western edge of
Utah Territory. They lived in the crude dwellings of Johntown, eking out a living
in Gold Canyon. In 1856 the population doubled when dozens of Chinese laborers were brought to help mine. They lived in "Chinatown," or Mineral Springs,
near the mouth of Gold Canyon. Gold Canyon showed promise, so the men of

Johntown and Mineral Springs continued to toil there, but no one had yet made a fortune—though the Grosh brothers seemed poised to do so.[1]

Two Pennsylvania brothers, Hosea B. Grosh and Ethan Allan Grosh, had gone beyond Gold Canyon and into the wretched Six-Mile Canyon. Like Hearst, the brothers had originally come to El Dorado during the gold rush, but they soon found California too crowded. In 1853, while prospecting in western Utah Territory, they discovered silver in Six-Mile Canyon. Hosea and Ethan returned the following years, but in 1857 they met with a series of fatal accidents. Hosea struck a pickax through his foot and died of blood poisoning. Ethan was trapped in a snowstorm and had to kill his mule for sustenance. Although he was rescued, both his legs had to be amputated, and he soon died.

No one quite knew where the Grosh brothers had been mining, or *what* they'd been mining, but the Johntown prospectors smelled a fortune. Such men included Joseph Kirby, who had first discovered gold in Gold Canyon; John F. Stone, a prospector from Nevada City; Patrick McLaughlin and Peter O'Reilly, Irish partners accustomed to roughing it; Nicholas Ambrose, or "Dutch Nick," who ran a tent saloon and boardinghouse in Johntown; Henry Comstock, otherwise known as "Old Pancake," whose nickname derived from the fact that he was too busy prospecting to bake bread, instead turning his flour into pancakes; E. A. Harrison, a friend of Comstock's; and James Fennimore, a hard-drinking Virginian who claimed two nicknames: "Old Virginia" and "Finney."[2]

"Almost everybody has a nickname here," Virginia City prospector Dwight Bartlett wrote his family.[3]

Ultimately, Comstock and his friends moved from Johntown to Gold Hill, closing in on the likely site where the Grosh brothers had been prospecting. McLaughlin soon located a silver vein, and a new town was created: Virginia. The name was taken from one of James Fennimore's nicknames. The story goes—put down in Dan De Quille's 1876 history of Virginia City, *The Big Bonanza*—that "Old Virginia and the other boys got on a drunk one night there, and Old Virginia fell down and broke his bottle, and when he got up he said he baptized that ground Virginia." Almarin B. Paul recalls Fennimore telling the tale differently. "I wanted it Comstock, and Comstock wanted it Virginia," Fennimore explained. "At the time I was carrying . . . two bottles of whiskey, and in our heated arguments was careless as to where I stepped, when suddenly I went down and broke one of the bottles. That settled the question, when it was declared the name should be Virginia, and so it is."[4]

The unofficial name for the bonanza was the Comstock Lode. No prospector in their wildest dreams imagined that more wealth than all the riches of California would be found in that concentrated spot, but that was precisely what was about to happen.

Hearst verified the rumors by getting ahold of a piece of melted Comstock ore and sending it to an assayer. The assayer told him it was worth $3,000 a ton. The fellow who'd been mining the stuff told Hearst there was a lot more where that came from.

"All right, I am going over there," Hearst told him.[5]

Hearst had been haunted by his failure to immediately leave Missouri for the gold rush. Certainly, he never forgot how the father of the girl he was sweet on had talked him out of immediately joining the forty-niners. When the man had pulled the book from the shelf, Hearst hadn't initially known it was *Coast Range*—he'd worked that out later. "It was of course the Coast Range, as I know now," Hearst explained. The loss of the store, the years he spent standing in cold creek water while looking for flakes of gold in a pan, the frigid nights spent huddled in a tent—throughout all of it Hearst must have thought about the timing. He'd come too late.[6]

This time Hearst was quick to act.

"The row made over the discovery of the Comstock silver mines in Nevada set the whole Coast wild," Hearst recollected. "I had been disappointed in the work I had been at, and found myself pretty nearly broke." Nonetheless, Hearst bought a mustang and started the 125-mile journey for Virginia City with about a dozen others. But, after several nights on the trail, the fire in Hearst's belly turned to ashes.[7]

> I wasn't feeling happy, because I'd worked and struggled and speculated for a good many years, and it struck me as rather rough that a man of my age should have to start out, as I did then, as a young fellow. There was about ten or twelve of us in the party, and as I was blue they let me rather alone, and my mustang being rather worn down, I stopped on the trail, put my arm through the bridle, and picked out a rock to sit on. The rest of the boys rode on, but I sat there.[8]

While he sat, Hearst took the willow switch he'd been using as a whip and began switching the dust in the trail. For about twenty minutes he switched and switched. "I thought it was about 100 miles to the mountains," Hearst related in his memoirs, "and this looked like a wild-goose chase amongst the Indians." He thought to himself, *Shall I go with them or go back?*[9]

> I saw behind me all the hard work I had done, all the chances I'd taken and lost on, and felt old and used up, and no good. My sense told me to turn back and make my fight where I was known. There was safety in that anyhow. But I'd been camping night after night with the boys ahead of me, and it made me lonesome to think of parting company with them. So after switching and switching the dust on the trail, and feeling weak and human because I'd yielded, I mounted my horse and rode after the party.[10]

Riding at full gallop, Hearst reunited with the boys. Days later they reached Virginia City. "Finally," Hearst noted in his memoirs, "we got on a great big mountain and saw below a tent where some people were working; that was the Comstock."

McLaughlin, O'Reilly, Comstock, and some others formed the Ophir Mine. It was a biblical name, referring to a port where King Solomon had received tribute every three years: pearls, ivory, silver, and gold. Considering such an auspicious name, the black stuff they were pulling out of the Ophir Mine was disappointing, but Hearst thought there was more to it than met the eye. Initially, Hearst began prospecting a half mile away with a fellow named Jim Southwell, but he kept close watch on the Ophir Mine.

Coming back to the Ophir, Hearst and Southwell were having a drink together while spying the Ophir men taking out large chunks of ore. After two or three more drinks, Southwell said to Hearst, "Do you know what this is?"

"I don't know except that it's metal," Hearst replied.

Taking Hearst off to one side, Southwell confided, "That is silver."

"How do you know?" Hearst asked.

"We are all sure of it."[11]

On the strength of that tip, Hearst bought from McLaughlin a share of the Ophir Mine on a month's credit. To Paul, Hearst wrote, "Now, Paul, you must go over and build a mill. It is the biggest opening you ever had or ever will have. You will see shipments of gold and silver going out every month, and now I will tell you I have bought 'Pat' McLaughlin's . . . interest in the Ophir for $1500 payable in thirty days, and you must let me have the money, or sell my interest in Lecompton and get it."[12] Hearst then loaded his saddlebags with the ore, got on his mustang, and with several others began the return journey to Nevada City.

On a slope, by the side of the Truckee River, they came across a man "shot all to pieces," as Hearst recalled. One man went for a doctor. The rest of the party waited awhile before pushing on.

In Nevada City, Hearst quickly sold out of the Lecompton Mine. He instructed Paul to use some of the leftover money to pay his debts, which Paul did. Together with his old partner on the Lecompton Mine, George D. Roberts, he set out again for the Washoe. On June 1 Hearst gave McLaughlin the money and made his share in the Ophir Mine official.[13]

Hearst was just in time. By mid-June, Comstock and the others felt it was time to have the black stuff assayed. To that end they sent E. A. Harrison to Nevada City. Harrison arrived in Nevada City in late June, carrying a bag filled with "black stuff," given to him by Comstock.

"It was not gold, but sometimes gold could be seen with it," Comstock had told him. Harrison delivered the bag to an acquaintance, Melville Atwood, who worked as a mill man and an assayer in Grass Valley, four miles south of Nevada City.

To Atwood, Harrison reported, "The ore given you was taken from the surface of the Ophir mine, by me. Comstock and his associates were grading the surface for gold, and taking out as high as $300 a day by cradle. I was on the mine on the 26d of June, 1859, and obtained the samples I gave you on this visit."

The contents were remarkable: $876 worth of gold and $3,000 worth of silver.

When Atwood determined that the "black stuff" was gold and silver, worth almost $4,000, his pronouncement was greeted with a hush. Cagey prospectors wanted to keep the news mum, but word quickly spread. A few days later, all of California knew. Paul sent an article to a San Francisco newspaper under his nom de plume, COSMOS, stating "that a vein has been discovered which can be traced for six miles, and all rich in gold and silver, and which by assay will pay $1,000 a ton." Parties quietly began slipping out of Nevada City and Grass Valley, heading east. Thousands were soon to follow.[14]

The next prospector to reach Nevada City carrying a bag filled with precious minerals was J. F. Stone. Stone called on two assayers: Atwood and John Sutter's cousin James J. Ott. On July 28, 1859, Ott claimed the ore was worth $968.96 in gold and $1,975.75 in silver. In a flash, every prospector who had thought Harrison's bag a fluke was kicking himself. Pat McLaughlin died a poor man, eking out his living as a cook. Hearst, on the other hand, had been given a new nickname: "Lucky."[15]

Meanwhile, Hearst began to demonstrate that luck was the residue of design. A note Hearst scribbled shows a small investment he made with a partner:

Hearst	$100
Sam Custis	$40

But a $100 investment was small potatoes compared to the riches that could be made. In November 1859, Hearst sold half of his one-sixth interest in the Ophir to a hot-headed lawyer named Henry Meredith for a quick $10,000 and purchased a heftier share of the Gould & Curry claim, three-tenths of a mile to the south of the Ophir.[16]

The most dramatic story of Hearst's rise to fortune comes from his own words:

> I may say here that my interest in the mine was only one sixth. We divided it into 12 parts and the size of the claim was 1500 feet. The good part of it was about 400 feet. In the meantime we got enough to pay expenses, $2000 a ton. We worked away till we got about 45 tons. Some people said it was no good, and nobody believed it was silver. Anyhow we knew the stuff was in it, but we did not know how to get it out, but we hired mules to get some of the stuff to San Francisco.[17]

After driving the pack of mules 150 miles through snows running twelve to eighteen feet deep, Hearst and his brave companions reached San Francisco. But a hero's welcome was not in the cards; no one believed the ore valuable. An Englishman named Davis offered to "ship it for you to England, paying you so much," but Hearst thought he could do better. They ultimately found a German smelter who offered to build a furnace and transform the thirty-eight tons into gleaming bars for $450 a ton. They struck a deal. They hauled it to the San Francisco Mint, but the bars looked so much like lead that no one believed it was silver. Rumors said that Hearst and the others had hauled the "stuff" up from Mexico and were trying to run a swindle.[18]

But the head of the mint was willing to take a look. After examining the bars, he sent word all prospectors long to hear: "Boys, come up here and I will give you some money." The silver bars netted $91,000 after costs.

"We went there and got our pockets filled," Hearst recalled, "and then went downstairs to see if it would pass for whisky, and they took it. Then there was great excitement. That was the actual beginning of the Washoe excitement."[19]

News spread east from San Francisco to Sacramento, to all the boomtowns and miners throughout California. It was printed in newspapers and cabled to Salt Lake City; Chicago; New York City; Boston; Philadelphia; Washington, D.C.; New Orleans; Richmond; St. Louis; even Franklin County, Missouri. Sailors voyaged across the world, spreading firsthand accounts of the bonanza. The race for the riches of the Comstock Lode was on, and Hearst had gotten there first.

"Lucky" George Hearst was now in his element, on pace to become King of the Comstock. Returning to Virginia City, he prospected and invested aggressively. Hearst dangled shares of the Savage Mine for $4,000, upped the price to $8,000 once investors were hooked, and used the profits to buy Charley Chase and Len Savage's interest in the Savage Mine. On February 27, 1860, the *New York Times* listed George Hearst, along with H. H. Raymond and Henry Meredith, as one of the principal owners of the profitable Ophir Mine. The Sierra Nevada Silver Mining Company was also formed. Partners included George Hearst, Joe Clark, Bill Stewart, George D. Roberts, and Hearst's fast friend Bill Lent, among others. Each mining company was soon hauling tons of silver to San Francisco.[20]

The world was Hearst's for the taking. "I got to the Comstock and in six months I made half a million dollars," Hearst bragged.[21]

On March 16, 1860, Joe Clark sent his cousin a letter:

> As Jack O'Brien goes over to Nevada today I send you this letter. I bought one hundred feet of ground from on the Sugar Loaf and Lady Bryan adjoining the Desert Co. for which I gave him an order on you for $2,300. I also Bot 100 feet of Arch McDonald on the same lead. He will not want his money for some time to come. Altogether I have bot 325 feet in this Co. I think it is the best Hill in the Flowery district. I have paid from $5 dollars to $25 per foot for. I can sell now for $40—I am frozed to go out prospecting but can't go. Can't leave here. Several parties are out now. I have got men at work on all our claims. Devil's Gate will be good. The Jumpers are getting good pay. In Hast,
> Joe Clark[22]

Everyone was soon getting good pay. Virginia City quickly boasted a population of about ten thousand. Hearst erected one of the finest houses in the area, located on D Street, also serving as the Gould & Curry superintendent's house. Hearst's white-banistered two-story house was a tenth of a mile from the Gould & Curry Mine. In the center of the city, Hearst could gamble faro and poker, eat and drink at "Dutch Nick's" saloon, and visit any of Virginia City's cathouses. The *Territorial Enterprise* wouldn't move from Genoa to Virginia City until late 1860, but beginning in April 1860, the Pony Express began delivering letters. Shotgun messengers, protecting the iron-rimmed treasure coaches from Virginia City to San Francisco, could also be seen on the makeshift roads—though the roads were fast becoming toll roads. Toll roads became big business for Virginia City's most avaricious businessmen, which included Hearst's friend George D. Roberts.

The landscape outside and underneath Virginia City was also changing. Piñon pine groves were chopped down to provide firewood, lumber for houses, and support for the mines. The mines themselves began to stretch for miles, dangerously honeycombing the area. More permanent residences were erected—and burned down when fire spread out of control. Snow sometimes disappeared. In the depths of the mines, temperatures could reach 110°F, so snow from the surface was brought down to give miners some relief before they clawed their way back up. Water was scarce, and initially no one could imagine a way of piping it in. Samuel Clemens, who wouldn't arrive in Virginia City until 1861, described the area as being "fabulously rich in gold, silver, copper, lead, coal, iron, quicksilver, marble, granite, chalk . . . thieves, murderers, desperadoes, ladies, children, lawyers, Christians, Indians, Chinamen, Spaniards, gamblers, sharpers, coyotes (pronounced ki-yo-ties), poets, preachers, and jackass rabbits."[23]

It was the only place like it on earth, where fortunes were won and lost overnight. Hearst survived it unscathed. Though he wasn't yet a Virginia City millionaire, he lived like one. It is not hard to imagine Hearst sitting on the deck of his two-story house, drinking whiskey and smoking cigars with his friends and cronies, overlooking his growing empire.

At forty years old, Hearst began looking seriously for a wife. Mary Dollarhide, who lived on Main Street, was one woman he courted. Her sister and brother ran a store, and Mary was on the market for a suitable bachelor. Hearst proposed marriage, but Mary's sister soured the play, telling Mary, "You can't marry that worthless Hearst!"[24]

Hearst may have continued his hunt for an eligible lady in Virginia City had his stepfather Joseph Funk not sent word. Hearst was to return immediately, for his mother Elizabeth was deathly ill. Having been in California while his sister Martha passed, and having not seen his mother in a decade, Hearst had no intention of letting his mother die while he was living it up in Virginia City. Leaving his mining interests in the hands of Joe Clark and Bill Lent, Hearst bid farewell to the Washoe. Once in San Francisco, Hearst sold his mules and began looking for passage aboard a ship to New York City. However, Hearst quickly found that though he had left Virginia City, Virginia City had not left him.

On April 5, 1860, Hearst received a letter from Lent. Despite his absence, Hearst's claims were doing well. For the first time, Hearst could brag that he was a millionaire. But others—including Lent—were struggling. Lent complained that "money is d—d tight" and asked for assistance. "If you can buy one of the claims on the Comstock, let us in for a share and we will try to get even with you."[25]

On April 28 Hearst received a letter from miner John O. Earle in response to a dispute involving Hearst, Henry Meredith, and the Washoe Company. Professing that he didn't want to get involved, Earl intimated, "In regard to the . . . ground, now belonging to the Washoe Co., I do not see what I can do in the matter . . . certainly it is much for Mr. Meredith's interest . . . Mr. Meredith being *now on the ground himself* . . . hoping this letter may find you well, and that I will have the pleasure of seeing you soon."[26]

Meredith, incidentally, was about to find himself on the wrong side of another dispute—this one between Paiute Indians and Washoe settlers. The short but bloody conflict, known as the Paiute Indian War, was the consequence of ten thousand prospectors disrupting the ecosystem on which the Indians depended. By 1860 the Paiute Indians had seen their grazing land invaded, their water stolen, Pyramid Lake overfished, their piñon pine groves—from which they harvested piñon nuts—chopped down. In response, on May 6, 1860, an Indian war party raided Williams Station—thirty-six miles east of Virginia City—killing two of the three Williams brothers and reducing the station to cinders. Ultimately, two militias were formed to battle the Indians. Hearst stayed out of it. By the time the war ended in early June, eight Paiutes had been killed. The pioneers had lost seventy-eight men, including "Hapless" Henry Meredith, shot off his mule and cut to pieces by Paiutes on May 12, 1860, at the First Battle of Pyramid Lake.[27]

Although Hearst did not lose his life, his enterprises suffered as a result of the Paiute Indian War. "This Indian War was playing the very Dickens with us. It cost me a good deal and I had to sell some of my ground," Hearst lamented.[28]

On August 1, 1860, Hearst booked passage in a first-class cabin, which he shared with the lord bishop of Victoria, aboard the *John L. Stephens*, setting sail on August 1. Ultimately, Hearst reached the Isthmus of Panama. After braving the Panamanian jungle and reaching the Caribbean, Hearst took a ship to New York City. His first time in Gotham, Hearst visited his friend J. B. Dickinson and took a trip to Niagara Falls before boarding a train to Missouri. After ten years, George Hearst was going home.[29]

— 4 —

CIVIL WAR

(1860–1862)

> I believe there is a certain equilibrium always kept up. Look at the war,
> for instance, no man had anything to do towards bringing that on,
> and no man stopped it. It was inevitable.
> —George Hearst

As the train pulled into the St. Louis station, Hearst must have been amazed. It had been a decade since he'd been in St. Louis, and the city had grown up in his absence. The population was 160,000, rivaled in his experience only by New York City. To determine why the city had grown so, all Hearst had to do was glance at the riverfront. St. Louis was crowded with boats, with some bows touching the shoreline but many docked two or three deep. In fact, more than three thousand boats landed annually in St. Louis. The reason was its central location on the Mississippi River, a natural hub between St. Paul and New Orleans. The mouth of the Missouri River was also nearby, and for steamboats along the Ohio River, St. Louis was an important destination.[1]

Glancing east toward the Mississippi River, Hearst could observe the grand sweep of progress. Just as the Capitol Building in Washington, D.C., was under construction, the cupola of St. Louis's Old Courthouse was being replaced by an Italian Renaissance–style cast iron dome, meant to mirror those of the Capitol and St. Peter's Basilica in Vatican City. A new sort of people also dominated the neighborhoods. Though most of Missouri was rural, St. Louis was a bustling metropolis, imbued with the Northern values of mercantilism and abolitionism. Additionally, St. Louis was home to a large population of German Americans, many of whom had fled Germany after the Revolution of 1848. Contrary to the slaveholding beliefs held by many rural Missourians, the "forty-eighters" were staunch abolitionists. All in all, half the population of St. Louis was of German descent.[2]

From St. Louis, Hearst rattled southwest, reaching the St. Clair depot on September 1, 1860. There he was greeted by his old friend James Inge. Inge informed Hearst of the sad financial state of his farm. Hearst had been betrayed. The good country doctor William N. Patton, whom Hearst had believed was "sterling" and "honest," had bequeathed the farm to his heirs before dying in 1857. Hearst and Inge stopped in Franklin County so that Hearst could begin attempting to pry his childhood home away from the doctor's heirs. He also called on several women, doubtless boasting of his great success in the Wild West.[3]

In Crawford County Hearst finally visited his mother. Hearst had presents with him, and though they were likely appreciated, no gifts from the West could help Elizabeth. Afflicted with tuberculosis, she was suffering badly. Hearst determined to stay at least until she passed and until the lawsuits over the farm were settled. When not at her bedside or speaking to lawyers, Hearst stayed with Inge and visited friends. At one point he acquired a horse and buggy and took Josephine Renfro to the county fair at Union, Missouri.[4]

Marriage was on Hearst's mind. A letter sent to him by J. B. Dickinson mostly concerns his Virginia City operations, but the last paragraph demonstrates that Hearst had confided in his friend his desire to marry:

> New York
> October 17/60
>
> My dear George,
>
> I duly received your letter a few days ago since and much regret to hear that your mother's health is so bad, and trust it may yet prove that your fears have made you look on the gloomy side.
>
> My last date from San Francisco is Sept. 22 by pony. Lent is still at Washoe. He says Central is greatly improving. They are taking out considerable quantity of the richest kind of ore—have the long tunnel in now, 900 ft., and expect next to advise that it is in the lead.

The crushing and stamping mill is completed. They have made a contract to reduce 4 tons per day by the Veitch process. The parties to be ready to commence in sixty days; they are to pay $60 per hours.

He says the Gould & Curry is a better mine than the Ophir and in less than a year will sell for more. The mining is improving daily—the quantity of metal is increasing. . . . In another letter they speak of the suit against the Ophir as "Black Mail suit" that . . . amount to nothing—they do not mention anything about the suit against the Gould & Curry. . . . I am inclined to think it is only to level Black Mail—that it will not amount to anything.

I am sorry to hear you have the Blues—that won't do—you must cheer up. We shall send you papers, and hope you will be able to get this way and spend a part of your time. I showed your letter to Mrs. Dickinson, she said tell Mr. Hearst I will introduce him to a young lady that will suit him when he comes here—she told me who, and I am inclined to think well of it.

With my best wishes, I remain, my Dear George,

Yours most truly,
J. B. Dickinson

In February 1861, Joe Clark sent him a letter. Like Hearst, Joe was trying to find a wife: "Girls—I don't know if I ever will marry in that country. I am greatly in love with a pretty girl of Carson." Joe also mentioned, "I am in favor of secession."[5]

Clark was safe enough in sending the letter, protected by nearly two thousand miles of desert and mountains. But most of Missouri was divided on the issue of secession, and as tensions heated up, speaking one's mind could have consequences. To friends out west, Hearst claimed neutrality. He was neither for or against secession. Most Southerners, however, were much more fervent in their beliefs.

The issue dividing the country was slavery. Many forward-minded Missourians considered their brand of slavery less barbaric than slavery on Southern plantations, but the reality was still a cruel life. Being "sold down the river" was a constant threat, and even in St. Louis—which had a small population of free blacks and an African American church—depravity and violence frequently erupted. William Wells Brown, an escaped St. Louis slave, recalled his fellow slaves being taken out into the streets and beaten. In 1824 a resident of St. Louis issued a public objection to the "shocking spectacle" of an enslaved woman dragging around her manacles as she crawled about the floor of her master's house. Fifteen years saw little change. In 1839 William Eliot, the founder of Washington University and a minister, witnessed his neighbor's slave being flogged by her owner while hanging by her thumbs.[6]

Outside Missouri, the issue was much more contentious. Since the Missouri Compromise, an uneasy truce had existed between proslavery and abolitionist forces: for every slave state admitted to the Union, a free state had to be admitted soon after, keeping a legislative balance of power in Washington. But a year after gold was discovered in California, President Zachary Taylor revealed himself to be a Free-Soiler, driving Congress to admit California as a free state without admitting another territory as a slave state. This engendered a series of individual laws that came to be called the Compromise of 1850, wherein California entered the Union as a free state and the Fugitive Slave Act was amended in favor of Southern slaveowners. To wit, all escaped slaves were to be tracked down, even across state lines, and returned to their masters.[7]

Adding further fuel to the fire was the *Dred Scott v. Sanford* case. Scott, born into slavery in Virginia, had traveled in 1837 with his master, Dr. John Emerson, into the free state of Illinois and Wisconsin Territory, where he married Harriet Robinson. In 1840, when Emerson was ordered by the army to Jefferson Barracks, just south of St. Louis, he leased Scott and his wife out for profit. Missouri precedent was that a slave who had lived for some time in a free state would continue to be free. But before resorting to the courts, Scott attempted to purchase his wife. Irene Emerson—her husband John having died—refused the $300 he had raised. Finally, in 1846, Scott sued Emerson for his freedom, his wife's freedom, and the freedom or their child, Eliza. Initially, Scott lost the case due to a technicality: he hadn't sufficiently proved he had been enslaved by Irene Emerson.

Scott fought for his freedom, first against Emerson and then against John Sanford, who had purchased him, until a final decision was reached in 1857. With this case, initially tried in St. Louis's Old Courthouse, Missouri was once again the center of the storm. Ultimately, after the U.S. Supreme Court took up the case, Scott lost in a 7–2 decision. Chief Justice Roger B. Taney espoused that black Africans were wholly "inferior, that they had no rights which the white man were bound to respect; and that the negro might justly and lawfully be reduced to slavery for his benefit." The decision fomented further hostility between North and South.

Further turbulence occurred along the Kansas–Nebraska border. If the Missouri Compromise had cracked in 1850, Stephen Douglas's 1854 Kansas-Nebraska Act shattered it. Douglas believed the question of slavery should be determined by popular sovereignty. The people of the territories of Kansas and Nebraska themselves would settle the question by voting for their representatives. "Bleeding Kansas" was the result. Antislavery Free-Staters from the East and proslavery Border Ruffians, most of whom hailed from northern Missouri, streamed into Kansas to try to tip the balance of power, causing violent clashes. John Brown and his sons, some of the most vehement abolitionists, created a focal point of rage by murdering five proslavery farmers with broadswords in what became known as the Pottawatomie Massacre. A further precursor to war was John Brown's Raid, in October 1859. He and his companions stormed the U.S. arsenal at Harpers Ferry, Virginia, to seize weapons they would need to liberate the Southern slaves. The incident ended with Brown's capture by Colonel Robert E. Lee and his execution.

The final catalyst to war was the election of 1860. When Abraham Lincoln defeated John Bell, John C. Breckenridge, and Stephen Douglas to win the White House, South Carolina had already been on the verge of secession. To the Palmetto State, this was the last straw. South Carolina officially seceded on December 20, 1860. The next to secede was Mississippi, on January 9. The next day Florida followed suit, and the day after that Alabama broke away as well. January 19 saw Georgia leave the Union. A week later it was Louisiana. On February 1, Texas added its immense size to the Confederacy, formed in early February.

Much of rural Missouri favored secession. But to the north, in the metropolises of St. Louis and Westport (present-day Kansas City), the Stars and Stripes proudly waved. During the election of 1860, Missouri had voted for Democrat Stephen Douglas, with only 10 percent of the vote going for Lincoln. But that 10 percent had come primarily from St. Louis, a city of immeasurable economic and strategic importance. Missouri, a slaveholding state and a border state, was also surrounded on three sides by Union states. Furthermore, whoever controlled Missouri would have access to its saltpeter mines, from which ammunition could be manufactured. In short, both Abraham Lincoln and Jefferson Davis needed Missouri on their side.[8]

But even as the country tore itself asunder, life in Franklin County went on. Invited to a picnic, Hearst determined that he would make the most of it and succeeded in accomplishing his twin goals in Missouri: spending time with his mother and courting a suitable young lady. Hearst invited twenty or thirty friends to the picnic and, to his mother's horror, hired a special carriage for the occasion. Clarence Greathouse recalled that Elizabeth "remonstrated him for his extravagance, but he told her he could stand it. . . . It was during this visit that he met his future wife, Miss Phoebe Apperson."[9]

In the spring of 1861, Phoebe Elizabeth Apperson was eighteen years old. For a country girl, she was well educated, and she had put her education to use. Recently she had graduated from teaching farm children to working as a schoolteacher at the Meramec Iron Works in St. James, thirty miles from the Apperson house. Phoebe was as intelligent as she was pretty. Buxom, dark-eyed, and brown-haired, with an oval face, Phoebe had her share of suitors. One such was Newton Crow, a Crawford County farmer and stock raiser who, when calling on Phoebe, dressed to impress. Recalled Randolph Apperson, "Newt Crow, who lived over there on the Meramec River . . . dressed in store clothes, high boots, a spur on each heel—and a rooster feather in his hat, just to see my Phoebe. He just looks killing!"[10] But it was plain-clothed George Hearst who struck Phoebe's fancy.

Phoebe's parents, however, thought Hearst too old: at forty years old to her eighteen. But Phoebe likely thought him experienced, capable of showing her the world. A poem she wrote to her best friend, Susan Ellen Patton (daughter of William Patton, who had willed away the Hearst farm), describes a young lady who yearns for more—and perhaps a secret suitor.

> Oh! heaven is where no secret dread
> May haunt love's meeting hour

Another reads:

> Few and by still conflicting powers
>   Forbidden here to meet,
> Such ties would make this life of ours
>   To fair for aught as fleet.[11]

One of Phoebe's biographers, Judith Robinson, uncovered hints that Hearst might have also looked seriously at Susan Ellen Patton as a suitable wife and may have even proposed. If so, it is odd that Phoebe would confide her love poetry to Susan Ellen. Whatever the case, after the picnic, Hearst began pursuing Phoebe more earnestly.[12]

Unable to meet her at the Apperson home, Hearst began to call on Phoebe at the Iron Works. Before long, he was calling on her three times a week. Oftentimes Hearst stopped at the home of Dr. Alexander Gibson in Steelville, not far from St. James. Gibson recalled that Hearst visited him so often that citizens of Steelville began to suspect he and Hearst were organizing a chapter of the Golden Circle, a secret society hoping to expand the Confederacy into Latin America. In fact, Hearst and Gibson were discussing a different campaign: how best to win Phoebe's heart.[13]

But strife interrupted the courtship. Hearst's mother was dramatically worsening. In response to a letter Hearst had written in the spring of 1861, J. B. Dickinson wrote, "I am sorry to hear that your mother is so low. It must indeed be a great comfort to her to have you near her." On April 1, 1861, Elizabeth Collins Hearst looked up from her sickbed and said to her son, "George, I will meet you in heaven." These were her last words before she died. Dutifully, Hearst buried her beside his father, brother, and sister. The same month, the South Carolina militia fired upon Fort Sumter, outside Charleston. The Civil War had begun. On April 17, within a week of Fort Sumter's capture by the Confederacy, Virginia joined the war on the side of the South.[14]

Initially, the Union seized the advantage in Missouri. In late April, General John Pope captured the Mississippi River strongholds of Island Number Ten and New Madrid, Missouri, imprisoning five thousand Confederates, 158 cannons, and a trove of war supplies—all without losing a single Union soldier. But the question of whether Missouri would declare for the Confederacy or Union was still unanswered.[15]

The answer came in the first two weeks of May. Secretly favoring secession was Missouri's newly elected governor, Claiborne Fox Jackson, a Border Ruffian who had participated in Bleeding Kansas. Jackson, a former Missouri state senator, had claimed to be anti-secession during the election but was actually plotting to tip Missouri to the Southern cause. Jackson quickly realized that the key to Missouri was its munitions, both in Franklin County and St. Louis.

Acting quickly, Jackson ordered an increase of production at the Saltpeter Cave Munitions Plant, near the old Hearst farmstead. Simultaneously, he called on Confederate sympathizers to bear arms. This divided Franklin County, but not in the way Jackson had anticipated. Of the sixty-seven hundred men from Franklin County who ultimately fought in the Civil War, only seven hundred supported the South. Rather than the Confederacy, it was the Union that seized control of the Saltpeter Cave Munitions Plant.[16]

More dramatically, St. Louis was home to the U.S. arsenal on South Broadway, three miles from the Old Courthouse and across the street from where Anheuser-Busch would one day build its distillery. Inside the arsenal lay sixty thousand muskets, forty-five tons of gunpowder, a million cartridges, and forty cannons. It was by far the greatest stash of weaponry inside a slave state. If the

Missouri Militia took the arsenal, they could outfit an army. From there, they could conceivably launch an invasion of their own.

Missouri senator Frank P. Blair, however, saw through Jackson. Recognizing that the arsenal's commander, Major William H. Bell, was in cahoots with Jackson, Blair relieved Bell of command, replacing him with Captain Nathaniel Lyon. By the end of April, Lyon had spirited most of the arms and munitions across the river to Illinois and outfitted seven thousand pro-Union volunteers, whom he personally commanded.

Almost a week after the Civil War began with the bombardment of Fort Sumter, on April 23, Jackson showed his true colors. "To attain a greater degree of efficiency and perfection in organization and discipline," he ordered the pro-secession Missouri Militia to establish a camp. Camp Jackson was thus formed outside St. Louis, presided over by Confederate brigadier general Daniel Frost. Two weeks later, on May 6, Arkansas joined the Confederacy as well.

By then Camp Jackson was gearing up to attack the arsenal and seize whatever munitions were left behind. Hearing of this, Lyon struck first, surrounding Camp Jackson with his seven thousand troops. Rather than fight, Frost surrendered. But while Frost's men were being marched under guard to the arsenal, enraged secessionists began throwing rocks at Union soldiers and shouting, "Damn the Dutch!" The Union soldiers responded with gunfire, and by the time the shooting stopped, twenty-eight civilians had been killed, seventy-five wounded. Among the dead were women and children. The effect on the populace was to deepen anger and resentment, particularly against German Americans.

Southerners depicting German Americans as "Hessians" and "mercenaries" became commonplace throughout the Civil War. Southerners were fighting for a noble cause, for their homeland, the message went; the ignoble Germans, who had fled their homes, were fighting for money, just as they had during the Revolutionary War while fighting for the British. Later on, Virginian Mary Stribling remarked, "It is nothing when they have only the dregs of society and those foreigners whose lives are not valuable to the Yankees." Nor were godly men immune to demonizing their German brothers. Georgia Methodist bishop James O. Andrew sneered at these one-time "inmates of foreign poor houses and prisons . . . the scum and offscourings of foreign lands." The tactic further pitted Missourians against each other. In many ways, Missouri served as both a battlefield and a microcosm of the Civil War.[17]

Further outrage for Missourians occurred on June 22, 1861, when *Harper's Weekly* published an illustration of Union general Winfield Scott's Anaconda

Plan. Scott, who wished to minimize casualties, thought the best way to subdue the South without creating a bloodbath was to blockade Southern ports, seize control of the Mississippi, and march an army through Missouri into Arkansas. The most terrifying aspect of the *Harper's Weekly* article was the illustration. In it, a great snake was seen constricting the South, with the head of the snake slithering through eastern Missouri.

By the time of the South's first major victory, at the Battle of Bull Run on July 21, North Carolina and Tennessee had joined the Confederacy, bringing the count of seceded states to eleven. The quick actions of Senator Blair and Captain Lyon had ensured that Missouri remained in the Union, but it remained a war zone. More than 130,000 Missourians ultimately fought in the war: more than 100,000 for the Union and at least 30,000 for the Confederacy. The political picture grew even more tense when Union general John C. Frémont, speaking in St. Louis on August 30, declared martial law.[18]

Living only sixty miles from St. Louis, Hearst was certainly safer than he would have been had Jackson's plan to attack the arsenal come to fruition. Of the hundreds of battles fought in Missouri, few ever threatened Franklin County. All Hearst needed to do was keep a low profile. He had enough to keep him occupied, battling Dr. Patton's heirs for the farmhouse and continuing his courtship of Phoebe. But Hearst had never learned to keep to himself. He was outspoken and, though not a fighter, had always been a leader. Above all, he was a risk-taker. The greatest threat he faced was himself.

So it was that in August or early September 1861, Hearst was arrested in St. Louis for sedition. After his release, Hearst sent word to his friends in Nevada City. The *Nevada City Morning Transcript* printed the following on September 12:

We learn that a letter has been received in this city from Mr. George Hearst, dated in St. Louis, Missouri, in which he says he was placed under arrest by the Federal authorities of that place, on account of alleged seditious language. In former letters written by him, Mr. Hearst represented Missouri as an intolerable place for a neutral man to live in. Indeed such a thing as neutrality was out of the question, neither Unionists or Secessionists allowing a man to occupy neutral ground. He must be for them, else he is against them. Mr. Hearst, it appears, expressed opinions in St. Louis deemed seditious by the authorities there, and hence his arrest. In giving vent to his opinions, he probably did not realize the effects of martial law, as he never before witnessed the workings of that institution. Mr. Hearst, as our citizens well know, is anything but a bad or dangerous man, and we hope he will be allowed to return to Washoe, where he can employ his time more profitably than with politics.[19]

Although Hearst could count on the support of the *Nevada City Morning Transcript*, any newspaper in martial law Missouri with a pro-Southern slant was subject to harsh consequences. Early in the war, the U.S. army suppressed the *St. Louis State Journal* and arrested editor Joseph W. Tucker for pro-Confederacy reporting. The *New York Times* had no sympathy for Tucker or the *Journal*, determining that "the chief Western organ of the Southern conspirators [had] given itself up to stimulating the mob of St. Louis to sedition and bloodshed, and inaugurating the reign of anarchy in the city and state." Federal troops also padlocked newspapers in the Missouri towns of Osceola, Platte City, Oregon, Washington, and Warrensburg; destroyed the offices of the *Girardeau Eagle*; and shut down the *Hannibal Evening News*. Mark Twain later reflected that he had fled Hannibal one step ahead of Colonel Ulysses S. Grant and the Twenty-First Illinois Infantry.[20]

Along with having to keep his thoughts to himself, mining was also off-limits to Hearst. In early to mid-October, Confederate brigadier general M. Jeff Thompson—the Rebel commander in southeast Missouri—marched with about fifteen hundred men to the mining region around Fredericktown, ninety miles south of Franklin County. Thompson's goal was to create a distraction, allowing Major General Sterling Price and the Missouri State Guard the opportunity to escape a large Federal force sent from St. Louis after Price's victory at Lexington. Thompson certainly created a distraction, severing the integral Ironton railroad from Missouri's mines to St. Louis and seizing sixteen thousand pounds of lead. The ore was promptly sent south.

What followed was the Battle of Fredericktown, climaxing on October 21. Most of the action took place in a cornfield just outside Fredericktown, where the Confederates attempted to attack from concealment. The Seventeenth Illinois Infantry and the First Indiana Cavalry weren't so easily fooled. The end result was a Union victory. Of the fifteen hundred Confederates, twenty were killed, forty wounded, and eighty captured. The Union dead totaled seven, with sixty-one wounded.[21]

The Union soldiers were incensed, not just over the loss of life but over the belief that local residents of Fredericktown had helped the Confederates. Before the commanders could restore order, seven homesteads had been burned in retaliation. If Hearst was willing to listen, there was a message there. Unless he was willing to be shot, the mining regions were forbidden.

If Hearst was desirous to immediately return west, there were two major obstacles. One was securing a pass to travel through Union lines to New York City, to take ship to Panama and another up to San Francisco. The other was the Great Western Flood.

The *Nevada City Democrat* reported that local Indians, fearing floods, had warned white people that "the water would be higher than it has been for 30 years, and pointed high up on the trees and houses where it would come." The Indians then left for the Sierra Nevada foothills.[22]

It was as the Indians predicted. For roughly three months, between November 1861 and January 1862, Washington Territory, Oregon, and California saw more rain than they had seen in a lifetime. The cause wasn't an El Niño. Instead, it was a series of atmospheric rivers, each one containing as much water as the Mississippi River. Over the course of those three months, California was hit by fifteen atmospheric rivers. Los Angeles recorded thirty-five inches of rain, which washed away settlements and drowned thousands of cattle. At one point, the Los Angeles River, the San Gabriel River, and the Santa Ana River merged, creating one great mouth. In January alone, San Francisco recorded twenty-five inches of rain. Anglers could catch freshwater fish on Market Street. Hardest hit was Sacramento, built dangerously close to the confluence of the American and Sacramento Rivers. On January 10, the newly elected governor, Leland Stanford, was inaugurated in California, accessing the Governor's Mansion through a second-story window after being transported there in a rowboat. The roughly thirty thousand people living in Sacramento largely abandoned the city. On January 22, the state legislature did so as well, convening in San Francisco for the next eighteen months.

In the Central Valley, many small towns, encampments, and shantytowns filled with Chinese laborers were completely obliterated. Large brown lakes formed throughout California; some even covering stretches of the Mojave Desert. The *Sacramento Daily Union* estimated that one-third of all taxable value in the state was lost. Many people lost all their belongings; everything they had squirreled away over the years washed away. Nor was the Washoe area immune. Virginia City and Carson City each recorded nine inches of rain, and Carson Valley turned into one great lake. To Hearst, the thought of trading the Civil War for the Great Western Flood might have seemed like a choice between Scylla and Charybdis.[23]

Letters from Bill Lent illustrated that though Hearst's finances were far from underwater, they weren't what they had been. Lent wrote that a man had come inquiring about Hearst's stock in the Gould & Curry, now that Hearst had become "an officer in the Confederate Army." Hearst hadn't, but Lent did not know that and panicked. The next day Lent sold some of Hearst's mining interests for $2,750. The next letter Hearst sent calmed the issue. A few months later Lent wrote to Hearst that he felt his letters were being tampered with—someone was working to paint Hearst as a Rebel to take advantage of his Virginia City mining interests. It seemed to be working. Lent also encouraged Hearst to sell all his stock in mining and buy bonds: "I am sick of mining and I am disposing of my stock as soon as possible. . . . It is hard to be poor, you are now rich and should take the advantage of it and place yourself in a position that you cannot be in danger of depending on any man."[24]

Certainly, it seemed Lent was not a man to be depended on. But Hearst determined he would wait it out. In the meantime, Hearst received a letter from Johnson's Island Military Prison in Ohio, sent by his cousin William Hearst, urging George to speak on behalf of his freedom:

> My dear Cousin,
>
> I received your kind address of the 2nd of which gave me much satisfaction to learn your whereabout and that you were well and doing well. I was much pleased with the great sympathy that you expressed for me while in my present and unfortunate condition. I am quite indebted to you for tendering your services in behalf of my release. You might accomplish something by getting those influential Amer of St. Louis of whom you spoke to exert their influence in behalf of my release. The time of intercession may have passed. I know not but should it be agreeable with you I hope you will converse with some of them upon this subject when an opportunity is afforded you. . . . I was quite glad to learn you were successful while in California. . . . I remain your cousin, William Hearst[25]

Nearly six hundred miles southwest of Johnson's Island, the fight for the Hearst farm was finally settled. Hearst won the battle in the district court but lost the war. In a compromise in 1862, his so-called friends James Halligan and James N. Inge were granted title to the land while Hearst was given $1,000.[26]

Hearst had been living in Missouri since the fall of 1860. In that time his mother had died, he had been arrested for sedition, his friends had stolen his family farm, he had lived through martial law, he had failed to secure his cousin's release from prison, and he had seen the country dissolve into war. But there was one bright spot in an otherwise bleak year and a half. Phoebe had agreed to marry him.

Randolph and Drusilla reluctantly agreed to the marriage. They still felt Hearst was too old for their daughter, but they were pragmatic enough to realize at this point they could not stand in the way. Their daughter wanted the marriage as much as Hearst. One additional benefit was that Hearst had agreed to a premarital contract. Phoebe would receive fifty shares of the Gould & Curry Gold and Silver Mining Company should Hearst die before her. Should Phoebe die first, which was unlikely, the shares would revert to Hearst.[27] It wasn't very romantic, but it was practical, fitting with their personalities.

Now all they needed was to get married and get the hell out of Missouri.

On June 14, 1862, Hearst and Phoebe went to the Steelville Courthouse, forty miles south of Franklin County, to have the stock contract drawn up. The next morning they met at the house of Captain Abraham Jefferson Seay on Steelville's Main Street. Seay had enlisted as a private in the Thirty-Second Missouri Volunteer Infantry, seeing action in the battle of Pea Ridge. Despite Seay being a Republican, Hearst and Seay were friends. It was in his house that the Reverend W. P. Renick, a Presbyterian minister, married the couple. It was a simple affair. None of Hearst's or Phoebe's relatives were present, and Phoebe wore a dress she herself had sewn.

The newlyweds stayed in Missouri for one more month, trying to secure passage to San Francisco. Hearst ultimately tracked down his old teacher, Dr. Silas Reed, working at a military hospital in St. Louis. Reed helped him arrange passage to New York City. Hearst also secured a passport that allowed him to travel through Union lines. In October the couple reached New York City and boarded the *Ocean Queen*, bound for the Isthmus of Panama by way of the Chagres River on the Caribbean. At the Pacific Ocean, they boarded the steamship *Sonora*, renting a first-class cabin.[28]

On deck, the Hearsts met Helen Peck and her three children: Helen, Janet, and two-year-old Orrin. Because Phoebe appeared seasick, the older Helen graciously brought Phoebe tea. The two struck up a lively conversation. By the time the *Ocean Queen* reached San Francisco Bay at 10 P.M., November 6, 1862, the two had become fast friends. Promising to visit often, Helen could offer tips on motherhood, for the truth was that Phoebe was not seasick. She was four months pregnant.[29]

—PART II—
THE GAMBLER

Luck is a very thin wire between survival and disaster,
and not many people can keep their balance on it.
—Hunter S. Thompson

— 5 —

DEAD SURE

(1862–1866)

I had rather live on pork and beans than answer such despairing letters and
if I am the cause of it, it must and shall be stopped.
—George Hearst

San Francisco in 1862 was still recovering from the Great Western Flood. The lights
of the gas lamps could be seen reflecting in mud puddles. But to Phoebe Hearst,
San Francisco must have looked magical. The gold rush had made San Francisco
possibly the most diverse city in the world, with Germans, Irish, Scots, British,
French, Italians, Russians, Chinese, American Indians, Spaniards, Mexicans,
Chileans, Australians, and a smattering of free blacks. The Comstock Lode had
made San Francisco one of the wealthiest cities in the world. Monterey Street
was lined with high-end shops, including Davidson's Department Store, where
Hearst bought Phoebe seven new dresses. All in all, thirty thousand men and
five thousand women called San Francisco home. It was a bustling, booming city,
and the Civil War was far, far away.[1]

Immediately, George and Phoebe rented rooms in the luxurious Lick House.
For all its splendor, Phoebe was most impressed by the ladies' parlor. For the rest
of her life, she could describe it in minute detail. Next the Hearsts moved to the
elegant but quieter Stevenson House. But it was Russian Hill that caught Phoebe's
eye. "That's where I should like to live," Phoebe told her husband. Initially she

was disappointed. Shortly afterward, George bought their first home, made of solid brick, on Rincon Hill.

Ten months after the wedding, on April 29, 1863, Phoebe delivered a healthy boy. They named him William Randolph Hearst. William was for George's father, William G. Hearst. Randolph was for Phoebe's father, Randolph W. Apperson. To baby Willie, Hearst sang "Oh! Susannah," which, with changed verses, had become the unofficial song of the forty-niners:

I sailed from Salem City with my washpan on my knee.

I'm going to California, the gold dust for to see.
It rained all day the day I left, the weather it was dry.
The sun so hot I froze to death, oh brothers, don't you cry!

Oh, California, that's the land for me.
I'm going to San Francisco with my washpan on my knee.

Phoebe's parents and brother—Randolph, Drusilla, and Elbert Apperson— decided to visit San Francisco in 1863, having fled Missouri and the Civil War. Not long after their arrival, the Appersons settled roughly fifty miles southeast of San Francisco in rural Santa Clara Valley. Both Randolph and Drusilla became prominent members of the Cumberland Presbyterian Church.[2]

While the Appersons were busy re-creating their religio-agrarian lives in Santa Clara, Hearst created a new identity for himself in San Francisco, that of a race-track owner. Signaling a lifelong passion for horse racing, in 1863 Hearst became the chief investor in the Bay View Park racetrack, five miles south of his Rincon Hill home. Located between Hunters Point and Candlestick Point, adjacent to the San Bruno Turnpike, the Bay View Park racetrack offered San Franciscans a welcome diversion. Naturally, Hearst spared no expense. Noted the *San Francisco Directory*, "A large and spacious hotel, with stables and outhouses attached, has been added, including the judge's stand and all modern improvements. . . . A beautiful shell road is being built from near the Mission to the Park, about three miles in length, and will cost probably $30,000."[3]

The track itself was egg-shaped and considered very fast. The who's who of San Francisco gravitated to Bay View Park, not just to bet on the ponies but to mix with different sets of people. There they could hobnob with the elite and rub shoulders with the salt of the earth. Those who met Hearst—turfman, hotelier, miner, and Missourian—realized in a flash that he belonged to both sets.

More than anything, Hearst was an adventurer. Once again, he looked toward Nevada to make another fortune. But family took precedent. Before leaving for Virginia City, Hearst hired Irish Catholic Eliza Pike as a governess to help with Willie's education. Eliza also had the duty of wet nurse, breastfeeding Will until he was fourteen months old. Willie, however, preferred his mother to any substitute. Habitually sleeping in his mother's bed, Willie became irritable when his father would return home and displace him. "He was very much put out when his Papa came home," Phoebe wrote, "because he could not sleep with me. I told him when his Papa went away again he could sleep with me. He said, well, he wished he would go."

With Eliza Pike, Phoebe got a little more than she wanted. One day Eliza informed Phoebe that she had taken the baby to church to be baptized by a Catholic priest.

"But Eliza, I am a Presbyterian," Phoebe protested.

"No matter, madam, the baby is Christian."[4]

Once in Virginia City, Hearst saw that the nature of mining had changed. In California, Hearst had experienced the transition from pans and rockers to hydraulic mining, pumps, and crushers. In Virginia City, these inventions had been largely replaced by compressors fitted for diamond-tipped air drills and ventilation shafts, underground rail cars to transport ore, and elevators carrying miners deep into mine shafts. Hearst's financial position had also declined. Although Bill Lent and Joe Clark had tried to keep his investments sound, without Hearst's commanding presence, mining disputes had blossomed into lawsuits. All in all, Hearst lamented that he had lost about $400,000. Clarence Greathouse contended that the figure was $500,000. Though Hearst had once been heir apparent to become the Silver King of the Comstock, other men were poised to seize the throne: William Sharon, James G. Fair, John Mackay, James Flood, Adolph Sutro, William C. Ralston. Even Bill Stewart had a piece of the action.[5]

No amount of prospecting improved Hearst's position. The wealth of the Comstock was concentrated, and the new Silver Kings seemingly owned it all. Hearst was undeterred. As he had done so many times in California, he sought out new ventures. One was in Nevada's Reese River district, 150 miles east of Virginia City. In 1862 William Talcott, a former Pony Express rider, had been tracking lost ponies in the Toiyabe Mountains when he discovered a ledge of what looked like silver. Dubbing the site Pony Canyon, Talcott showed the ledge to a nearby rancher named O'Neill, who took some of the ore and had it assayed in Virginia City. The ore contained iron, copper, antimony, and traces of silver. The town of Austin was soon platted, and the rush for the Reese River district commenced. Hearst invested in mid-1863, becoming president of the Lander Silver Ledge Company.[6]

Coincidentally, around the time Virginia City prospectors were shouting "Ho! For Reese," another former Pony Express rider, Johnny Moss, discovered silver in a different canyon. This was El Dorado Canyon, four hundred miles southeast of Virginia City. In that inhospitable stretch of desert—midway between Fort Mojave in Arizona Territory and present-day Las Vegas, Nevada—Hearst, Lent, and Levi Parsons invested in five mining claims. These included the Queen City Mine, the Wall Street Mine, and the Techatticup Mine. Another was the Moss Mine, of indeterminate value.[7]

But Virginia City was where Hearst spent his time carousing. Sticking around, he rubbed shoulders with the *Territorial Enterprise*'s brilliant reporter Samuel Clemens, who went under the nom de plume Mark Twain. The transplanted Missourians became fast friends.[8]

In one Virginia City incident, Twain arrived prematurely to a party at a hotel where Hearst was staying. Twain knew he was underdressed for the occasion, his suits having burned up in a fire. In need, Twain stole into Hearst's room. What Twain found hanging in the closet was a "biled" shirt. Popular at the time, such shirts were white, generally boiled for extra starchiness, with an extravagantly high buttonless collar. Carelessly donning the shirt, Twain went to join the festivities. Sometime later, Hearst appeared, wondering who had robbed him. The moment he noticed Twain's high collar, the mystery was solved. For decades, the pair of jokers delighted in retelling the "biled whitey" story.[9]

Years later Twain, recalling Hearst as his "partner . . . in the days of long ago," described Hearst as a prospector: "It was George's habit to take up a brief residence . . . start a dignified drunk, pack Johnny [Hearst's mule] with bacon, flour, baking powder, and depart at the end of one week to the exact hour, returning to the tunnel he is running to display the glories of his vein to some 'Eastern gent' with thousands."[10] Along with Twain, Hearst rekindled old times with Bill Lent, Cousin Joe, and other mining friends. When he heard that stagecoach driver Hank Monk had made a fool of Horace Greeley—with Greeley commanding Monk to "go quick" and Monk responding by driving at breakneck speed—Hearst suggested they buy Monk a gold watch. Nine others went in on it, purchasing for $1,500 an eighteen-karat gold watch made by San Francisco's S. S. Shreve.[11] The inscription inside the watch case read:

Presented to

Hank Monk

as a testimonial of appreciation of his friends for
his skill and carefulness as a "WHIP."

W. Thompson, Jr.	Alex O'Neil
Joe Clark	John S. Henning
H. P. Wakelee	W. M. Lent
J. O. Earle	Geo. Hearst
W. W. Stowe	H. H. Raymond

"Keep your seat, Mr. Greeley, I'll have you there."

Dec. 1, 1863[12]

Such a gift speaks to Hearst's generous nature, but his time may have been better spent looking over his El Dorado Canyon mining investments. Hearst, Lent, and Parsons had sent H. S. Allen to work the five claims. Allen determined that the Moss Mine was "valueless," and Hearst and his partners sold their one-half interest on his recommendation. But according to the *San Francisco Journal*, "The Moss claim was exceedingly valuable, some of the ore yielding as much as $20,000 to the ton." When Hearst learned that the Moss claim was actually profitable, he sued Allen for fraud.[13]

Though his finances were beginning to look dicey, Hearst still spent money like water. In early 1864, Hearst bought a luxurious house north of Russian Hill, on the corner of Chestnut and Leavenworth Streets, overlooking the bay. Although not quite a mansion, it contained a master bedroom, a greenhouse, a garden, a basement, a bathroom, several guest rooms, and a billiards room, where Hearst enjoyed shooting pool with his friends on a $150 table. The home was an easy mile walk from 712 Montgomery Street, where Hearst and Lent shared an office. But the new house did not usher in marital bliss. In fact, the strain of Hearst's collapsing financial position, and his long absences, caused hardship for both George and Phoebe. Neither was happy when in the spring of 1864, Hearst determined that he would make another stab at winning back the family farm—a journey that could take months.[14]

This time Hearst decided that an overland trip—despite the Civil War still raging—would be more promising than braving the Isthmus of Panama. In spring 1864, war-torn Virginia was the center of the storm. While Grant and Lee ordered armies of Americans against each other, Missouri was mostly quiet. In

Franklin County, Hearst allied himself with Austin Clark, who was still fighting for the family farm, but there was little he could do. On June 25, Hearst threw in the towel, sent Phoebe a telegram, and boarded a westbound train. Phoebe learned that George planned to stop in Virginia City on June 27 and expected to be home June 29 or 30. After reading the telegram, she wrote to Eliza, "I am so lonely I don't know how to live. . . . I am glad he is coming home."[15]

On July 28, 1864—back in San Francisco—Hearst received a letter from Uncle Austin. Beyond sending his love to Phoebe, Will, and Joe, he also asked Hearst to send $306 to continue the fight. Two months later Hearst was in Virginia City, overseeing a lawsuit and likely checking up on the Gould & Curry Mine, whose stock had been depressed among rumors that the bottom had fallen out.[16] To Phoebe, George scribbled a raw letter.

Fascinatingly, the letter was filled with a kaleidoscope of conflicting emotions. In it, Hearst alternately expressed confidence and trepidation regarding the lawsuit. Self-pityingly, Hearst wished that Will would have an easier time in the world than his father—"if he lives"—and then began mulling if their lives would actually be better without material wealth. He sympathized with Phoebe's unhappiness at their long separations, at the same time wishing he could hide away from the world. He professed his love for her while expressing exasperation. With little punctuation and written as one complete paragraph, the letter reads almost as stream of consciousness.

> Virginia, Sept. 14, 1864
>
> My dear wife. This leaves me in great health. . . . I am glad you are having a pleasant time but am sorry you are so low in spirits. I have been very home sick since I have been up here this time at best and [when] those Blue letters come I feel like giving up every thing and letting it all go. We can [go] into some valley and live on beans better. I am shure it will not take much to do me and if the Boy can be edu-cated, should he live, that will be sufficient. He can go in to the world and make his own living. I hope he will have an easier time than I had before I succeeded. I will come home as soon as this case is decided. It is going on first rate and I have no fears of them getting the best of it yet. If it was not well attended too we would loose sure and I have too much in it to loose unless I conclude that I have too much and then I had rather give it to some Hearst people than to have a pack of

thieves have it. As I am here I will do the best I can for this Time, all
though I feel very low spirited and feel just like I would just as soon
be in some out of the way place wherein I could not see any person in
a month as any other way. Just so I had enough of something to eat if
it was only bacon and beans. . . . You are unhappy because I have to
be away looking after what we have and I am not happy for this is no
company here for me and if we had nothing it might be different. If it
was beans we could appreciate we had had and been. If were Happier
we would be glad of it. At all events, I am tired of this way and am
agoing to change, for 200 dollars a year will do me and I had rather
live on pork and beans than answer such despairing letters and if I
am the cause of it, it must and shall be stopped, you can rely on that,
that I am shure. I will stay until this suit is about over. . . . You say
in your letter you are sorry that you are a fool for loving me as you
do. I am sorry you think so. I do not know I had done any thing so
unworthy of your love. I know I am sorry to have done any thing
rong and I am not sorry I love you and hope I never will be . . . but
enough of this. I fear as you say I have wrote too much. But I have
the Blues and feel very bad. As to the Carage, I am glad you got it.
I told you to get it if you wanted. . . . I am going to try after this to
please you, your husband G. Hearst

Kiss the boy for me
I wish I could kiss you for myself
G H[17]

Fortunately, cash-strapped Hearst soon invested in a gold claim much more
substantial and closer to home than the far-flung silver mines. On October 8,
1864, he made a deal with George W. Seaton, a state senator and one of the partners of the Drytown Quartz Mining Company. Outside Drytown, thirty miles
south of Sutter's Mill, Hearst purchased six-tenths of Seaton's interest in the
Seaton Mine for $6,000. It was a good investment, for the mine was bringing up
around twenty tons a day with a value of $50 per ton. The following year Hearst
bought out William Hooper's share, making his share one-twentieth of the entire
operation. Hearst also became principal owner of the nearby Loyal Lead Mine
and the Hearst Claim. Seaton, who had brought in Hearst by selling shares, now
began buying shares from the Ritchmeyer investment group.[18]

In April 1865, Hearst, Seaton, C. H. Bradford, William Thompson Jr., and W. W. Stowe transformed the Drytown Quartz Mining Company into the Seaton Mining Company, with Hearst a major shareholder. Soon the Seaton Mine had a twenty-stamp mill, a boardinghouse, a stable, and a water ditch.[19]

April 1865 proved momentous for other reasons. On April 2, with the fall of Petersburg imminent, Jefferson Davis abandoned Richmond. The following day, Grant seized Richmond. After four bloody years and half a million men dead, the Confederacy was on the verge of collapse. On April 9, Grant surrounded Lee's Army of Northern Virginia at Appomattox, and Lee officially surrendered. The Civil War was nearly over. But the horror was not.

On April 14, while sitting next to his wife, Mary Todd Lincoln, at Ford's Theater, President Lincoln was shot in the head by actor-turned-assassin John Wilkes Booth. News of the president's assassination created a furor around the country, manifesting itself through angry mobs of Unionists. One such mob arose in San Francisco. On the day Lincoln was pronounced dead—April 15, 1865—violent San Francisco rioters destroyed the offices of several Democratic newspapers: the *Occidental*, the *News Letter*, the *Monitor*, and the *Democratic Press*.[20]

Hearst had no way of knowing it, but the destruction of the *Democratic Press* would make an extraordinary difference in his life. Outraged by the destruction, a forty-niner from Virginia named Benjamin Franklin Washington—whose great-granduncle had been President George Washington—resurrected the *Democratic Press* as the *San Francisco Evening Examiner*. The name was likely an homage to the *Richmond Examiner*, whose offices had burned to the ground on the night of April 3, 1865, after Confederates fleeing Richmond had set fire to a tobacco warehouse—intending to keep the goods from Union soldiers—and the fire had spread out of control.

Serving as the four-page paper's editor, Washington published the *Examiner* every evening, except Sunday. An individual paper cost ten cents. A subscription for three months cost $3. A yearly subscription cost $10. The first issue of the *Examiner*, published on Monday, June 12, 1865, was distributed gratis to subscribers of the *Democratic Press*. In that first issue, Washington wrote, "It is a trite, but nevertheless true remark, that the freedom of the press is the palladium of conditional liberty. . . . We expect to make our paper first an exponent of correct principle. In this regard we will speak boldly and fearlessly."[21]

Washington made good his promise to speak boldly through the *Examiner*, though his principles were more aligned to the Deep South than California. As the country began to heal from the nightmare of war, the *Examiner* supported candidates who pledged to vote against emancipation. One such candidate was George Hearst.

By mid-1865, Hearst was looking to expand. Bolstered by the success of the Seaton Mining Company, Hearst also added to his budding empire the Rancho Piedra Blanca, a nearly fifty thousand–acre cattle ranch outside San Simeon, 250 miles from San Francisco. It was there, on Camp Hill, on a rise between the sea and the Santa Lucia Mountains, that Hearst liked to camp. To advance his racing program, he also built barns, stables, sheds, stalls, and a racetrack measuring three-eighths of a mile, the outline of which can still be seen from the air above Piedra Blanca. When copper was discovered nearby, Hearst naturally staked a claim in the Phoenix Mine. A local paper described Hearst and his activities in San Simeon: "He is a man of means and energy and having invested of late in real estate here, and the copper prospects having been brought to his notice, he determined to try his hand. . . . He has six or eight men employed, driving a tunnel, which is being worked night and day." Although the Phoenix Mine proved a bust, Hearst enjoyed Rancho Piedra Blanca.[22]

Phoebe also liked to travel. On July 2, 1865, she wrote Eliza a long letter from her parents' home in Santa Clara:

> I have been out of town four weeks. We are having our house made much larger, it will be yet a month before it is finished. You know me well enough, to know that I will be glad to get home again, although I have been having a very nice time. The first week I was at Ma's . . . I enjoyed the drive over the mountains to Santa Cruz. The scenery is beautiful. I think it is a lovely place. I only stayed two days. The fare at the hotel was so wretched that I could not stand it, baby ate little or nothing, if we had not taken some chicken and crackers with us I don't know what the child would have done. . . . I went to stay there three or four weeks, the place is crowded with people from the City. . . . You will wonder where Mr. Hearst is all this time. He has been on several little trips and the rest of the time in the City. He did not go to Santa Cruz but comes to see us once a week when he is in the City. I am very well this summer. Willie keeps well and fat though he grows tall. He is as brown as a berry and so active and mischievous, he is a very good boy—you have no idea how much he talks. You would be astonished. He seems to understand everything. He often talks of you. He likes his books so much. Can tell you about

Cocky Locky and Henny Penny, knows more of Mother Goose than ever. . . . Grandma has several little kittens. She has given us one, we will take it with us when we leave. . . . Before I came away we had been going out a great deal, there was a splendid operetta troupe at the Academy of Music. We went six or eight nights (not in succession), saw the best operas. I enjoyed it very much. . . . I think we will go to the Sandwich Islands [Hawaii] sometime. It must be a delightful climate, but you know how foolish I am about leaving Mr. Hearst.[23]

With his domestic and financial life more settled, Hearst decided to pursue a political career, becoming a candidate for the California State Legislature.

On the night of September 4, 1865, Hearst spoke at the Democratic Ratification Meeting in Platt's Hall at 216 Montgomery Street in San Francisco. Even the *Examiner* had to admit that Hearst was not impressive: "[Hearst] was no speaker in this kind of place; he might have been on a rock or a log, but not here." In his speech, Hearst claimed that George McClellan had lost the election of 1864 to Lincoln only because of "terrorism at the polls" and urged Democrats to vote in the next election. "If we are successful, all right; if not, we can endure defeat for we have endured it often."[24]

The following day Hearst endured a different sort of defeat: his Bay View Park Hotel burned to the ground. The day after that, a wit for the *San Francisco Chronicle* added insult to injury by making a pun of his name. On page 3 of the *Chronicle*, under the caption "Dead Sure," the reporter quipped, "One of the candidates is not only dead, but *hearsed* (Hearst)."[25]

The election was held mere days later. On September 11, 1865, the supervisors canvassed the election returns. The next day the newspapers announced that George Hearst had officially been made an assemblyman.[26]

As part of the California Legislature, Hearst naturally served on the Committee on Mines and Mining Interests. This required more and more time in Sacramento, keeping him from prospecting. Although George divided his time between San Francisco and Sacramento, Phoebe was pleased. She routinely took the ferry from San Francisco to Sacramento and back, enjoying the voyage as much as visiting her husband. Naturally taking to traveling, Phoebe set her sights on greater horizons.

About a month after the election, disaster struck George W. Seaton, Hearst's chief partner at the Amador Gold Mine and a Democratic ally in Sacramento. On the night of October 12, 1865, the state senator was aboard the steamer *Yosemite* at Rio Vista, sixty miles south of Sacramento, as it made its downward voyage on the Sacramento River, when the boiler burst. The explosion injured forty or fifty people and killed thirteen. George W. Seaton was one of the dead.[27] Moving quickly, Hearst and the other partners capitalized on the tragedy, purchasing from Seaton's widow, Phoebe Seaton, his shares in the company.[28]

On December 6, 1865, Hearst was in Sacramento. The Thirteenth and Fourteenth Amendments—which abolished slavery and granted *all* citizens equal protection under the law—was put to a vote. Hearst voted against the constitutional amendments. Of all the men named George who signed the document, Hearst was the only one to write out his full name. The others all wrote "Geo." The historical implication is that Hearst, a transplanted southerner, was proud of his vote. Irrespective of Hearst's vote, the constitutional amendments were made into law.

In 1866 Phoebe made good her desire to travel to the Sandwich Islands, leaving Willie under the care of his grandmother. Her younger brother, Elbert Apperson, accompanied her. Hearst and a party of friends came down to the dock to wish her good-bye. Together, Phoebe and Elbert explored Honolulu, Hilo, Diamond Head, and the crater of a volcano. Willie enjoyed himself with his grandparents at Santa Clara. Decades later, William Randolph Hearst recalled, "I was devoted to my grandmother [Drusilla] and she thought pretty well of me too—not that I deserved it, because I must have been considerable of a nuisance around the place—but because she was dear and sweet and I was her grandson."[29]

Randolph Apperson also delighted in his grandson, whom he called Prince.

But financial difficulties began to plague the Hearsts. On June 12, 1866, Hearst received a letter informing him that the fire insurance policies on the Bay View Park Hotel had been canceled. On August 21, he was back to prospecting in the wilds of California, 250 miles north of San Francisco in Lewiston. He returned on November 1. "His trip was by no means profitable, he does not think of returning to that rough country," Phoebe wrote Eliza Pike.[30]

That year, financial constraints prompted Phoebe to write in her diary, "I feel that we must live more quietly and be economical. . . . I have sent the horses to Pa's. . . . We have sold the Rockaway [carriage] for two hundred dollars. The coachman goes away tomorrow. By doing this we will save $100 every month."

That Sunday she was forced to miss church. "Have no carriage and the mud is terrible." Two weeks later she hired a carriage, but the wait was dreadful. She missed the "team very much, but I must not complain for we must live according to our means."[31]

Having seen his fortune recede, Hearst determined that he did not want to "live more quietly." He wanted to make another fortune. To that purpose, he did not run again for the California Legislature. Politics could wait. The Wild West would not.

— 6 —

THE GILDED AGE

(1867–1871)

The tendency was to buy today and sell tomorrow.
—George Hearst

By 1867 Hearst and Lent moved into separate offices—Lent at 402 Montgomery Street and Hearst at stone's throw away at California and Sansome Streets—but the two remained friendly. Not a pair to linger in their offices, the Comstock companions ventured seven hundred miles north into Idaho Territory. On May 1, 1867, Lent induced an old friend from New York, James M. Classen, to install a mill on Gold Hill, near a mine Hearst had acquired. Before developing the Pioneer property any further, Lent and Classen collected specimens and asked for Hearst's expert opinion. When Hearst announced he was satisfied with the property's strength, Lent and Classen began purchasing more mines in the area. To Phoebe he wrote on August 29, 1867, that though he thought the area had potential, he was "home sick," that he missed her and "the Boy," and that "life is so short."[1]

In September 1867, Hearst sold his last mining interests in Virginia City.[2] Other than occasional ventures outside California, Hearst stayed close to home, concentrating on his mining interests in Amador County. To the Seaton Mine he added a new forty-stamp mill, powered by a forty-foot waterwheel.

Hearst was able to alleviate Phoebe's lack of companionship by adopting a Scottish daughter. Her name was Alice Booth. Her parents, who were related to friends of Hearst's, had died, and the girl was in need. The adoption was supposed to be temporary—relatives were planning to take her to Canada—but Phoebe thought the Scottish lass would be happier in San Francisco living with them. Phoebe was glad for the company.[3]

In a letter to Eliza Pike written on September 15, 1867, Phoebe described Alice Booth: "Instead of getting a Chinaman we have a girl about 16 years old. She was from Glasgow, Scotland, her mother died four years ago. . . . She has a very good, gentle disposition, is as steady as an old woman but very childlike, has no pert independent ways. . . . She is an exception. . . . Her name is 'Alice Booth,' she is quite pretty, fresh, good face."[4]

Despite the presence of Alice, Eliza, and Willie, Phoebe's loneliness was palpable. On November 20, 1867, Phoebe sent George a lonesome letter from San Francisco:

> My dear husband, I was both surprised and pleased to hear from you
> & very glad to know you were well so far, since that time it has been
> raining here & I fear storming where you are. I feel very lonely. . . .
> Cousin Joe did manage to get out here . . . for dinner Sunday, so stayed
> that night. Why is it that he will not stay with us more; do you know?"[5]

Although Phoebe enjoyed the company of Alice, Eliza, and Cousin Joe, it was Willie who kept the family entertained. It soon became evident that Phoebe and Eliza were having an effect. Before Willie turned five years old, he knew how to spell, could count to one hundred, knew that Sacramento was the capital of California, and had developed a love of learning. Phoebe and Eliza had succeeded in making it a game, something to be enjoyed. Willie was also being groomed to be a man of station. His first riding lesson occurred as a baby, and tutors were hired to teach the boy fencing, drawing, and dancing.[6]

In the meantime, Hearst continued to be active. On March 12, 1868, he was in Sacramento. One week later the California State Assembly authorized Hearst to build a wharf in San Simeon. No one in San Simeon suggested that the timing was more than coincidental. Hearst didn't stick around to draw attention. On March 22, he was seen in Salt Lake City en route to Idaho Territory.[7]

In May 1868, Hearst and the other investors in Rising Star Mine in Owyhee County, Idaho Territory—John Mackay, William M. Lent, Alexander W. Baldwin, and George D. Roberts—were thrilled to learn that the silver found there, 135 miles south by southwest of Lent's quartz mine on Gold Hill, was being hailed as the richest since the Comstock Lode. In July Hearst was there himself. In a letter he groused to Phoebe that they could have gotten by with a mine half the size, reaping greater profits. Hearst ended the letter tenderly: "Kiss the Boy for me. I wish I could kiss you in reality . . . your George"[8]

Doubling down, in August Hearst established with Mackay and John W. Gashwiler the Hearst Silver Mining Company. The capital stock was set at $1.2 million. Three and a half months later, on the last day of November 1868, Hearst also became a trustee to the Golden Chariot Mining Company in Idaho Territory. Ambitions were high. The capital stock was set at $1 million. Shares were valued at $100 apiece. Along with Hearst, James G. Fair also invested. So too did "some of those Comstock fellows," as Hearst recalled. But the Chariot proved no Comstock. In particular, Hearst, Fair, and the others had difficulty smelting the ore that had been assayed so highly. Hearst lost $92,000 on the venture.[9]

Phoebe—writing George from Reading, Pennsylvania, in 1868 while traveling by train with Willie from New York City to St. Louis—lamented the loss. "I am *very sorry indeed* that Death *always* manages to have things his own way—am afraid the *big* Idaho mine will never benefit *us*, I was thinking matters would be different, however it is no use to worry about it."[10]

Regardless of any financial difficulties, the Hearst home was still the place to be. That year, the Hearsts played host to a wedding. The groom was Hearst's first cousin Caleb Bowles. The bride was Phoebe's childhood friend Sue Ellen Patton. Concerning the loss of the family farm (and possibly Hearst's proposal to Patton), all was forgiven though not forgotten.

In January 1869, George traveled to Hamilton, Nevada. On January 30, he wrote Phoebe a letter:

> My dear wife,
>
> I arrived here all well and have been in good health ever since came, eat first rate and am well pleased with the place. But miss you very much. If I could carry you around in my pocket I had just about as soon be here as any place. But you do not know how much I think of you. It is a horable life for me to live without you. I have a good place to sleep in . . . and have as good a time as I could have without you. But this place will not do for you as the cold wind and light atmosphere would be hard for your throat. . . . We would make plenty money. But I do not know that I can stand it to stay here without you.
>
> . . . There are some women here, but Oh, what hard looking ones. . . .

This is a great place for small folks to make money. . . . The whiskey
bars and restaurants are crowded . . . they are taking in piles of gold.
Many persons cannot get a bed and have to set up all night or sleep
in a chair or on a stool and some have no money to get a bed. But no
one need go without money as all can get work that will. But there
is more broken down businesses here than any place I ever saw. But
if they will leave off whiskey and will try, they will make money. . . .

If I don't come out with plenty, you can blame me for it. . . .

Your
George[11]

On February 27, 1869, Hearst and Phoebe registered at Phoebe's beloved Lick
House in San Francisco, Hearst having returned from White Pine County, Nevada,
and Phoebe having returned from Santa Clara Valley, doubtless visiting her
parents and brother. "Eppy," as she referred to her brother Elbert, had become a
problem, being rude to her parents. Phoebe also disliked Bill Lent, considering
him reckless and a drain on their finances. That February, Phoebe wrote Eliza,
"Lent offers to pay up what he owes . . . in old notes and 'wild cat' mining stock. . . .
Lent ought to be sent to the Penitentiary for life." But enjoying themselves at the
Lick House, free of distraction, they could be together. Phoebe greatly desired
another baby, preferring a girl. In a letter to George she wrote, "I am so very sorry
we have no other children. We love babies so dearly. Why we are not blessed I
cannot understand. I have tried to be careful of myself . . . hoping for *something*,
but no change yet. I suppose we must be patient."[12]

With the wolf at the door of their Chestnut Street house, Hearst secured a
$30,000 loan. This he invested in a mine in Kern County, 150 miles east of San
Simeon. The mine proved lucky, yielding $160,000, temporarily replenishing
Hearst's coffers.[13] This put him in contact with two men who had baronial interests in the area: Lloyd Tevis, whom Hearst knew from the Comstock, and his
brother-in-law James Ben Ali Haggin.[14]

Like Hearst, Tevis and Haggin were Southerners who came to California
during the gold rush. Tevis had been born in 1824 in Shelbyville, Kentucky,
350 miles east of the Hearst farmhouse. In 1848 he traded the Bank of Kentucky
for an insurance company in St. Louis and the following year joined the argonauts
heading west. In October 1850, Tevis partnered in a Sacramento law office with new
friend Haggin, who also hailed from the Blue Grass State. The two pivoted from
law to investments, where they demonstrated shrewd talent. In a ten-year stretch

they invested in the California Steam Navigation Company, the Western Union Telegraph Company, the Gould & Curry Mine, the Central Pacific Railroad, and the Union Pacific Railroad. In 1869 Tevis succeeded Leland Stanford as the president of the Southern Pacific Railroad, becoming one of the most affluent and powerful men in California. The following year Tevis was elected vice president and director of Wells, Fargo. Haggin branched out as well, purchasing hundreds of thousands of acres of "desert land" throughout Sacramento, San Joaquin, and the Kern River valley. After Haggin successfully irrigated the land, he sold it for a fortune.[15]

Attracted to Hearst's industry and uncommon mining abilities, Haggin and Tevis agreed to back him. Hearst would seek and purchase new mining claims on their dollar, provided they received a strong percentage. Fellow prospector Asbury Harpending commended Haggin and Tevis on backing Hearst: "Nothing could keep Hearst down in a mining region. Any capitalist was only too eager to back a man with such surpassing talents.[16]

Letters had been pouring in from prospecting friends in Mineral Hill in Eureka, Nevada. Grubstaked by Haggin and Tevis, Hearst set out. By March 1869, Hearst was back in the Silver State.[17]

Charles A. Sumner, a former member of the Nevada State Senate, recounted that he shared a stagecoach with George Hearst, and several other passengers, including Joe Clark and Nevada state senator Samuel Wilson, who would die of a morphine overdose later that year. The stage was bound from Eureka, Nevada, to Pioche, Nevada.[18] Through Sumner's lens, their winter road trip comes into focus.

The wagon set out from Eureka in the snow, with the thermometer reading 30°F in the shade. Sumner recalled seeing rolling hills and a broad valley from the window. There was little else.[19] At 10 A.M., five or six miles away from the mining town of Hamilton, they determined that the road was impassible for the carriage. Hearst, Clark, Wilson, Sumner, and the others transferred to a sleigh while a small party began beating a path through eight inches of snow in "avalanche-ready" conditions. An argument between the passengers and the foreman, whom Sumner described as "slow moving," was headed off by Clark and Wilson, who kept the conversation full of good humor. At noon, the party finally arrived at Hamilton.

At Hamilton they found there was no connecting stagecoach ready for them. They would have to lay over at least a day. The weary passengers were happy to do so. They ate at Barnum Restaurant, popular throughout the mining camps. Sumner marveled that Hamilton was rapidly becoming a ghost town. A few years before, the population of Hamilton had been twelve thousand; now only one in five houses was occupied, "some of them ignominiously going to rack and ruin."

They looked upon the two-story Wells, Fargo building, the $80,000 courthouse, and the Catholic chapel, which had once seated two hundred people every Sunday and now gave a service once every six weeks or so, when an itinerant priest visited.

The next day at noon they set out from Hamilton on a sleigh, passing Treasure Hill, while Clark passed the time telling of his experiences in the nearby Mountain Maid Mine, the Sailor Boy's Delight Mine, and the Queen of the Hills Mine. A burned mill was noted on the side of the road. Afterward they transferred to a mud wagon, then back to a sleigh, which during a steep stretch tipped over and deposited all of them in the snow. No bones were broken, but the sleigh once again tipped as they got started. Sumner then took on an "I mean business" attitude. He took the front of the sleigh and a pioneer took the rear, intent that the sleigh would not tip again. While they engaged in this hard work, Sumner quasi-facetiously noted:

> George Hearst and Senator Wilson did the talking. It is always agreeable to hear rich men converse about their respective biographies when they are at leisure. They love the reminisces for themselves; they love to fondle over their lucky plans; they don't object to have attentive listeners. So it was a pleasant ride from the second overthrow to within six miles of the foot of the descent and the end of the gorge or valley, through which the road passes into the meadows at Washburn's.

They reached the Washburn station by the light of the full moon. There they transferred to a coach, which proved almost as difficult as the sled. During one stretch, the stagecoach driver steered the team up and down slopes where the rock gave way. The passengers felt gravity leave them in the pits of their stomachs. Afterward, Hearst mentioned Horace Greeley. The passengers were set at ease, waiting for Hearst to launch into the famous Hank Monk/Horace Greeley anecdote, when an earthquake seemed to strike the stagecoach. Hearst clamped his mouth shut as the driver yelled, "Slide 'em, Fannie; slide 'em! Hi! Yi!!"[20] Ultimately, the stagecoach reached Washburn's Hotel at 9 P.M. There the stagecoach driver asked if they wanted to stay the night or press on. Sumner noted that, hungry and tired, everyone wished to stay the night: "All except George Hearst. He was glad for more. He was fairly churned into decent candor of confession. As he stretched down he declared that 'this might be for a good sort of thing for a mile or two, but for an all night's business, it would be monotonous.' So the proposition to move on from the station that night instead of laying over, did not meet with decisive favor."

Washburn's Hotel was a single-story structure, resting above the throat of the gorge, made of wood, mud paste, and thatch. After supping, sleeping, and breakfasting, the passengers boarded the coach again. At 8 A.M. they started off. They reached Patterson station around 11 P.M. Sumner recalled:

> Patterson's station is situated within about a mile of the eastern foot of the mountain. We roused the landlord; injudiciously ordered supper; ate heartily, and camped down in close quarters, heads and points, on the barroom floor in true traveler's style.
>
> A chinaman woke us up at five with loud stamping and shrieking announcements for breakfast: "Here! get up; get up, you—! What you sleepee allee day for? Never getee to Pioche. Bleckfast getee allee—cold."[21]

At 7 A.M. they departed for Pioche, reaching the mining town that day.

A few months later, in spring 1869, Hearst backtracked to Treasure Hill in Lincoln County, Nevada, as it began drawing more and more silver-seekers in droves. Among these miners was Johnny "the Buster" Skae, a mining legend whose mansion on San Francisco's Nob Hill was the envy of all. Another was Gashwiler. Bill Lent—who by this time owed Hearst $200,000—was also seen on the slopes of Treasure Hill.[22]

In early March, Hearst established in White Pine the Treasure Box Mining Company with Tevis and A. E. Head. Simultaneously, Hearst formed the Hearst Mining Company in White Pine's Treasure City. John O. Earle, who like Lent had inscribed the Hank Monk watch, was named a trustee. Lent likely had a piece of the action. The *San Francisco Directory* listed Lent's offices at 402 Montgomery Street as headquarters for the Hearst Mining Company in Treasure City. Three weeks later, Hearst was named a trustee of the Independence Consolidated Mining Company, also operating in White Pine. The capital stock was set at $1 million. Shares were valued at $100 each. Shades of the Chariot lode, this proved overly ambitious. But Hearst did not give up. In early June, Hearst was named a trustee to the Bromide Flat Mining Company, also located in White Pine.[23]

Meanwhile, disaster had occurred in Amador County. Though the Seaton Mine processed ten thousand tons of quartz in 1868, profits declined and the company filed bankruptcy. In 1869 it was sued for back taxes and the mine was sold at auction for $97.50. To recoup losses, Hearst began dabbling in San Francisco real estate. On June 9, 1869, he became president of the Nevada Consolidated Blue Gravel Company, once again firming up ties in Nevada City. One week later, on June 16,

Hearst was named a director of the Potrero Homestead Association. Two days after that, Hearst and the eight other directors advertised shares.[24]

One of the main draws—which Hearst was counting on—was the southward improvement supposed to take place on underdeveloped Montgomery Street. Championing "Montgomery Street Straight" were the directors of the Montgomery Street Real Estate Company, Silver King William C. Ralston, and prospector Asbury Harpending, among others. The Potrero Homestead Association's duties included guiding bills through the state legislature, made more difficult by the unpopular plan to level Rincon Hill in the process of expanding Montgomery Street. Although an estimated $35,000 went to the bills' managers, along with $400 to grease assemblymen, the plan was stopped cold when Governor Henry Haight vetoed the measures. As one wag put it, "Montgomery Street Straight" became "an Unpleasant Corpse." Though the southern extension was dead, the following year Ralston managed to extend Montgomery Street to the northwest—which did nothing to help Hearst. All Hearst had to show for his real estate venture was a couple of Potrero lots.[25]

In this manner Hearst lost "all the loose money I had." But a real estate venture Hearst made in 1869 eventually would pay off—ultimately in a manner Hearst never could have envisioned. He rekindled his interest in the San Simeon property, and from Don Juan de Jesus Pico purchased the remaining half interest—an additional five hundred acres. The wharf Hearst had been authorized to construct now extended over the Bay, improving sea trade. Hearst could not imagine what would one day be built on his beloved Camp Hill.[26]

While Hearst was losing money at real estate, he was also suffering bad luck at mining. Hearst's creditors' patience was all but exhausted. On September 27, 1869, Hearst received a letter from an individual in Silver City, Idaho, saying that he owed $550.[27]

On a cloudy November morning he left his wife and six-year-old son for another mining camp—this one in Elko, 150 miles north of Treasure Hill. He did not stay long. After passing through Salt Lake City, where he observed Mormon settlements, Hearst reached Wyoming Territory, where on November 11 he wrote Phoebe, "I had the Blues badly as you felt so when I left. I felt bad all day and thought of you and the Boy often and felt terable, hope you have got over your Blues."[28]

Phoebe too felt lonely but had learned to take her husband's absence in stride. To Eliza, she joked, "You know how fond he is of rocks."[29]

As it turned out, 1870 proved a quiet year for Hearst. Although he established the Mauntauck Silver Mining Company in White Pine and began dabbling in a company that promised to create gas pipes throughout San Francisco, it was San Simeon that drew most of his focus. Hearst opened a lawsuit against Domingo Pujol, whom he accused of cheating him out of 160 acres of land there. By this time, Hearst had acquired 1,340 acres. He wanted to make it an even fifteen hundred acres. The case would drag on for another six years, eventually reaching the Supreme Court of California. It was at this time that Hearst made a lifelong friend, Clarence Greathouse, a lawyer who hailed from Kentucky. Mining claims invited lawsuits, and it was convenient for Hearst to have Greathouse at his beck and call. The money Hearst paid him also made it convenient for Greathouse.[30]

At the same time, though Hearst's business ventures were quiet, his home was becoming wilder and wilder, courtesy of his headstrong son. To interact with children his own age, Willie was sent to a Presbyterian Sunday school and to a private school. As always, Phoebe praised her seven-year-old son. In a letter to George, Phoebe wrote, "We feel very proud of our boy. The teacher has 12 little scholars and says Willie is the favorite of them all. He is such a mimic, sings, dances, plays, so as to much amuse them all."[31]

His teachers' approval did not last long. The mischievous streak that W. R. Hearst displayed throughout his life was developed at a young age. As a boy in San Francisco, Willie and a friend, Fred Moody, skipped a dancing class taught by a Miss Estrada, a friend of Phoebe's. Estrada caught the boys in the garden and irritably ordered them to class. This prompted Willie to stick out his tongue at the teacher.

"I won't go!" Willie declared.

"You bad boy!" retorted Estrada.[32]

Willie capped his offense by turning on the garden hose, deliberately spraying Estrada's afternoon dress with water. He acted even more monstrously toward a Monsieur Gallivotti, who was attempting to teach his class the polka. This was all part of Phoebe's desire to raise her son as a gentleman. The problem was, Willie did not want to be a gentleman; he wanted to be a pirate. As he watched Gallivotti gallivant about the Academie de Danse in dancing pumps, silk stockings, and black silk knee breeches, Willie asked himself, *What would Captain Kidd have done?* The answer came to him: "*Sumpin fierce,*" of course.

Instead of pointing his toes as Gallivotti instructed—one, two, three—*un, deux, trois*—Willie walked into the street. There he picked up a large cobblestone and smashed it through the window of the Academie de Danse. Willie was not invited to return.[33]

Later, Willie incurred the ire of his father by playing an April Fool's Day prank in the home of the Hearsts' friends the Addisons. The Hearsts had been staying with the Addisons on Nob Hill while their Chestnut Street house was being redecorated. Willie had purchased six Bengal lights and, while the family slept, touched them off on tin pie plates.

As the rockets ignited, Willie roused the house by yelling, "Fire!"

The family came running, seeing the red glare under Willie's door. Soon smoke was pouring into the hall, and Willie could hear the adults attempting to batter down the door. Meanwhile the Addisons' cook had raised the alarm. In short order, a fireman with a hose pried the window open and showered Will and the fireworks. Dripping, Willie opened the door. Delighted by the sensation he had caused, he explained that it was all an April Fool's Day prank. Phoebe must have been more relieved than angry, for she issued no lectures. Hearst, however, felt he needed to play the disciplinarian—a difficult part for the old miner, given his gentle demeanor.

"Were you very warm in that room while the fire was going on, Willie?"

"No, Papa, I wasn't warm at all."

"Well," Hearst said, placing the boy across his knee, "you're going to be warmed now, son, where it will do you the most good."[34]

Later in life, W. R. Hearst recalled his early childhood in a "Little Willie" poem:

When Willie was a little boy,
Not more than five or six,
Right constantly did he annoy
His mother with his tricks.[35]

Around the time Willie was seven, Hearst decided to take more of a hand in his son's education. Hearst, who was raised as a hardscrabble pioneer, did not want his son staying in private school indefinitely. It was time Willie learned that life was not one big laugh. Phoebe, on the other hand, worried about what might happen if her "delicate child" enrolled at a public school. One morning over breakfast, Hearst finally put his foot down. "He seems to have more than the usual amount of mis-directed youthful energy. If the public schools are rough-and-tumble they will do him good. So is the world rough-and-tumble. Willie might as well learn to face it."[36]

Soon after, Willie began attending public school. Biographers and newspapermen give differing accounts of which school or schools he attended. The North Cosmopolitan School, the Geary Street Grammar School, the Hamilton Grammar School, and the Lincoln Grammar School are all mentioned. Because the Hearsts moved so often—and because of Willie's tendency to cause mayhem wherever he went—it may well be that he attended each. In grammar school, Willie learned the Spencerian system of penmanship. The future newspaper proprietor dutifully copied down sentences—"Honesty is the best policy" and "Evil communications corrupt good manners"[37]—making sure to shade carefully on the downstrokes and bear lightly on the upstrokes.

Meanwhile, while Phoebe devoted her time and energy to their son, George's reputation suffered. On September 10, 1870, he received from Hamilton, Nevada, a pointed letter from a respected Irish mining engineer and friend, Samuel McMaster, whose operations included mines in South America and Australia. "Where are you, and why have you not answered my letters?" McMaster demanded. Shortly afterward, Hearst was reduced to borrowing.[38]

Although Hearst had suffered losses through real estate and mining, in the spring of 1871 his would-be political career received an uptick when he was appointed a delegate of San Francisco's Second Ward. But a financial boon rather than a short-lived political success was what the family needed.[39]

On May 20, 1871, it was reported that Hearst was made a trustee of the Star Milling and Mining Company in Eureka as well as the Wide West, Blue Star, and other claims.[40] One of these other claims was the Eureka Mine. Hearst describes the contentious purchase of this mine in his memoirs:

When I got over there and looked at the mines I wrote back to San Francisco to these fellows to get some money as I had made a trade for them. It was $400,000 to be paid down, and $600,000 afterwards. We, that is I and my partner, got $80,000 and a piece out of it. This was known as the Eureka mine. I got this mine from a lot of Irishmen, and bought it for myself, Bill Thompson, George Roberts and some others.

Hearst and Thompson had been partners in Virginia City and Amador County. Roberts and he had been close since the days of the Lecompton Mine. But the Eureka Mine did not pan out. Hearst further relates, "I borrowed $40,000 for my part from Haggin. Then those outside got to quarrelling and said we were stealing and I got mad and sold out."[41]

Hearst next traveled to Pioche, 150 miles southeast of Eureka. There he got embroiled in a scheme with John W. Gashwiler. Hearst and Gashwiler were thick as thieves, underscored by the fact that in San Francisco, eight-year-old Willie Hearst had attended the thirteenth birthday party of Gashwiler's son, Jared. In early November 1871, the *San Francisco Chronicle* published a rumor surrounding Hearst, Gashwiler, and stock prices: "Dame Rumor says that since General Gashwiler and Colonel Hearst joined the Young Man's Christian Association, all the young Christians have been dabbling in stocks—buying 'long' and selling 'short.' There is a method in some people's madness, says Colonel John F. Boyd."[42]

Two and a half weeks later, on November 19, 1871, the *Chronicle* returned to the subject in a damning article, illustrative of the Gilded Age:

> The stock market has been considerably excited during the week, the bulls and bears becoming frantic in their efforts to elevate or depress certain stocks, particularly Raymond & Ely and Eureka Consolidated. . . . The Eureka Consolidated rejoices in 50,000 shares, and a few weeks since under a strong bull movement, went up to $31, at which quite a number purchased. The regular $1 dividend for October was declared, and then EUREKA BEGAN TO CRAWFISH. George Hearst had gone up meanwhile to look after the Haggin interest, and it was soon rumored that although Hearst telegraphed "bully" to the office, he said "sell" to Haggin . . . then it oozed out that Haggin was selling, and Eureka gently dropped peg by peg.[43]

Lloyd Tevis was also in on the action. On September 26, 1871, Tevis sent a Western Union telegram addressed to Hearst: "Have sold down to three thousand shares join account Shall I continue to sell or buy back."

The same day Tevis sent Hearst an additional telegram regarding the Hermes Mine and the Raymond and Ely Mine. Hearst had established the Hermes Mine on a silver-bearing ledge near William Henry Raymond's Raymond & Ely Mine. The Hermes Mine ostensibly claimed part of the ledge undeveloped by the Raymond & Ely Mine, particularly the rich Panaca Shaft. According to an Englishman who had recently spoken with Tevis, "All their rich ore is on our ground." Tevis instructed Hearst to determine if this was the case. Unsurprisingly, Hearst determined it was, though many Pioche men—in particular William Henry Raymond—disputed that claim. Sensing an easy killing, lawyers began gathering around the Panaca Shaft like vultures.[44]

Never one to gather moss, Hearst was in Montezuma, Nevada, 125 miles northwest of Pioche, by mid-December 1871. To Phoebe, he admitted he wouldn't be home for Christmas. He professed his loneliness and, in a rare admission, his inability to turn a profit. "I have traveled on the outside of this camp some 2 or 3 days, found nothing that will do for an opperation and hate to go home without something to put on the mantle. It would be nice to start something the first of the year."[45]

As for Idaho Territory, Hearst knew he would get nothing to "put on the mantle" by partnering with Cousin Joe. That same December, Sam McMaster sent him a letter from Idaho with the despondent news: "Clark's Idaho mines will not do."[46]

Back in San Francisco, Hearst spent more and more time at the San Francisco stock boards, in Duncan's Building and Hayward's Building. Most of the heaviest speculators were Hearst's friends. The *San Francisco Chronicle* noted that the big operators, who could make or lose $5,000 or $10,000 at a turn, included George Hearst, J. B. Haggin, J. W. Gashwiler, William M. Lent, A. E. Head, William Sharon, John P. Jones, George D. Roberts, William Thompson Jr., John O. Earle, and Jasper McDonald. Though Joseph Clark was mentioned as a "smaller operator," he did quite well for himself.[47]

The winners of the day indulged in fine cigars and frequented saloons. The losers went home to lick their wounds. Ultimately, Hearst "dropped his wad" at the stock boards. Despite the backing of Haggin and Tevis and whatever double-dealing Hearst had undertaken in eastern Nevada, by early 1872 he was in financial freefall, out of pocket $125,000. It was the same situation Hearst had found himself in during the gold rush—when he had lived off credit and promissory notes—but with key differences. During the gold rush, Hearst had been in his thirties; now he was in his fifties. During the early lean years, Hearst had owed $40 here and there, mostly to merchants. Now he was heavily in debt to millionaire financiers. He was also single and unattached when he first arrived in California. Now he had a wife and son to support.[48]

For his part, Hearst never appeared down at the mouth. It was said that he drank "good wine," just as he had when on top. A favorite expression of his—"He saw no necessity to go into mourning"—was often on his lips. But inside, he was driven to recoup his losses. He needed one more great score. He hungered for another Comstock Lode, hidden somewhere in the great Wild West.[49]

In the meantime, Hearst needed a personal loan. Already in debt to Haggin and Tevis for $125,000, he couldn't ask them for help. Instead, he borrowed $5,000 from John T. Bradley of San Francisco. When he could not repay, Bradley went to Haggin and Tevis to make good the note. The brothers-in-law told Bradley they would happily repay him—but at seventy-seven cents on the dollar. Their terms to Hearst were more ominous. Hearst had one last chance to find a paying mine. Otherwise, he was on his own.

According to the *Oakland Tribune*, Hearst "then took Haggin & Tevis's last backing and went out to put it all upon the touch for a permanent fortune or permanent poverty." In other words, Hearst had one last throw of the dice—boom or bust.[50]

George Hearst, circa 1888. Courtesy California Historical Society, San Francisco. *Photograph by George Prince, Washington, D.C.*

Lloyd Tevis, circa 1899. Tevis was one of Hearst's business partners in the Ontario Mine in the Black Hills and the Anaconda Mine. *Courtesy Wikimedia Commons.*

James Ben Ali Haggin, circa 1914. Haggin was one of Hearst's business partners in the Ontario Mine in the Black Hills and the Anaconda Mine. *Courtesy Wikimedia Commons.*

Henry Janin, Hearst's secret ally during the Great Diamond Hoax and a business partner in the Black Hills. *Courtesy Huntington Research Library, San Marino, California.*

Almarin B. Paul, Hearst's business partner in Nevada City and Sacramento. *Courtesy Huntington Research Library, San Marino, California.*

George Hearst. *Courtesy of Bancroft Library, University of California–Berkeley.*

Phoebe Elizabeth Apperson Hearst, circa 1897. *Courtesy Wikimedia Commons.*

Phoebe Elizabeth Apperson Hearst. *Courtesy California Historical Society, San Francisco. Photograph by J. Ludovici.*

William Randolph Hearst. *Courtesy California Historical Society, San Francisco.*

Bust of George Hearst, by James Paxton Voorhees, circa 1897. *Courtesy Hearst Castle Visitor Center. Photograph by Chris Stewart.*

= 7 =

THE GREAT DIAMOND HOAX

(1872)

I would have staked my life that the diamond stories were reliable.
—George Hearst

This time it wasn't silver or gold Hearst sought, but diamonds.

Rumors of a mysterious diamond field, located somewhere in Wyoming Territory or Arizona Territory, had been circulating since November 1870, ever since two prospecting cousins from Kentucky—Philip Arnold and John Slack—had arrived in San Francisco carrying a grubby bag of uncut diamonds and gems. They initially entered the office of George D. Roberts. Roberts had been mildly successful in Virginia City, but as the silver and gold played out, he sought greater fortune elsewhere. Showing initiative, he reinvented himself as a land speculator, working for the Tide Land Reclamation Company. Now he sought to reinvent himself again, as a Diamond King. After being hooked by Arnold and Slack, Roberts confided the potential of the diamond find to William C. Ralston, who had used the fortune he'd made off Washoe silver to found the Bank of California. Ralston was quickly brought in, along with another man who had been a partner to George Hearst: William M. Lent.[1]

Like Hearst, Lent lived in San Francisco. Lent's son Eugene, called Gene, was nearly the same age as Willie. Even more than Hearst, Lent had been abysmal at retaining his original Washoe fortune. Now that the scent of diamonds was on him, he was looking to cash in. To this end, Lent partnered with Ralston and Roberts on the diamond venture. But to be sure the diamond mine hadn't been salted, they need a prospector to vouchsafe Arnold and Slack and the veracity of the claim. If Roberts and Lent floated George Hearst's name, it did not go very far. After all, Hearst worked for Wells, Fargo men Haggin and Tevis, whereas William C. Ralston was a Bank of California man. Additionally, on January 27, 1871, the Bank of California notified Hearst by letter that he had overdrawn his account by $2,462.55. Whatever the case, Lent, Ralston, and Roberts commissioned a different prospector to examine the diamonds: Asbury Harpending.[2]

Like Arnold and Slack, Harpending had been born in Kentucky. Thirteen years earlier he had attempted to join up with the famous filibuster William Walker. Fortunately for Harpending, Walker was shot to death by a Honduran firing squad in 1860 before Harpending reached him. The following year, when Kentucky became a neutral state during the Civil War, Harpending was arrested for his part in a piratical scheme to raid Union merchant ships along the Pacific coast. President Lincoln had granted him parole. In 1870, when Lent, Ralston, and Roberts needed his prospecting expertise, Harpending was in London, attempting to drum up interest in a California mining company.

In his 1913 memoir, Harpending described his early impressions of Philip Arnold and John Slack: "I had some knowledge of the prospectors. Arnold generally had borne a good reputation among the mining fraternity. Slack seemed to be a stray bird who had blown in by chance, probably picked up by Arnold because of a marriage relationship. It seemed they had told a straight enough story. It was impossible to tangle them in any detail."

Harpending did not reach San Francisco until May 1871. By then the San Francisco and New York Mining and Commercial Company had already been formed by Ralston, Roberts, and Lent. The three financiers grubstaked Arnold and Slack with $50,000 and sent them to collect more specimens from their secret location. Harpending met Arnold and Slack in August 1871 at a train station at Lathrop, California, seventy-five miles east of San Francisco. Harpending noted that the cousins looked "travel-stained and weather-beaten and had the general appearance of having gone through much hardship and privation." With the cousins was a buckskin bag. The cousins told Harpending that they had originally had two bags, both filled with diamonds and gems, but one of the bags had fallen overboard as they rafted across a flooded stream. "As the other contained at least a million dollars' worth of stones," the cousins told Harpending, "it ought to be fully satisfactory."

To Ralston, Roberts, Lent, and Harpending, the bag proved more than satisfactory. In conference with the others, Harpending spread a sheet on his billiards table, opened the bag, and poured out the glittering contents. "It seemed like a dazzling, many-colored cataract of light," Harpending recalled. The contents of the bag were soon made public. Potential stockholders were brought in, though Ralston, Roberts, and Lent determined they would hold on to three-quarters of the stock. Their goal was raise $10 million in capital and to locate and purchase the diamond field. Excitement was terrifically high. Not since the early days of the Comstock Lode—since George Hearst had brought to San Francisco tons of silver through the Sierra Nevada in the winter of 1859–1860—had such a bonanza been struck.

Ralston, Roberts, and Lent quickly brought on Major General Benjamin Franklin Butler, who had fought for the Union during the Civil War and was currently a Republican congressional representative from Massachusetts. Earlier that year, Butler had scored a significant political victory by authoring the Ku Klux Klan Act of 1871. Signed into law by President Ulysses S. Grant, it gave the federal government authority to prosecute and combat the white-hooded champions of the Lost Cause. Butler was looking to follow up his political success with a financial killing. He was made a stockholder. Harpending was general manager. Lent was named president. Samuel L. M. Barlow, an attorney living in New York City, was brought on as general counsel.

The next order of business was to take the diamonds to the world's authority on such matters: Charles Tiffany. Lent, Harpending, Arnold, Slack, and two other board members took the transcontinental railroad to pay Tiffany a visit in New York City. They met with Tiffany and Butler at Barlow's house, along with several others who wished to profit from the extraordinary find: General George B. McClellan, Brevet Brigadier General George S. Dodge, and the editor in chief of the *New York Tribune*, Horace Greeley, whose name had been bandied about as the Democratic nominee for president in 1872.[3]

Tiffany looked over the sapphires, rubies, emeralds, and diamonds, sorting them into heaps and holding them into the light. "Gentlemen, these are beyond question precious stones of enormous value," he declared. "But before I give you the exact appraisement, I must submit them to my lapidary and will report to you further in two days."

After two tense days, Tiffany made his pronouncement. One-tenth of the bag's contents had been examined and found to be worth $150,000. Lent and the others quickly surmised that the entire bag might be worth well over a million dollars. Now it was time for Arnold and Slack to reveal the location of the diamond field. According to Harpending, Henry Janin was then brought in. Janin had a sterling reputation as a mine appraiser. It was said that he had examined more than six hundred mines without steering his backers wrong. Janin asked for the following terms. He would be paid $2,500 for his expertise, would have all his expenses paid, and would be given the option to buy one thousand shares of stock. Lent did not like the terms—possibly thinking Hearst could do it for less—but was overruled.[4]

Harpending also held Hearst in high regard, made clear in his memoir:

George Hearst was probably the greatest natural miner who ever had a chance to bring his talents into play on a large scale. He was not a geologist, had no special education to start with, was not overburdened with book learning, but he had a congenital instinct for mining, just as some other people have for mathematics, music or chess. He was not a man of showy parts, liked the company of a lot of cronies, to whom he was kind and serviceable—when he wasn't broke himself—was much inclined to take the world easy, but if anyone mentioned mines in his presence, it had the same effect as saying, "Rats!" to a terrier. Hearst became alert and on dress parade in a moment.[5]

Despite Lent's reluctance, Harpending relates that in June 1872, a party set out from New York City to the fabled diamond fields. The members included Arnold, Slack, Harpending, Janin, Dodge, and Alfred Rubery, a swashbuckling Englishman and a friend of Harpending's. Arnold and Slack revealed to Ralston that the diamond field was not in Wyoming Territory or Arizona Territory but in Colorado Territory, roughly three hundred miles northeast of Salt Lake City. They spent four days on pack animals, cutting a labyrinthine route from the railroad depot at Bridger—in present-day Wyoming—to the diamond fields.

"The country was wild and inhospitable. . . . Everyone wanted to find the first diamond," Harpending recalled.

After a few minutes Rubery gave a yell. He held up something glittering in his hand. It was a diamond, fast enough. Any fool could see that much. Then we began to have all kinds of luck. For more than an hour diamonds were being found in profusion, together with occasional rubies, emeralds, and sapphires. . . . Mr. Janin was exultant that his name should be associated with the most momentous discovery of the age, to say nothing of the increased value of his 1,000 shares. . . . Two days' work satisfied Janin of the absolute genuineness of the diamond fields. He was wildly enthusiastic. . . . Janin pointed out that this new field would certainly control the gem market of the world and that the all-essential part of the program was for one great corporation to have absolute control.[6]

The *Salt Lake City Herald* gives a different rendition. According to an article published in 1884, in April 1872 Arnold and Slack revealed to Ralston the location of the diamond field. According to the *Herald:* "One morning in April, 1872, four disguised figures crept down in the dawn to the Oakland Ferry. They were Arnold, George D. Roberts, Henry Janin and George Hearst."
The article continued:

Janin was the most accomplished geologist and mining engineer in the city, and Roberts and Hearst were the best practical miners in California. The party took the cars and Arnold piloted them to Green River, Wy. T. There they left the train, got mules and an ambulance and struck for the Green River Mountains, forty-five miles south of the railroad. They were on the ground a week. The "diamond field" did not seem to be more than fifty acres in extent, and was at the base of a low range of barren red sandstone hills. They found diamonds in the greatest quantities scattered about in the low beds of dry gravel.[7]

The *Salt Lake City Herald* account conflicts with Harpending's and garbles its details. At the same time, holes appear in Harpending's memoirs concerning Hearst. Harpending relates that after Hearst and Joe Clark struck it rich with the Ophir Mine, Hearst suggested a "blow out" in Europe, and while the two were looking over "the effete monarchies of the Old World," Bill Lent watched over their investments. In fact, Hearst never visited Europe, as he made clear in his memoirs. After his success with the Ophir, Hearst traveled to Missouri, not Europe.[8]
Though the *Salt Lake City Herald* article strikes a false note, it rings true in broad terms. As much as anyone involved, George Hearst had caught diamond fever. In fact, he had been searching for the diamond fields as early as April or June of 1872. Contrary to the *Salt Lake City Herald* article, which appeared a dozen years after the fact, Hearst was not working with Lent and the other members of the San Francisco and New York Mining and Commercial Company. Hearst

was working against them. He based himself out of Salt Lake City, probably for its centrality to where the diamond fields were supposed to exist: Wyoming or Arizona. In this respect, Salt Lake City would be Hearst's Nevada City. The diamond fields would be his Comstock Lode.

From that central location, Hearst partnered with diamond expert and miner James F. Berry, who lived in Salt Lake City. "Mr. Berry and George Hearst," noted the *Cincinnati Enquirer* in late 1872, "determined to find the location of the Lent-Harpending claim. To this end they worked like beavers." They sent men in all directions. To Washington, D.C., a man was sent to bring back maps, which would help them secure a patent on the claim. To San Francisco, men were sent to "pump" Lent and the others. In this manner Hearst and Berry got hints as to the location of the diamond field. To a mountaineer named Taber, Hearst reportedly promised, "Find the location of this Roberts Company and I'll give you $10,000." Taber was only one such expert Hearst sent throughout the country.[9]

During these months Hearst resembled nothing so much as a spider, spinning a web in hopes of catching prey. The web expanded from San Francisco to Washington, D.C. At its heart was Salt Lake City, where Hearst, eating bacon and fried mush, was poised to strike.[10]

Recalling this time period, the *San Francisco Chronicle* reported an "amusing" story "at the expense of George Hearst." Taber returned to Salt Lake City, supposedly having located the diamond field, and shared his findings with Hearst. "All right," said Hearst, "come here in the morning and I will give you a check for your money." The next morning, when Taber came for the check, he discovered Hearst had left the city. "An important telegram from San Francisco require[ed] his absence from Salt Lake and he left on the morning train. And as no man can be in two places at once in the same identical period of time, Hearst was not on hand to meet Taber." Taber began swearing "like a trooper . . . he is daily seen at the railroad depot with a shotgun slung across his arm. It is loaded with buckshot and he is looking for that check. Should Hearst return to the land of the Saints Taber will interview him."[11]

As focused as Hearst was on the diamonds, the telegram must have been important. Something else was going on.

Whatever the case, Hearst kept up the pressure to locate the diamond mine. On October 10, Janin—playing his own double game—telegraphed Hearst in Salt Lake City: "Can you arrive Winnemucca trade if so will join you." The following day, Janin telegraphed, "Lent boyd and Dodge insist upon my going to

Sanfrancisco first will have these Monday If Everything satisfactory I must have ample time for Examination."[12]

Joe Clark was also keeping tabs on the San Francisco and New York Mining and Commercial Company. On October 15, 1872, Clark sent his cousin a letter, stating, "The new party of Diamond hunters have returned (Roberts party) and seem to think they have the bigist thing in the world. It is not in Arizona or New Mexico. I don't know exactly where it is but I think I could find it."[13]

A few weeks later, in early November, the shadow game Hearst and Berry were playing came to fruition. When Arnold and Slack left Salt Lake City with the others for Bridger on the Union Pacific Railroad, tailing them were Berry, a man named McClelland, and another confederate. Berry and his party were "fully equipped and armed to the teeth."[14] If Arnold, Slack, Harpending, Janin, Dodge, and Rubery realized they were being followed, they never mentioned it. On horseback, they traveled thirty miles through the wilderness to the mountains visible from the tracks.

Meanwhile, Janin had appraised the diamond field, declaring it financially sound. To his partners he wrote, "I consider any investment at $40 per share, or at the rate of $4,000,000 for the whole property, a safe and attractive one." Jubilant, the men returned to Bridger with more bags of diamonds, sapphires, emeralds, and rubies. From there they entrained, their ultimate destination San Francisco.

While the key members of the San Francisco and New York Mining and Commercial Company were aboard their train, each flush with excitement—but for different reasons—Berry, McClelland, and the others located the diamond field. They spent two or three days in the wilderness, plucking diamonds and gems from the ground. Berry himself located twenty-six diamonds.[15]

Berry quickly realized two problems with the diamonds. "The stones seemed to him like old acquaintances. . . . He at once recognized the stones as African or Cape of Good Hope diamonds of rather inferior quality," reported the *Cincinnati Enquirer*. On November 11, rumors that the fabled diamond field had been salted began to swirl. It appeared that Arnold and Slack had played for suckers the San Francisco miners and New York City diamond experts—and gotten away with it. Upon reaching San Francisco, they had cashed out, to the tune of $600,000, and disappeared back south.

When on November 12, Haggin telegraphed Hearst, "Write me all you know about diamonds. It is important for me to know everything," Hearst could give him a full report.[16]

Lent and the others commissioned another mine appraiser, Clarence King, to make a further pass at the diamond field outside Bridger. King and Hearst had been rival mine appraisers for years. Hearst disliked King's high-minded northern sensibilities; King considered Hearst two-faced but praised his toughness. Said King, "Hearst was bitten on the privates by a scorpion; the latter fell dead."[17]

King was unimpressed by the diamond field. A German in his party said to him, "Mr. King, this is the bulliest diamond field that never was. Not only does it generate diamonds, it generates cut diamonds." On November 22, a reporter for the *San Francisco Chronicle,* realizing that Hearst and Berry were traveling together on a train from Salt Lake City to San Francisco, got aboard the train at Pleasanton—forty miles from San Francisco—and managed to conduct an impromptu interview with the two mining operators. Hearst and Berry attempted to be cagey—after all, there were stocks involved, and they had precious information—but it was too great a secret to keep to themselves.

"You see," explained Hearst to the *Chronicle* reporter, "Mr. Berry is a diamond broker and understands the subject thoroughly. He and I have been hunting after this thing for the last five or six months. Up to within the last month I would have staked my life that the diamond stories were reliable—you couldn't make me believe that Janin could be fooled or induced to misrepresent anything of that kind."

"I can't tell you what our object is," Berry told the reporter. "Mr. Hearst and myself have been working this thing up together. He has several friends in this city who may want to buy or sell diamond stock, according to the nature of our report. Of course, we want them to have the first information."

When the reporter mentioned that a man in Santa Fe had a big ruby from the diamond fields, Berry and Hearst were amused. Berry scoffed that Tiffany's jewelers couldn't accurately tell the value of any such a stone. "I'll bet a hundred dollars to fifty that the stone proves to be no ruby," Hearst challenged. "There's a man aboard here now who has got a whole sack full of stones. He thinks they are all rubies, and I'm certain there isn't a ruby in the whole boodle."[18]

Whether Hearst and Berry were paid by stock speculators for their information, or whether they shorted the market, went unreported. Instead, the papers were soon filled with the travails of Lent, Roberts, and Ralston, who were caught holding the bag. Butler, Dodge, and McClellan had also lost money. Furthermore, the supposed experts in their field—Henry Janin and Charles Tiffany—were exposed as having been duped. But for Hearst, the Great Diamond Hoax of 1872 had a silver lining.

8

PANIC!

(1872–1874)

I am going to stay right here and watch this little mine.
—George Hearst

The *San Francisco Chronicle* article claiming that Hearst left Salt Lake City so he could read a telegram is verified in Hearst's memoirs. Hearst writes, "I . . . went to Salt Lake. I lay around there, but I did not see much that I could do; so I went back home and there found a telegram awaiting me about the biggest mine in the World." This was the Little Emma.

"There was great excitement," Hearst recalled. "I said I would go up to look at it. Several others looked at it but said it was a failure." Wanting to look for himself, Hearst and Gashwiler journeyed thirty miles southeast of Salt Lake City into the Wasatch Mountains, near Deer Valley in what was then called Parley's Park, now Park City. Though the Little Emma was attracting substantially more attention, particularly from England, Clarence Greathouse recalled Hearst describing it as "like a turnip turned upside down. He said it would probably be found to be only a pocket, or a large lump of ore, and that it would not last. . . . The result was as Hearst predicted. They were working on the top of the turnip. They soon got to the bottom, and the result was that thousands were ruined."[1]

Dodging that catastrophe, Hearst and Gashwiler decided to investigate the McHenry Mine, which they had bonded sight unseen from San Francisco. Seeing it up close, they were disgusted. "When I got there," Hearst recalled, "I found an immense reef of quartzite, with occasional scattered nests of ore and saw at once that it was no good." Hearst and Gashwiler had just begun the arduous trip back to Salt Lake City when they ran smack dab into Marcus Daly. Of Daly, the *Anaconda Times* noted, "Marcus Daly was Irish, and all that the word implies. His veins were full of red blood and his nerves were like electric wires." In 1872 Daly was living in Salt Lake City, making a living as a "boss foreman" of a mining company.[2]

Daly mentioned that a half mile away, down a canyon, a few men had established the Ontario Mine. Unwilling to admit defeat, Hearst ventured with Gashwiler, Daly, and others into Ontario Canyon to appraise the mine. They located it next to an old pine tree and a fine spring, nothing more than a hole about six feet long "and as deep as your shoulder."[3]

When Hearst began digging, one of the mine owners called out from a nearby bank, "You can tear that down all you want to." Emboldened, Hearst continued digging. Encouraged by Hearst's apparent interest, the mine owner confided to Hearst, "I had a chance to make a stake and go home three times since I came here and I must get some money out of this thing now. I am going to sell."[4]

Hearst quickly learned that the Ontario had three owners: Rector Steen, John Kane, and Gus Dawell. Daly, Gashwiler, and the others were not interested. They told Hearst that in the morning they were headed for Pioche, but Hearst had other ideas. "I am going to stay right here and watch this little mine," he told them. Hearst stayed for three weeks, until the owners sank another hole. Hearst gathered some of the ore they brought out and had it sampled. Without waiting any further, Hearst offered $30,000 for the mine. The exact date of the acquisition was August 21, 1872. On August 26, the *Morning Oregonian* reported that Hearst had purchased the Ontario Mine for $25,000, all in cash ($5,000 less than what Hearst claimed he paid).[5]

Hearst also offered $3,000 for a nearby mine, simply to "get his out of the way." Although Hearst described this off-handedly, considering the law of the apex, it was a shrewd calculation. Since the gold rush, the rule of thumb had been that mining claims belonged to individuals who first located the apex, or outcropping, of gold, silver, copper, or cinnabar. The law of the apex had been modified earlier that year when the General Mining Act of 1872 passed on May 10. In addition to using the term *valuable mineral deposits* rather than *gold, silver, copper, and cinnabar*—with Benjamin Butler expending political capital to make the change, so that the fabled diamond fields he'd been hunting would be similarly protected— the General Mining Act of 1872 declared that should a vein snake beneath another miner's claim, the owner of the wayward vein would own the mineral rights. With this in mind, and with the potential he saw in the Ontario, Hearst didn't want to leave anything to chance.[6]

Hearst additionally picked up the Daly Mine from Marcus Daly. "I staid here a while and organized and started the works but kept prospecting all the time," Hearst reflected. Thomas Edwin Farish, whose brother William would one day work for Hearst as a superintendent, recognized that Hearst was at his best with his back against the wall. Said Farish of Hearst, "The energy of the man was never more conspicuously displayed than when the tide of fortune was against him."[7]

At long last, the tide was about to turn. The Daly and Ontario Mines appeared to have unlimited potential. They contained lead, zinc, copper, and gold but primarily silver. All Hearst needed to do was build up the mines, and if luck was with him, he would be able to rebuild his fortune. Ironically, had Hearst not stationed himself in Salt Lake City, tracking the movements of the San Francisco and New York Mining and Commercial Company, he might never have looked into the neighboring Ontario Mine.

Silver King James G. Fair, who was no slouch at mining himself, sent Hearst a letter of hopeful congratulations from Virginia City on September 27, 1872: "I hope you have got a good thing. Nothing would please me better than to know that you and Daly had struck another Comstock."[8]

Feeling lucky, Hearst took another stab in Idaho Territory in January 1873, this time in the Caribou Mountains, becoming trustees for the Lane & Kutz Caribou Mining Company, along with Haggin, Greathouse, and Joe Clark.[9]

The Hearsts were feeling particularly happy on the last day of February 1873. There, in the Hearst's home on Chestnut Street, Alice Booth was married. The groom was Marios Jasper McDonald, who was said to have been descended from Scottish nobility and went by his middle name. McDonald was a local business-man, a friend of Hearst's, and a "bull" at the San Francisco stock boards. The *San Francisco Chronicle* reported, "Although the marriage was ostensibly a private one, there were present a select number of ladies and gentlemen, who were all either relatives or intimate friends of the parties. . . . As we expected, the wedding gifts were alike numerous, costly and tasteful, as benefited the wealth, culture and high social standing of the principals interested, and the scene presented was strikingly brilliant. Shortly after the ceremony the young couple . . . departed for their future home, which is a handsome residence on O'Farrell Street."[10]

With Alice happily married, Phoebe and Willie decided to embark upon on a grand tour. They would visit relatives in Missouri, see the sights in Boston,

Washington, and New York City, and ultimately sail for Europe. With Phoebe, Willie, and Alice out of the house, George began renting out the house on Chestnut Street for $125 a month. Just a half mile from San Francisco Bay, on posh Russian Hill, it was quite the catch. In the meantime, Hearst listed his San Francisco residence as the Grand Hotel. Mining camps and hotels would be the center of life for him.[11]

Phoebe and Willie set out at 7 A.M. on March 18, 1873, in a palace car of the Central Pacific. They reached St. Louis at 11 A.M. on March 24. Mother and son spent Easter with relatives before vacationing in Washington, D.C., and New York City. Boston followed. There, Phoebe's childhood friend Clara Anthony was waiting at the station. "Mr. and Mrs. Anthony have entertained me very handsomely," Phoebe wrote her husband. Afterward, Phoebe and Willie sailed for Ireland. For the next year, Hearst would receive letters addressed to the Chestnut Street house and postmarked from Dublin, Belfast, Glasgow, Edinburgh, London, Antwerp, Brussels, Ghent, Cologne, Hanover, Dresden, Prague, Vienna, Geneva, Milan, Florence, and Paris, among other European cities.[12]

In a letter to Eliza Pike, Phoebe confided, "I had hoped Mr. Hearst would come abroad, but business has been in such an unsettled state this year, he finds it impossible to leave. He has been away from S.F. nearly all the time since we left. When he is there, he seems much more lonely than when he is in the mines."[13]

On the other side of the world, at the Nevada mines, events finally came to a head. Hearst's underhanded manipulation of Pioche stock two years earlier proved only the opening act of what the *Pioche Daily Record* called "The Great Mining Suit." The trouble concerned the Panaca Shaft, claimed by both Hearst's Hermes Mine and William Henry Raymond's Raymond & Ely Mine. The Panaca Shaft had originally been sunk by Stephen Sherwood and his crew of Mormon miners. It was later sold to Raymond, who established the Raymond & Ely Mine in 1864. Wanting in on the silver-bearing ledge, Hearst had formed the adjoining Hermes Mine under the auspices of the Hermes Company in 1871. Painting Hearst as a robber baron, Raymond filed a lawsuit.

The great robber barons of the American West were almost all railroad magnates: Mark Hopkins, Charles Crocker, Leland Stanford, and Collis Huntington. John D. Spreckels was involved in railroads as well but was better known as the Sugar King. Lloyd Tevis engaged in railroads, banking, and—like J. B. Haggin—real estate and whatever mining enterprises Hearst could dig up. William Sharon and William C. Ralston made money through banking, real estate, and Virginia

City silver. Sharon and Ralston were particularly efficient at loaning money to mining companies, foreclosing on them, and seizing the mines for themselves.

More robber barons lived in New York City, the center of American finance. Some of the most notorious included Jay Gould, John Jacob Astor, John D. Rockefeller, Andrew Carnegie, J. P. Morgan, and Cornelius Vanderbilt. Their countless investments included fur, oil, steel, railroads, real estate, banking, and Wall Street stocks.

Whether the robber barons held court on Nob Hill or in Manhattan, they played the capitalistic game by the same crooked tactics: acquire semi-monopolies or outright monopolies through piratical means—attacking rival companies through a combination of lawsuits, political pressure, and stock depression—and squeeze the customers until exorbitant prices seem standard. Some, like Stanford and Sharon, went into politics. Most preferred to manipulate events from behind the scenes. All of them lived like royalty, eternally seeking to expand their kingdoms.

Though George Hearst liked to style himself as a man of the people, the moves he made in "The Great Mining Suit" demonstrated his capacity to become as great a robber baron as Stanford or Gould. Hearst's lawyers—William W. Bishop, J. S. Pitzer, and Judge Delos W. Lake—attempted to invalidate the Raymond claim through a variety of arguments. First, Bishop introduced the notion that the Mormon miners who sank the Panaca Shaft had been operating under Brigham Young's Mormon law instead of U.S. law. Pitzer concurred, arguing that the laws governing the initial Panaca Shaft were "made in the interest of the Mormon Church."

Next the Hermes lawyers argued that the Raymond & Ely had abandoned the mineshaft between 1864 and 1870 and that it was therefore up for grabs when the Hermes Company formed in 1871. When Raymond's attorney, H. I. Thornton, insisted that the Raymond & Ely miners only left the area to recruit reinforcements to fend off Paiute Indians, the Hermes lawyers pounced. Pitzer wondered aloud, "Now, was it 'local insurrection,' or 'rebellion,' when mother Lee put the five Indians to flight with a billet of wood?" Lake jumped in, sarcastically dubbing the friction "the Indian war in 1864–1865 . . . as notorious a place in the history of the country as some of the battles of the civil war."

At nearly 4 P.M. on April 30, the twelve-man jury deliberated the manner. That evening, rumors spread that Hearst had "purchased like sausages" some of the jurors. A few gamblers made bets on just how many men Hearst had placed in his corner, ranging between five and nine. The jury reached a decision at half past eight. Afterward, the jury foreman, A. O. Wilcox, made the announcement that seemingly all of Pioche had waited for "with breathless interest." To the satisfaction of the Hermes Company, Wilcox intoned, "We the jurors in this case find for the defendant." As for the side bets, nine jurors had sided with Hearst, only three for Raymond. Additionally, the court ordered that Raymond & Ely pay $4,987.24 for the cost of the Hermes defense.

In response, Raymond's lawyers met at the courthouse the next morning, filing a motion for a new trial. Nearly two months later, Judge Mortimer Fuller granted the motion, citing "insufficiency of the evidence to justify the verdict" and "irregularities in the proceedings of the defendant and of the jury." It was a small victory for Raymond, who did not relish the idea of once again facing Hearst's sharp-tongued lawyers and greasy palm. Instead, Raymond decided to settle with Hearst out of court, offering to purchase from Hearst the Hermes Mine.

Hearst accepted Raymond's offer, and though the "high figure" was never disclosed to the newspapers, Hearst mentioned it and the Pioche misadventure in his memoirs: "Just knocked around a bit. Got in with some men who had a set of Pioche mines, sunk a shaft down, struck a bed of ore, got into a big lawsuit over it, got out of that, making some $250,000." In a retrospective of the entire affair, the *Chronicle* wrote that "George Hearst, who came here [to Pioche] in September, 1871 . . . immediately concocted the scheme . . . to reap the reward of Raymond's perseverance and energy." As luck would have it, Hearst had big plans for that money.[14]

Back in San Francisco, in a letter to Phoebe dated May 30, 1873, George noted that dinner at "Allice's" brought home how much he missed her, and how much he hated homelessness.

> I hope you are having a good time for I have missed you very much since I have been back. We have been together so long I have been weaned from nearly everyone and scarsley know anyone and find the Hotel a very stupid place and nothing to interest me. A man without a home is just about no man at all. Be shure to write me all about your travels. I am very anxious for you and the Boy for fear you will never get home safe. I think the time long until you return. I hope I may get off and meet you yet.
>
> Your husband,
> George.[15]

Friends noticed that George, whose regular prospecting garb included a slouch hat, high-topped boots, and a cutaway coat, was even more careless with his appearance without Phoebe. Multiple letters from overseas concerned sartorial matters: "Tonie wrote me she saw you and your clothes looked like 'Pioche.' You had no necktie, etc., and looked 'don't care.' I felt very badly and wish you would be more careful with your appearance for my sake." And: "I hope you go home with Mr. Greathouse, you have *clean* clothes. However, I shall not fret about things I cannot change. I know you are good, but *careless*."[16]

If Hearst was dressed "like Pioche," it's because he lived and breathed mining at this time. The earnings of the Hermes sale, and his boundless energy, poured into the Ontario mine. Hearst began by renting a mill. Later he built a mill, strong enough that it lasted fifteen years. He also hired Robert C. Chambers, a prospector from Ohio who, like Hearst, had reached California in the summer of 1850. When Hearst hired him shortly after purchasing the Ontario Mine, Chambers was managing the Bully Boy and Webster Mines in southern Utah. Managing the Ontario Mine soon became his full-time job and raison d'être. Soon tons of silver were being extracted from the Ontario Mine. All of this took money. Aggravating Hearst's money struggle were financial policies first adopted by Europe, then the United States, deflating the price of silver.[17]

With the Atlantic Ocean between North America and Europe, the Franco-Prussian War initially seemed like it would have little effect on the United States. But when Otto von Bismarck captured Paris and was declared chancellor of the German Empire, one of his first moves was to disrupt the world's financial system. In November 1871, Germany began shifting from bimetallism to the gold standard. The effect was the worldwide deflation of silver. Within two years, thriving stock markets and banks—which had been dependent on the high price of silver—found themselves insolvent. In May 1873, the Vienna Stock Exchange crashed. On September 18, Jay Cooke & Company—headquartered in Philadelphia, New York City, and Washington, D.C.—declared bankruptcy. Two days later, the New York Stock Exchange closed for ten days, attempting to stave off a panic. But the Panic of 1873 had already begun. Banks failed as struggling families demanded their money, prompting bankers to call in their loans. By 1875, more than eighteen thousand businesses had shuttered. It was estimated that in California alone, unemployment had leaped to a staggering 20 percent—even higher in the cities. In San Francisco, more than seven thousand people were out of work.[18]

A few members of Congress had recognized the danger, most prominently Senator John Sherman. The Coinage Act of 1873, put forth by Sherman in 1871 and signed into law by Ulysses S. Grant on February 12, 1873, ended bimetallism, putting the United States on the gold standard. Cities dependent on silver—such as San Francisco and Virginia City—were hit hardest. To them, the Coinage Act of 1873 became known as the "Crime of '73."

But Hearst did not panic. On June 30, 1873, he wrote Phoebe that joining her European holiday was "about the only trip I was anxious to make" and that he was "very lonely with no Boy" and also relating a story demonstrating his charitable nature, even in the face of Armageddon. He explained that he had "met a nice little boy about Willie's size who had his foot smashed by a wagon running over it."

Hearst continued: "He was going on one foot and a crutch, so I gave him money enough to send to Philadelphia and have a cork foot made for him. If he had been left to grow up that way, he would have been all out of shape. But if he gets good attention from this on, he will hardly miss his foot, as it is only off from the instep."[19]

Though Phoebe wrote often, George's letters were infrequent. In October 1873, from Milan, ten-year-old Willie even scolded his fifty-three-year-old "Papa," writing that he and Phoebe had become "very uneasy" because they hadn't heard from him in so long. In the postscript, Phoebe mentioned, "I have allowed Willie to write this without assistance from me, although the writing is bad, he can express himself moderately well. He reminds me of you in his aversion to writing but if practice and perseverance can change him, I will try it." Clearly, Phoebe wanted an update from her husband. After all, it had been eight months since she had seen him.

Hearst wrote back that he had returned from Portland, Oregon. In November 1873, Phoebe replied to her "dear husband" that she was "glad that he was thus far safe & well." Phoebe also related her concern about finances:

> I have bought for myself a very handsome Geneva watch . . . medium size, plain & elegant, warranted by one of the most reliable companies. I have paid $105 for the watch & have my monogram engraved on it, in beautiful large letters, & for an odd new style paid $40.
>
> I also had to get another suit of clothes for Willie here and some shoes, for myself a plain woolen dress and a little warm jacket for traveling. I was sorry to spend anything on clothes for myself as I want to wait until I go to Paris, & get some to bring home, but I needed what I have bought. Traveling is rather hard on clothes, & I must appear

respectably dressed. I spent about $65 for us both, for those things. I only write this to let you know I am not spending my money foolishly.

I will write again, & hope to hear from you often.

Your loving wife

P. E. Hearst[20]

On December 3 Phoebe wrote from a hotel in Milan, reminding George that it was her birthday and wondering whether he remembered. Phoebe added, "We are both growing old, but I hope we may enjoy many happy years together!" Phoebe was only thirty-one, her husband fifty-three.[21]

Hearst's reluctance to write may have had to do with his dismal finances. Despite the promise of the Ontario Mine and the Daly Mine, the Crime of '73 was causing him grief. The San Simeon property was also proving irksome. In 1873 he successfully subdivided San Simeon Bay, piped in mountain spring water, and leased lots for $2 a year. But this was just a drop in the bucket, and the lawsuit concerning the 160 acres continued to drag on.

Hearst also opened another lawsuit in 1873, this one against his old friends James Halligan and James Inge over the family farm. This suit lasted years and would ultimately be all but fruitless. In his memoirs, Hearst bitterly estimated that though the property was worth at least $10,000, the entire eight hundred–acre Hearst farmstead was sold for a meager $228.[22]

As 1874 dawned, friends warily observed Hearst still trying his hand at new investments. On February 9, Hearst and a smattering of others incorporated the California Vinegar and Wine Company in San Francisco. Hearst also invested in Nevada's Blackhawk Ledge, located in the Indian District. But as these flash-in-the-pan investments proved mediocre, Hearst began cutting the fat. On March 9, he let the Hall and Van Dyke Consolidated Coal Company in Rock Springs, Wyoming Territory, slip into delinquency.

In April 1874 Hearst visited St. Louis, doubtless to oversee litigation. Shortly afterward, George wrote to Phoebe, who was then in Paris, that he had taken ill. On April 20, 1874, she wrote back that she was "uneasy" about the state of his health and that "I must come home immediately." In the same letter, Phoebe professed anxiety about what they would come home to: "Mr. Tevis says, if I decide to remain until Oct., he will arrange for me to have a little money, for I shall not have enough to keep us that long, but shall do the best we can, if we stay and anything should turn out good in your business, can I get some nice things to bring home. I mean, if you can spare the money. Though I fear everything is very dark for us, unless Ontario or Caribou should prove very rich."[23]

Unfortunately, Phoebe and Willie had no home to come back to. With his debts far outstripping his income, Hearst was forced to sell their beloved home. While he fled San Francisco for the camps, Phoebe and Willie shuffled between a boardinghouse and the Appersons' Santa Clara home. Settling into their new life, Phoebe put on a brave face. Although their would-be real estate empire had crumbled, and her husband's mining empire was underwater, they still owned the ranch in San Simeon. To Eliza Pike, Phoebe wrote:

> Mr. Hearst is going down to San Luis Obispo to look after the ranch a few weeks. He has sent some of his Missouri relations down on a small part of it & gives them a start. Mr. H. has not suffered by the panic, excepting that he made arrangements to sell a mine to a N.Y. Co. and they could not take it so he feels that it is difficult to carry so much that does not pay, for one must spend money on a mine to get more out of it. Money is close, but times not bad.[24]

The Missouri relations were almost certainly George W. Hearst and Richard S. Hearst, who traveled to California in 1873 and resided six miles south of San Simeon, in Green Valley.

As for Phoebe, she must have wondered, with businesses shuttering, banks closing, and silver coins no longer being minted, how long the "times not bad" could last.[25]

Although Hearst's long-term plan involved the Ontario paying off, in the short term he needed to cut expenses to the bone. On June 4, shares of the Techatticup Silver and Gold Mining Company—which Hearst, Lent, and Levi Parsons had owned since 1863—were sold at auction. For once, Hearst refused to throw good money after bad, spending the rest of 1874 concentrating on building up the Ontario.[26]

Ultimately, Hearst's industry paid off. Despite the Crime of '73, Hearst's silver mines in the Wasatch Mountains brought in riches unimaginable. The Daly provided $30,000 a month in silver—$360,000 a year. The Ontario Mine was much more lucrative. On average it yielded $75,000 a month—$900,000 a year. Not bad for a mine Hearst had originally bought for $30,000. "From that $30,000 everything else came," Hearst noted. He quickly repaid the $125,000 he owed Haggin and Tevis.[27]

While the Great Diamond Hoax of 1872 cost Ralston, Roberts, Lent, and the others a fortune, and the Panic of 1873 caused a worldwide depression, George

Hearst walked away a rich man—the principal owner of the greatest silver mine in Utah Territory.

Their trust restored, Haggin and Tevis backed Hearst on the Sheep's Head gold mine in northern California. Haggin and Hearst got along particularly well. The *Annual Mining Review and Stock Ledger* noted:

> George Hearst and James B. Haggin, in stock matters, are like man and wife, and they agree splendidly—better than the average of hymenial conjunctions. Haggin swings the capital, Hearst the genius, to examine a mine. . . . The latter is so unpretending a man of the people, that he was once elected by the Legislature by a Democratic majority. He prefers the wilds of the mountains, the terrors of the deserts, the dreary alkali plains and the withering sage-brush to the comforts of civilizations—always provided there is a mining "prospect," at least, at the end of the rope.[28]

This passage underscores a secret to Hearst's success. Other than his much lauded "genius" at mining, it may be that no other millionaire in history ever spent so much time in mining camps and desert wastelands. Industry as much as instinct fueled Hearst's achievements.

Although Hearst was certainly down to earth, he wasn't about to let his wife and child stay in at her parents' place while he was living high on the hog. To make amends, Hearst purchased a luxurious Nob Hill home at 734 Sutter Street. His new house was a half mile from the corner of Taylor and Washington Streets, where Haggin and Tevis held court in their mansions. Once more, Hearst was a man on the make. He almost had enough capital to play in the same political sandbox as his friend Leland Stanford, whereupon he could trade the view from Nob Hill for one in a different city. Sacramento perhaps. Even Washington, D.C.

But that was getting the cart before the horse. First, Hearst needed to make another fortune.

9

DEATH VALLEY

(1875–1877)

I have confined myself to mining since I was 21 years old.
Everything else was incidental.
—George Hearst

Searching for another El Dorado—but also checking up on the Ontario—Hearst traveled to Utah Territory in January 1875. On January 23, he purchased fourteen hundred feet of the Ashland vein in the West Mountain Mining District, near Salt Lake City. The next month, Hearst arrived by stagecoach in Darwin, a fledgling mining town in California's Inyo County. Darwin neighbored Panamint, just inside the bounds of present-day Death Valley—a blasted hellscape where in summer the mercury soared to 134°F and in the winter prospectors shivered beneath 11,043-foot Telescope Peak. In this cruel country, silver and lead had been discovered. As a result, hardscrabble mining towns sprang up like barrel cactus: Darwin, Resting Spring, Cerro Gordo, Keeler, Lookout, Wildrose. The largest was Panamint, containing some two thousand silver seekers, including Hearst's old friend Bill Stewart. Stewart, now the junior U.S. senator from Nevada, invested heavily. So too did the senior U.S. senator from Nevada, John P. Jones.[1]

Although Hearst wanted in on the action, he didn't immediately pull the trigger.

On May 18, 1875, Hearst was back in San Francisco at the first official meeting of the Pacific Stock and Exchange Board, colloquially known as "the little board"—distinguishing it from the San Francisco Stock and Exchange Board. Hearst and seventy-seven others paid an initial $5,000, making for a cash capital of $390,000. The president and driving force of the new stock board was Elias J. "Lucky" Baldwin, a man who would soon become a friend and business partner to Hearst. Serving as vice president was one of Hearst's nemeses during the Great Diamond Hoax, General George S. Dodge. As for Hearst, he was named secretary of the Pacific Stock Board along with Lent and dozens of others.[2]

Whatever money Hearst frittered away at the Pacific Stock Board didn't make a dent or distract him from his purpose. Less than a month later, on June 5, Hearst, Greathouse, and Joe Clark formed the Consolidated Leopard Hill Mining Company, operating in Nevada's Elko County, midway between Carson City and Salt Lake City. But it was Panamint Valley that would come to dominate Hearst's attention.[3]

On July 21, the *Panamint News* announced that Hearst had bought several mines twenty-five miles from the camp. Shortly after, it was rumored that Hearst, Haggin, Janin, Roberts, Lester Ludyah Robinson, and a Sacramento River steamboat captain with whom Hearst was friendly, George W. Kidd, were interested in the New Coso Mining Company. Robinson struck first, nabbing one of Darwin's best prizes.[4]

With the low-hanging fruit already picked, Hearst looked elsewhere. Specifically, the west wall of the Panamint Valley, ten miles east of Darwin, held promise. There, on Lookout Mountain, part of the Argus range, Hearst poured his energy. On August 5, Hearst and Captain Kidd purchased from Jerome S. Childs and his partners the Lookout Mine and the Confidence Mine for $15,000. In short order, Hearst boasted five neighboring mines—Confidence, Lookout, Hearst, Keys, and Modoc. Hearst combined his newest mines into the Modoc Consolidated Mining Company. A week later, Hearst and Captain Kidd bought from respected San Francisco mineralogist "Professor" William D. Brown, a slice of a mine near Darwin, producing $60 of silver per ton. The Balance Consolidated Gold and Silver Company was formed, with Hearst, Brown, and Kidd serving as directors.[5]

Connecting the Modoc mines to the Balance mines would take some doing. Ten miles in the blazing August heat could be as deadly as ten thousand. On August 19, the *Pioche Record* speculated that the Modoc's two neighbors—Eels and Dolan—could let Hearst use their circuitous roads to Darwin "at a low cost." That might do for a spell, but it wasn't the Hearst way. "Mr. Hearst, however, is building a trail from his mines to Darwin, a distance of ten miles, over very rough country. This, we presume, is to more intimately connect his Lookout with that of his Darwin property." The Pioche reporter did *not* presume that Hearst would rather build a road than rent one or that allowing his silver to move through another's property was inviting trouble.[6]

In August 1875 Hearst was in Salt Lake City. He had grubstaked "a wild fellow who was always broke," as Hearst recalled in his memoirs, who had just returned from Dakota Territory's Black Hills. Lieutenant Colonel George Custer's Seventh Cavalry had confirmed the presence of gold in 1874, igniting a war between the United States and the Lakota Sioux and spurring a gold rush to the Black Hills. Not wanting to be shot or scalped, Hearst had so far avoided the contested lands. But he was intrigued by the ore the wild fellow showed him in Salt Lake City. "I could see gold," Hearst recalled. "I took it and had it assayed."[7]

Whatever its value, Hearst determined the Black Hills could wait. Back in San Francisco, Hearst returned to the real estate game. He still owned two lots on Potrero, but with Montgomery Street Straight dead in the water, they were all but worthless. At least that was before James B. Haggin entered the fray. Before Haggin was through, the Potrero property would be worth considerably more, although Hearst would be involved in another San Francisco real estate scandal, this one known as the Mission Creek Tide Land Grab.

The plan was simplicity itself. Through an understanding with certain members of the Board of Tide Land Commissioners, Hearst, Haggin, and a few other capitalists began looking to monopolize property surrounding the gurgling Mission Creek. Although Mission Creek belonged to the city and was considered public land, with the land commissioners in their pocket they figured once they owned all access points they could privatize the creek. To this purpose, on November 17 Hearst purchased from J. T. Bonestell lots 207 and 235 on the Potrero block—between Center and Santa Clara Streets—for $1,000 apiece.

"Now what does Hearst do with his acquisitions?" asked an indignant *Chronicle* reporter. Three days later Hearst sold the property to Haggin for $40,000, though he retained his initial Potrero lots, 236 and 242. Although a few diehards refused to sell out, George W. Ellis, Charles P. Duane, and Ezekiel Tripp bought the lion's share of the remaining property.[8]

With most of the land surrounding Mission Creek privatized, on the first day of 1876, the *San Francisco Chronicle* reported the combination's next steps. First Haggin, Hearst, and the others would pressure the remaining landowners bordering Mission Creek to sell. Next they would replace Mission Creek with a street. Finally they would extort the city to build a sewer. The *Chronicle* also described Hearst and company in terms generally reserved for eastern robber barons: "This combination embraces men of great wealth, of powerful political influence, of more skill of developing schemes, of intimate relations with officials at the State Capital, lawyers of ability and shrewdness; politicians, whose ambition is to acquire wealth; speculators who have no hesitancy as to means employed, so long as they gain their ends and make money, and needy and seedy adventurers."[9] Dabbling in shady real estate ventures was all very well, but Hearst's true passion had always been mining, and he wasn't about to hang up his spurs. "I have confined myself to mining since I was 21 years old," Hearst reflected. "Everything else was incidental."[10]

In early May 1876, Hearst, Haggin, and Kidd went in on the Consolidated State Range Gold and Silver Company of California. On May 15, Hearst and Robert Chambers placed a patent for the Banner Mine in Utah Territory. During the same week, the Modoc Consolidated Mining Company reincorporated, with Hearst and Kidd still directors. The road was coming along well, with no short turns and plenty of room for wagons to pass each other. This was good news, for Lookout Mine was thriving.

As his chief superintendent, Hearst hired Samuel McMaster. Under McMaster's sharp eye, a 175-foot crosscut tunnel was created in Confidence No. 4. The ore shipped from there sold for $250 a ton. The Inyo County assessor, after a careful examination of Lookout Mine, placed its value at $200,000.[11]

With Chambers working the Utah Territory mines and McMaster the Darwin mines, Hearst found he could conduct most of his business at his Nob Hill home or his office at 309 Montgomery Street. But at fifty-five, Hearst still liked to travel. On July 16, he met Chambers at Salt Lake City's Townsend House to discuss a new Banner Mine mill. Hearst and Chambers also discussed the excitement up north. Custer, along with 261 other men in the Seventh Cavalry, had been killed at the Little Bighorn in Montana Territory on June 25, 1876 while battling Sioux Indians. To avenge the military humiliation, every red-blooded prospector predicted that President Grant, despite the 1868 Treaty of Fort Laramie, would send an army to crush the Indians.[12]

Thinking the timing was finally right, Hearst made arrangements for Chambers to visit the Black Hills. Chambers had other ideas. In his memoirs Hearst noted, "The Indians got so bad it was worth as much as a man's life to go there." Chambers stayed in Utah Territory instead, and Hearst once again bided his time.[13]

In September 1876, Hearst received some bad news from Missouri. The United States Circuit Court, East Missouri District, finally determined the matter of the Hearst family farm, ruling against Hearst. He also received a hurried letter from Phoebe in Philadelphia, where she and Will were taking in the World's Fair. "Yesterday there were 257,000 people at the exhibition . . . it was dreadful. . . . Your loving wife *Puss*."[14]

Hearst also received a letter from a different family member: J. C. Clark.

Although Hearst and Cousin Joe remained close, he and J. C. had drifted apart. Correspondence from Uncle Austin to George carried the usual greetings to Joe, Phoebe, and the boy, but mention of J. C. was conspicuously absent. One factor to the rift could have been J. C.'s temporarily trading mining for law enforcement, taking him out of Hearst's orbit. In September 1864, J. C. won the Washoe election to become sheriff of Storey County. "Jake Clark is a good man," Almarin B. Paul had written after the election, but the sentiment was not universal.[15]

Eventually, J. C. skidded to Salt Lake City, where, on December 11, 1876, he scribbled a letter to "Cousin George." In the letter, J. C. implored Hearst to invest in mining property in Cottonwood, just outside Salt Lake City: "I think it one of the best chances for us both to make some money and we ought not to loose it."[16]

Shortly afterward, Hearst received a letter from attorneys William W. Bishop and G. M. Sabin, informing him that "J. C. is in great trouble and destitution and wishes you to fund us for him five hundred dollars." If Hearst did "fund" his cousin any money, he did not extend with it his friendship. Afterward, J. C. disappeared from Hearst's life.[17]

Toward Phoebe's brother Elbert, on the other hand, Hearst showed extraordinary generosity. Hearst landed him a job at the San Simeon ranch, where he and his fiancée could begin a new life. On December 13, 1876, Phoebe wrote Eliza Pike, "Eppy is to be married the last of the month. . . . He writes that he is doing splendidly at the ranch—will make from 8 to 10 thousand dollars per year from Mr. Hearst. Eppy receives a salary of $100 per month and board."[18]

Two months later, on February 15, 1877, Hearst and Dodge filed articles of incorporation for the San Francisco Steamboat and Transportation Company. Their goal was to create for passengers an alternative to the "railroad line" of steamboats traveling between San Francisco and Sacramento on the Sacramento River. Less than a month later, Hearst and Lent began looking into the Peck silver mine, seventy-five miles north of Phoenix. Liking what they saw, they bonded it in early March.[19]

On March 3, 1877, San Francisco capitalists received a gift. Congress passed the Desert Reclamation Act, intending to promote western desert expansion by allowing any U.S. citizen to purchase desert land at a price of twenty-five cents an acre, so long as the purchaser intended to improve the land. The limit was

640 acres. Hearst purchased 640 acres in Kern County for a mind-boggling $160. Haggin, Tevis, and Greathouse all bought hundreds of acres of Kern County desert as well. At that price, why not? Hearst's Kern County land was later valued at $30 an acre, worth $19,200 altogether.[20]

Hearst's property in the neighboring county was also thriving. "The mine in Inyo Co. called 'the Modoc,' is doing well," Phoebe wrote to Pike. Unfortunately, Hearst found that smelting the ore hundreds of miles from civilization was troublesome. Initially, Hearst established two great charcoal furnaces for smelting. With the furnaces proving inadequate, in the spring of 1877 Hearst instructed S. B. Morrison to create the great Wildrose Kilns—ten beehive-shaped limestone ovens reaching twenty-five feet high, spanning thirty feet in diameter, and each capable of holding forty-two cords of wood chopped from piñon pine groves.[21]

During the summer of 1877, Hearst came down ill. With his mining empire largely running itself, he let the telegrams pile up on the table while he recovered. But when he saw that John Sevenoaks, a well-known mining operator, had sent him $400 worth of telegrams, he looked through them. Sevenoaks, as it turned out, had started a lead mine in the Black Hills. He encouraged Hearst to make the journey. There was a fortune to be made.

Hearst still wasn't prepared. Instead, in June 1877 he telegraphed Chambers and instructed him to send north Ludwig D. Kellogg, an experienced Ontario mining engineer, to check out the place. "He fixed him up and sent him off," Hearst recalled. Hearst also spoke to Gashwiler about the potential bonanza, asking him to send mining engineer William Farish to scope it out. Feeling better, on September 1 Hearst partnered with Tevis on the California Trading Company, engaged in buying and selling land and stock. Certainly Hearst had money to burn. Working at full capacity, the Ontario mine was now bringing in more than $100,000 in silver bullion a month.[22]

Hearst was probably in his office when he received a telegram from Kellogg in early October. The mining engineer had taken his time assaying the Black Hills, particularly the Washington area, which would soon take the name Lead, three miles southwest of Deadwood. Kellogg ultimately determined that the Homestake Mine there "was a good thing." The site on which the mine was built had been discovered by Cyrus Engh and the Manuel brothers—Fred and Moses. Deadwood Merchant H. B. Young had shrewdly offered to finance construction for a one-fifteenth share, netting himself one hundred feet of the Homestake Belt.[23]

Kellogg negotiated with Engh and the Manuel brothers, and a deal was struck. Hearst would buy 1,075 feet of the Homestake Mine for $60,166.66. Wasting no time, Hearst telegraphed Kellogg to post a thirty-day bond and meet him in San Francisco. Kellogg did as bidden. The purchase agreement was drawn up on October 3, and on October 4 Kellogg took a stagecoach 275 miles south to Sidney. In that Nebraska city, Kellogg boarded a Union Pacific train to San Francisco.[24]

After meeting with Kellogg, Hearst went to Haggin to see if he would invest. "It is too far off," Haggin told him. "I don't want it."

Hearst next spoke to the brothers Leo and Jacob Ash about investing, professing that he would take only a quarter. However, after one of the brothers was thrown into an asylum for drunkenness and the other bailed him out, Hearst learned they weren't content with leaving Hearst a quarter. They wanted it all. "Then there was a regular row about it as I found they wanted everything and this made me mad," Hearst remembered. Without any financial backing, Hearst realized he'd have to put up his own money if he wanted to keep his share of the Homestake. "I then went to Haggin and said I am going to the Black Hills tomorrow morning," Hearst recalled. The next morning, Hearst boarded an eastbound train to impose his will on Dakota Territory. Hearst's destination was a city that had sprung up in a Black Hills gulch, conspicuous for burned-out dead trees, about fifty miles north of where Custer's men had confirmed gold.[25]

Deadwood, people called it.

—10—

THE BLACK HILLS

(1877–1878)

And it is quite possible that I may get killed but if I should, I can't but lose a
few years and all I ask you is to see that my wife and child gets all that is due
them from all sources and that I am not buried in this place.
—George Hearst

Prospectors and pioneers began flooding into the mining camp that became
Deadwood as early as 1874. The army chased some of them off—after all, they
were violating the Treaty of 1868, which granted the land to the Lakota Sioux—
but there were too many. What's more, with the country suffering from the Panic
of 1873. America desperately needed an influx of gold, and the incursion was
largely winked at.

By 1877, Deadwood boasted more than three thousand residents. Having produced around $2 million in gold in two quick years, the mining town attracted
western heroes and villains. On August 2, 1876, James Butler "Wild Bill" Hickok
was shot in the back of the head by Jack McCall in Nuttall & Mann's No. 10
Saloon while playing poker. Legend had it that Hickok was holding aces and
eights; the two pair became known as "the dead man's hand." Hickok's friend
Martha Canary, commonly called Calamity Jane in the hills, grieved over his
death. That same month, Seth Bullock, a Canadian who had served as sheriff of
Montana's Lewis and Clark County, began a hardware store with Sol Starr. In

the winter of 1876–1877, Wyatt and Morgan Earp tried their luck in Deadwood before returning to Dodge City. In the spring of 1877, Al Swearengen—a Pacific Coast miner who had helped lay out Custer City in 1875—opened the notorious Gem Variety Theater. At the Gem, along with procuring prostitutes, Swearengen demonstrated his ability with a handgun by shooting glass balls out of the air in competition with his friend Silas Adams. Around the same time Swearengen opened the Gem, Bullock was appointed Lawrence County sheriff. As violent murders became an everyday occurrence, Bullock was kept busy.[1]

In mid-October 1877, Hearst, Kellogg, and Henry Janin's elder brother Louis—who occasionally worked for Hearst as a mining engineer—reached Deadwood. Hearst got right to work. On October 16, Hearst assessed the Golden Terry Mine. Liking what he saw, he bought the mine and formed the Golden Terra Mining Company. Serving as directors were J. B. Haggin, J. W. Bailey, Henry Janin, Mark L. McDonald, and George Hearst.[2]

As for the Homestake, Hearst could not immediately offer to purchase it. On November 1, Hearst dictated a letter to Haggin and Tevis, explaining, "We have secured only the interest we had under the bond, owing to the fact that other parties had bought the balance, except about 100 feet, before we got here. The purchasers live east. . . . We have been in communication with these eastern people."

While negotiating with Engh, Young, and the Manuel brothers, Hearst seemingly paradoxically shut down the Homestake Mine. To his San Francisco partners he explained his machinations: "As a mine always appears at best advantage when being actively worked we have shutdown all operations and will keep the mine closed until these people are settled with in some way. We hope they will all take the money instead of stock."

Hearst kept his cards close to his vest, confiding in Kellogg but not Janin that he'd made an arrangement with the Homestake superintendent to purchase a large share of the gold mine for $50,000. "I am also using other means to secure a good trade," Hearst explained cryptically. "I want to close up Homestake matters before I leave as I am afraid some blunder might be made by those that I should have to leave in charge which would cost of us a large sum of money."[3]

H. B. Young, who owned one hundred feet of the Homestake, accepted Hearst's offer of $10,000 plus the right to work the Homestake for an additional twenty days. This proved a good move, netting Young an additional $8,000. The others, however, held onto their shares. Hearst had a notice of transfer and assignment drawn up. Transferring Kellogg's share of the Homestake to Tevis, the notice was finalized on October 25. The Davenport and Black Hills Milling and Mining

Company held onto 325 feet of the Homestake. It sold 175 feet of the mine but contended that it owned the remaining 150-foot interest to the north. So far, Hearst and the Davenport Company were at loggerheads.[4]

The owners of the Golden Star Mine were also reticent to sell. Hearst offered $50,000 for the mine but was refused. "The Star people," Hearst groused, "contend that they are entitled to all the ground next to us . . . while we maintain that our title being the oldest we are entitled to the full width of our vein without any regard to surface lines. I want to settle this dispute before I leave and do whatever else is necessary to give us good title."[5]

Haggin and Tevis received good reports on the Golden Terry and the Homestake. But Hearst wasn't content with two gold mines. He wanted the Father de Smet Mine, located on the north slope of the bluff above Deadwood Creek. "This mine," Hearst marveled, "I assert is the *greatest* gold mine yet discovered in the *world*. . . . In this lode, all the other veins to the south seem to have come together and the result is such a deposit of ore as I never saw or dreamt before." Hearst learned that unfortunately, the owners had previously been offered $700,000 for the mine—and had refused.

Having to be content with the Homestake, Hearst and his partners formally incorporated the Homestake Mining Company on November 5, 1877. Its directors included George Hearst, Henry Janin, George S. Dodge, Mark L. McDonald, and Lloyd Tevis. The capital stock was valued at $10 million. Shares were immediately listed at the San Francisco Stock and Mining Company. Despite having two experienced and reliable superintendents in McMaster and Chambers, Hearst wanted them working the silver mines for now. Hearst hired William Farish as superintendent, Dan Rathburn as mine foreman, Jake Siegrist as master mechanic, and J. D. McIntyre as surveyor. One Mr. Nelson, whom Hearst personally thought "a humbug," began construction of a mill. Although things were not well settled in the Black Hills, Hearst traveled home for Christmas, arriving in San Francisco on December 7.[6]

To his son, Hearst told stories of elks, deer, and grizzly bears. To his friends, which included a San *Francisco Exchange* reporter, Hearst gave his impression of the Black Hills:

Why it beats anything in the way of gold quartz you ever saw. It made me open my eyes, you hear me. Talk about your Hayward mine, your Plumas, Eureka, Black Bear, your Sierra Buttes—why they are all babies, and small ones at that, compared with the Homestake, the De Smet, the Golden

Terra, the Arius, and other properties over there at the Black Hills. Take the Homestake alone, and there is a profit of a million a year in sight, and it will last for 25 years at that rate of profit, and the Homestake is perhaps not the biggest mine in the camp, but I wouldn't give it for any other.[7]

In early 1878, Hearst was back in Dakota Territory. Expanding the front office, Hearst hired L. H. Edelen to keep the Homestake books. With the Darwin mines on solid footing, Sam McMaster came along to assist in the overall development of the Black Hills mines. On January 17, the Davenport Company sold to Hearst 175 feet of the Homestake Company for $5,000. Six days later, as part of the deal, the disputed 150 feet—which would become known as the Segregated Homestake Claim—was deeded back to the Davenport Company.[8]

Thus began Hearst's plan to accumulate as much of the Homestake Belt as possible. To that end, in February he seized the Golden Run Mine for $3,000 and successfully negotiated with the Golden Star owners. For $1,000, he purchased Tim O'Leary's fifty feet; for $1,666.66, he acquired James M. Woods's fifty feet. The remaining 1,375 feet of the Golden Star he bought piecemeal from more than a dozen men, including Angus McMasters, a talented mining foreman, whom Hearst hired.[9]

Hearst certainly needed the manpower. To go along with the Homestake, Golden Run, and Golden Star, Hearst added the Deadwood Mine, Terra Mine, and Giant Mine to his Black Hills empire. Each mine proved contentious. Hearst quickly lost faith in the Deadwood Mine, though McMaster thought it would prove valuable. Hearst ordered his men to perform more crosscuts to determine value. The Terra Mine, too, was soon found to be off the main quartz belt. The Giant Mine in particular was plagued with problems. Although it had been purchased for $42,500, Hearst realized that someone had made $7,500 on the side, for the price should have been only $35,000. Furthermore, part of the Giant had been deeded elsewhere, the result of the original owners having signed it away at gunpoint. Complicating the issue even further, one of the owners ended up dead.

Problems at the Homestake Mine engendered additional grief. Hearst had demanded that an eighty-stamp mill be constructed. Instead, the Homestake was making do with a thirty-stamp mill. Poor weather and a bad road had also thwarted the gold mine's potential. Although Hearst narrowed his eyes at Nelson, it was the head of superintendent Farish he called for on March 1, 1877. Hearst personally blamed Farish for the inaccurate survey work conducted between

Homestake and Giant, which ceded good Homestake ground to the rival Old Abe and American Flag Mines. Hearst fired Farish that day. On March 5, the Homestake board of directors approved Farish's termination and appointed Samuel McMaster as agent and superintendent over the company's properties.

On March 29, Hearst received a letter from his son, one month shy of his sixteenth birthday. The boy was Willie was no longer. He now styled himself "W. R."

> My dear Papa,
>
> It seems a long time since you left us, and we miss you very much. As you have already reached the mines we hope you are more comfortable. Mama said last night she wished you were at home again. I wish so too. I spent most of the vacation with Andrew at the springs and enjoyed it very much.
>
> We killed a few rabbits and squirrels, though game was very scarce. . . .
>
> I wish I could spend a few days in the Black Hills, I would like to have a shot at some of those deer, elk, and maybe grizzly bears I heard you talk about.
>
> Bunny took some champagne last night and it made him tight; Mama was very much provoked with me but mad as she was she could not help but laughing at him. He has learned to open his cage and now we can hardly keep it fastened.
>
> As the bell will ring for school in a few minutes, I must close.
>
> With much love,
> Your affectionate son
> W. R. Hearst[10]

While W. R. yearned to shoot a grizzly bear, "Papa" was after different game: the Father de Smet Mine. For $400,000, Hearst bagged the enormous gold mine. On May 4 he personally examined it. To his horror, Hearst realized that the legendary Father de Smet Mine didn't hold a candle to the Homestake. Like the Terra Mine, though it had enormous amounts of ore on the surface, underground was a different story. Instead of being part of the Homestake quartz vein, the interior of the Father de Smet intersected with a split or a fork. To work it, Hearst turned back to Farish as superintendent. Although Hearst remained suspicious of Farish, he allowed him stock in the company, his policy with mine superintendents.[11]

Later that day, Hearst wrote Haggin a letter from Deadwood.

"I have delayed writing this," Hearst explained, "for the reason that things had not sufficiently matured in our matters and various interests. First, things were going to bad as fast as possible and more than you can imagine."

Hearst explained to his business partner the trouble with the Giant, Terra, Deadwood, and Father de Smet Mines. He now planned to sell the Father de Smet, if possible, for the $400,000 they had paid for it. He suggested that Haggin not discharge Nelson until after the mill was completed but cautioned, "When completed I think the amount of money it will cost will make your hair curl."

Hearst also discussed the difficulties of securing water rights. He had bonded the Montana Ditch, which diverted water from Whitewater Creek. Through Whitewater-Montana water, Hearst planned to let his Black Hills ambition blossom. "All of which I think can be done inside the law," Hearst added.

The fly in the ointment was the Boulder Creek Company, which had been established well before Hearst's Montana Ditch had bought rights to Whitewood Creek at a higher elevation, before the creek flowed into the Montana. Securing the high ground gave the Boulder Creek Company the power to turn the Montana Ditch dry. Without water, the Homestake Mine wouldn't be able to operate, entombing the millions in gold Hearst knew were locked underneath.

Although Boulder Creek had the clear advantage, Hearst saw one point of weakness and sought to capitalize on it. To service its diggings, Boulder Creek had shifted its own ditch to a new position. Beforehand, Boulder Creek had had its ditch below where the Montana Ditch was dug. Now it was above the Montana.

"Now," Hearst asked Haggin, "can the Boulder sell a water right and take it out in a younger location than the one spoken above?" It seemed a question to which Clarence Greathouse and Bill Stewart—who had recently formed a law partnership in San Francisco—might have an answer.

Anticipating Haggin's reaction to the storm of lawsuits and expensive claims, Hearst noted, "No don't think all of the country has gone to H., but to the contrary. Homestake, so far as gone, has proved better than supposed and still continues to do so and from present appearances will make perhaps the largest and best gold mine in the world."[12]

On May 15, 1878, an actual storm hit the Black Hills. Almost all work slowed to a crawl. On May 19, Hearst traveled by horse from Lead to Deadwood through snowdrifts four to eight feet deep, alternatingly driving and leading his horse. "It was laughable," Hearst wrote Haggin, "to see the horses floundering and rolling through the snow. It seemed so ridiculous."

Hearst's mood had definitely improved. Small wonder, for the Deadwood and Terra were now making money, and the Homestake more than ever. The Giant was still an issue, however. Hearst finally learned exactly why the original Giant owners had deeded away part of the mine. To Haggin, Hearst related, "They were forced to do so by being overpowered in numbers, their opponents holding the ground with rock forts and rifles, and they supposing they had better give a part and hold a part, or they would lose all, so a deed was given, with no consideration." In other words, "shotgun mining." Hearst had been sure he could beat the scoundrels in court, but then they complicated things further by selling part of the Giant to a second party.

"I am not sure that will cure the fraud," wrote Hearst. "At least I am preparing to make it very hot for them."[13]

Making things "very hot" in court for his mining rivals, as he had in 1871 during the Great Mining Suit in Pioche, had become habitual. Although in this case Hearst seemed on the side of the angels, his penchant for filing lawsuits did not impress one of his employees, Arthur DeWint Foote, who had begun working as a mining engineer for the Homestake Mine under McMaster. In an interview decades later with *Mining and Scientific Press*, Foote dished on Hearst: "His principal business was lawsuits. . . . He said, if he went to a dump he would be sure to pick up the only piece of good ore that was on it. . . . He himself was dirty, slovenly, and extremely vulgar."[14]

With Haggin, Hearst also discussed the issue of water rights. At first it appeared great headway had been made. In the midst of the snowstorm, the *Black Hills Daily Times* reported, "The ditch known as the Montana Boys ditch has been purchased by George Hearst. The ditch taps the Whitewood in the vicinity of the Ten Mile ranch, on the Cheyenne Road, and running down that stream to Lead." But Hearst could smell trouble coming.[15]

Among other worries, Hearst suspected that the Homestake Belt, deep underground, would eventually run into land owned by the Old Abe and American Flag. Because of this, Hearst reviewed the shoddy survey work for which he had fired Farish. A fraud had been perpetrated, though to the best of his knowledge Farish hadn't been in on it. Hearst reviewed the book of record for the original Homestake claim, made on January 7, 1876, finding that the latest survey was off by more than four hundred feet. Knowing he would need more than dusty papers in court, Hearst scouted the area himself.

"I commenced inquiry," Hearst related in a hastily written May 22 letter to Haggin, "and finally dropped on a man that of course the survey is wrong. He pointed out a house and said the center end stake does not stand 60 feet from your office and you will find the stump of a sapling that was marked as witness." Hearst slept on it, but in the morning he and the man located the sapling stump that served as the original border. This infuriated Hearst. To his mind, an area measuring fifteen hundred by six hundred feet had been stolen from the Homestake Mine—land that could conceivably be worth millions.

To Haggin, Hearst wrote:

> You can bet your life I have made up my mind to fight the thing out on the old line at all hazards, as it shows the most damnable fraud ever perpetrated in any country. I will hurt a good many people, as I wrote you, if we succeed in finding out the fraud and maintain our rights there would be more squealing than ever was heard before. And it is quite possible that I get killed, but if I should I can't but lose a few years and all I ask is that my wife and child gets all that is due and that I am not buried in this place.

Although his lawyers in the Black Hills felt he faced long odds, Hearst differed, confiding, "I am sure a strong fight can be made on it with a pretty good chance for winning and will have the survey made 1500 × 600 but will not publish until I hear from you by telegraph." For a second opinion, Hearst suggested that Haggin speak to Greathouse or Stewart. Hearst concluded, "This is a beautiful day. Crosscut in Deadwood still continues, now 4 feet in vein good ore. All things looking well. McMaster expects you to lay away 2000 shares of Homestake for him. Don't fail to do so. Yours, G. Hearst."[16]

The next day Hearst deployed his own surveyors and six witnesses to look up the original location of the Giant Mine. J. D. McIntyre was also sent to conduct a new survey of the Homestake Mine. To Haggin, Hearst wrote: "You must wake up Tevis to the importance of protecting our interest here, for while the quartz is not very rich, the amount of quartz that will pay a profit is enormous. You nor your children will never live to see the end or the time when this property will not be worked for a profit. But, as you are aware, it will take time, patience and money to perfect a title to so large and widespread a property as this, as we have all kinds of people to contend with and all on the make."[17]

By the end of May, Hearst had relocated from Deadwood to Lead. Although Deadwood was more well established, Lead—closer to the Homestake—was springing to life, with more than one hundred buildings under construction. Hearst men. To newspapermen, the boss spoke favorably about the Father de Smet Mine, downplaying the Homestake. But anyone with eyes and ears knew the truth. To a large degree, the men of Lead made their livelihood through Hearst's Homestake Mine and its thirty-stamp mill, which crushed gold from quartz day and night.[18]

With full faith in the Homestake Belt, Hearst didn't mind spending exorbitantly to secure every inch of it. Having sued the American Flag Mine unsuccessfully, Hearst went ahead and bought it on June 19 for $75,000. That same month he bought a further interest in the problematic Giant Mine, to which he had also attached several lawsuits. Hearst also had his lawyers battling against the Old Abe Mine, with his old friend J. W. Gashwiler overseeing strategy.[19]

Whether the shifting survey work was fraud or not, employee Arthur DeWint Foote was disgusted by Gashwiler's tactics, eventually quitting—and laying the blame on Hearst. "One point of particular technical interest . . . was whether the Homestake and the Old Abe veins came together in depth," Foote recalled, "but the mines were not opened sufficiently to warrant an opinion. It was thought finally that they would come together, so Hearst bought out the other parties, after trying to beat them in a lawsuit. I was not sorry to leave Deadwood, in '78, to go to Leadville."[20]

By autumn of 1878, Hearst had succeeded in buying the entirety of the Giant Mine, which was reincorporated in September as the Giant and Old Abe Mining Company, with J. B. Haggin, A. E. Head, Henry Janin, T. Bell, and Joe Clark as directors. That Hearst, Haggin, and Tevis were never listed together as directors seemingly indicated that they did not work in concert. But that was far from the truth. The game was to have one or more of the directors buy stock in a competing company until acquiring a controlling interest, then driving the stock down by selling shares at bedrock prices. Hearst, Haggin, or Tevis could then swoop in and buy the stock at a reduced rate.[21]

Having tied up the Boulder Creek Company with lawsuits—ensuring that for the time being the Homestake Mine could divert Whitewater Creek through the Montana Ditch—Hearst left McMaster in charge and boarded a train west. As Hearst's train pulled into the San Francisco station, a grand reception, led by Haggin, was there to greet him. But Hearst was not on board. Without telling his business partners, Hearst had stopped in Virginia City. After climbing back into his calèche—a horse-drawn carriage with a foldable hooded cover—Haggin was heard to remark, "Just like George, never on time. Home to dinner and meditation."[22]

Phoebe and Will celebrated the bonanza by setting sail in September 1878 from New York to Liverpool aboard the RMS *Russia*. Hearst, too, splashed some

Black Hills gold around by ordering construction of an eighteen-room Victorian ranch house at San Simeon, a half mile inland and on a rise near the Arroyo del Puerto Creek. Built with redwood and serving as headquarters for the ranch managers, the house also afforded Hearst and his family rooms whenever they chose to drop in.[23]

With his wife and son at sea, Hearst set his eyes on a dusty town in Arizona Territory near Tucson. On September 21, 1878, Hearst, Greathouse, and Joe Clark established the San Pedro Mining Company to mine silver in the Tough Nut Lode outside Tombstone. With his reputation at sizing up mines second to none, Hearst's investment helped lure more and more westerners to Tombstone. Lawman or cattle rustler, everyone was trying to get rich.[24]

Hearst would return to Arizona Territory in the days when the Cowboys were looking to assassinate the Earps, but for the time being, he could enjoy himself properly. While Phoebe and W. R. made their way across Europe to Florence and Rome, Hearst purchased the Blue Range gold mine near Downieville—forty miles north of Grass Valley—and a ritzier Nob Hill residence, this one at 726 California Street. Hearst kept the same office on Montgomery Street, but the *San Francisco Directory* now listed him with different occupation, one more befitting his new station: capitalist.[25]

— II —

CALIFORNIA ASSASSINS

(1879)

I found all our troubles at fever heat, and most of them at a culminating point.
—George Hearst

Lounging in the Homestake office in Lead on January 17, 1879, Superintendent
Sam McMaster bristled when Deputy Sheriff James Lynch pushed open the door,
flanked by A. L. London and Abe Cohen. As the rival owners of the Pride of the
West Mine, London and Cohen were the last people McMaster wanted to see.
Even less welcome was the cease and desist order Lynch delivered, insisting the
Homestake men halt all work on the Grand Prize Shaft, which the Pride of the
West claimed as its own.

"You needn't bring a regiment to give notice," McMaster sniggered. "You'd
be perfectly safe by yourself."[1]

McMaster's reputation said otherwise. "Mc"—as Hearst called him—had
searched the world for a rich strike, and now that he owned stock in the greatest
gold mine in the Black Hills, he wasn't about to let anybody talk him out of his share
of the spoils—especially not with Hearst, Haggin, and Tevis paying him to ensure
operations ran smoothly. He'd sooner start a war than cease and desist. As soon
as the intruders left, McMaster stormed from his office to the Grand Prize Shaft.
Unsurprisingly, he found the mineshaft boarded up. McMaster was in the midst
of removing a plank when Joseph Lewis, a Pride of the West tough, intervened.[2]

When McMaster threatened to bludgeon Lewis, Lewis drew a revolver. McMaster backed off, but once in Lead, he too called in the law. Warrants for malicious trespass were quickly served to the Pride of the West owners. While Abe Cohen's brother Pincus "Pink" Cohen bailed them out, McMaster returned to the Grand Prize Shaft with his foreman, Angus McMasters, and four of his roughest employees—Tom Lee, John Clark, Lee Smith, and William "Buffalo Bill" Travis—armed with pistols, shotguns, and rifles. The mineshaft was still covered, but McMaster wasn't about to let the dozens of lingering Pride of the West men keep it that way—not without a fight.[3]

What the Homestake boys didn't have in numbers they sought to make up in position. Angus McMasters posted himself near the front door of an old cabin. The foreman hadn't yet drawn his pistol, but there could be no mistaking it on his hip. Meanwhile, Clark, Smith, and Travis positioned themselves inside the cabin, taking up firing positions from one window. Yards away, Tom Lee—who may have been the deadliest of the bunch—kept close to Samuel McMaster.

To the Pride of the West men, Angus McMasters called out, "Stand aside if you don't want to be shot."

A split second later, one of the guards in the cabin fired a shotgun filled with buckshot. Caught in the neck, twenty-two-year-old Pride of the West employee Alex Frankenberg toppled as two more shots rang out from the cabin. Charging, the Pride of the West men overpowered McMasters, Lee, and McMaster. By the time they breached the cabin, Clark and Smith had slipped out the back window. Travis remained, but he wasn't about to shoot his way out. Holding Travis at gunpoint, the Pride of the West men confiscated a rifle and a double-barreled shotgun recognized as McMaster's.

The Homestake men were quickly arrested. The next day Clark and Smith surrendered as well. After it was officially determined that neither McMaster, McMasters, nor Lee had fired the shotgun, charges against the trio were dropped. But the trials of Clark, Smith, and Travis were just beginning.[4]

Still, the imprisoned men fared better than Frankenberg. Initially treated by Dr. W. C. White, Frankenberg appeared to be recovering until shortly after midnight on January 23. After his neck hemorrhaged, Dr. J. W. Coombs performed emergency surgery. No dice. Hours later, the young man died from blood loss. It was at that point that the groundswell of rage against the Homestake Mine boiled over. That morning townsfolk of Lead called a community meeting, distributing placards branding Clark, Smith, and Travis "California Assassins."

To bring the assassins to justice, jurors were selected from throughout Lawrence County. If it looked grim for the arrested men, there was one comfort. The principal owner of the Homestake Mine, George Hearst, was set on returning to the Dakotas.[5]

Phoebe didn't like that one bit. Writing from Florence, Italy, on February 5, 1879, she warned her husband, "I hope you will avoid 'Black Hills' and all Indian countries where there may be danger. We don't want anything to happen [to] you. The money would be of little value if you could not enjoy it with us."[6]

Nevertheless, with the murder trial under way, Hearst traded San Francisco for the Black Hills. He headquartered himself in the Samuel McMaster's office in Lead instead of Deadwood. Hearst inspected not only the mines—having long conversations with Louis Janin, who was writing a report about the gold strike—but the courtroom as well. Presiding over the murder trial was Judge Gideon Moody—a Civil War veteran who had fought in the Ninth Indiana Regiment (called the "Bloody Ninth" by newspapers)—whom Hearst deemed "a very stern and upright Judge."

Fortunately, Hearst's law team was the best in the Hills. Despite McMaster's reservations, Hearst thought highly of lawyer A. D. Thomas. Along with being thoroughly organized, Thomas was the son-in-law of Alanson H. Barnes, a justice of the territorial supreme court and a good connection to have. Hearst also thought well of Thomas's law partner Dighton Corson, a former district attorney of Milwaukee County. Furthermore, the team included W. H. Claggett, who knew fine points of mining law and was a solid orator.

Hearst certainly needed all the legal talent he could get.

On March 6, he wrote the following on McMaster's letterhead:

My dear Haggin:

I arrived here in good health. Had a cold trip but the weather has been very good since my arrival and is now quite warm. I found all our troubles at fever heat, and most of them at a culminating point. The shooting scrape, combined with the various civil suits, made it pretty lively around the Court House.

We have all the boys out of jail except three [Clark, Smith, and Travis] and they are there for murder and will be tried this term of court. Their trial was to come off this week but the most important witnesses could not be found.[7]

One of the most important and slippery witnesses, a man named McCullough, had gone missing. Rumor had it McCullough had been "gobbled."[8]

In California matters, Hearst was concerned about the San Simeon ranch. He asked Haggin to send to the ranch between two hundred and three hundred small trees, either yellow pine or Monterey cypress, to act as a windbreak. Hearst also expressed interest in purchasing Nipomo Ranch, sixty-five miles south of San Simeon. "I want that property to make a magnificent estate and home out of. It is a fancy place and a valuable one and the last chance to get such a one." As for the mines, Hearst inspected the Homestake, determining that it was "looking first-rate." The Terra, Deadwood, and Highland Chief were "looking pretty well." Even the Giant showed potential. Hearst also smelled potential in a large body of coal, already in use at the blacksmith shop, that had been discovered twenty-five or thirty miles from Lead. Recognizing that building a railroad was inevitable, Hearst wanted to capitalize on the find. "I intend looking into the matter carefully," Hearst wrote Haggin, "as fuel will soon be a serious question with us and this coal is good and can be mined for not to exceed $1.50 per ton, and to be delivered here for a like sum."

Not all of Hearst's mining enterprises were going well, however. Hearst expressed irritation with Gashwiler for buying Old Abe for more money than he needed to, subsequently giving "outsiders confidence in thinking they could at any time force us to pay out money. And I certainly think the effect of it all has been stupendous and outrageous."

Encouraged by Gashwiler's largesse, Hearst faced enemies everywhere. All told, he had more than thirty different lawsuits, both civil and criminal, to contend with. Although Hearst quickly settled a lawsuit with the Prince Oscar Mining Company for $5,000, it was a drop in the bucket. Hearst acknowledged Haggin's warning "about me not getting killed" but wasn't about to back off. Instead, Hearst asked Haggin to send Greathouse to the Black Hills to bolster the legal team.[9]

Hearst also started a rumor that he intended to stay in the Black Hills. It had the effect Hearst hoped for. Three days later, Hearst wrote Haggin, "Since my arrival here the hostility towards our people in the way of lawsuits and threats of violence, I think has very much died out, as I tell them I have brought my blankets and intend to stay here and run for Congress and many have come to me and fairly thrown up the sponge and signified a willingness to take anything I will give them. I think they are getting tired of fighting."[10]

Nine days later, on March 18, 1879, a jury deliberated on whether Clark, Smith, and Travis were guilty or innocent. Of the twelve jurors, only Captain Oliver

Dodson and Frank Kelly voted guilty. The other ten voted for acquittal. They cited a lack of evidence and witnesses. Whether Hearst or his people had bribed the jurors, or whether they made the evidence and witnesses disappear, went unconfirmed—though speculation in the papers was rampant.

Judge Moody reluctantly declared Clark, Smith and Travis to be innocent but found the jury guilty. To the ten who had voted for acquittal he reprimanded, "If a cold-blooded murder can be committed here, in broad day-light, and the witnesses can be spirited out of the country, and all the evidences of the crime hidden and destroyed—as has been done in this case—why I would as soon trust my life and liberty to twelve Piegan Indians as to a Lawrence county jury."[11]

Judge Moody also ordered the names of the jurors stricken from the record. Thereafter the jurors became known as "The Pagan Indian Jury."[12]

Hearst wrote Haggin the good news on the day of the acquittal: "The parties who were indicted for killing the man—Frankenberg—in the mill site were today acquitted, but the hostility of the Judge seems to be very great, as he took the jury very much to task and dismissed them from the venire. What other trouble may arise from it we don't know."[13]

With the murder trial put to bed, Hearst could more fully concentrate on maximizing Black Hills profits. But his mind turned back to California and his ranch in San Simeon. On March 23, Hearst wrote to Haggin:

> There are some odds and ends among my cattle on the ranch which will be fat early and perhaps are now, and I think that early beef will bring a pretty good price and if so all that will do well for beef ought to be sold. My lambs ought to be sold in April. They are large and very fine and ought to bring a good price. Also the Wethers and Bannen ewes, if mutton is a fair price.
>
> G. H.[14]

Hearst boarded another train, reaching the Golden State on April 15. Hearst might have felt like he'd jumped from the frying pan to the fire, for California politics had heated up in his absence. Bending to pressure exerted by rabble-rousing Irish demagogue Denis Kearney, on May 7, 1879, California ratified a new state constitution. It gave teeth to the sentiments expressed by Kearney's Workingmen's Party of California: anti-Chinese, anti-monopolist, anti-capitalist. The law now forbade corporations from employing "any Chinese or Mongolian." Kearney imagined that without Chinese competition, the railroad barons would have to pay their employees higher wages, a first step toward curbing the power of the railroads, an unchecked monopoly that charged exorbitant freight rates.[15]

Although Hearst did not abandon the Democratic Party for the Working-men's Party as many men did, he agreed with the WPC's platform concerning Chinese immigrants, holding that by working harder and for less money than white Americans, Chinese laborers had a detrimental effect on the labor force. Hearst believed that instead of Chinese labor, Californians should turn to child labor. Commented Hearst, "I believe that the labor of children should be utilized. The great objection I have to the Chinese is, they work so cheap, and do a great deal of work that might be done by our children. If there were no Chinamen in California, a great deal of the fruit . . . would necessarily have to be gathered by the children, and this would make them industrious."[16]

Child labor laws aside, Hearst complied with the new constitution, forbidding his California mining corporations from hiring Chinese workers.

Awash in gold and silver, overseeing an empire that stretched from the Pacific Ocean to the Black Hills, Hearst could afford to pay good wages. If his profits shrank because he paid his employees more than what Chinese labor would have cost, they did not shrink by much.

The WPC was not as powerful. During the elections of 1879, both the Demo-cratic Party and the Workingmen's Party of California were trounced. Along with losing ground in the state assembly and state senate, they lost the governorship to Republican George C. Perkins. Had the Workingmen's Party not split the anti-Republican vote, Perkins, who won the election with only 42 percent of the vote, wouldn't have had a chance.

Having backed the wrong horse, Kearney's followers deserted the demagogue and slunk back to the Democratic Party. Hearst, who hadn't been swayed by Kearney, appeared prescient for remaining with the Democrats. Sure, Hearst also appeared villainous and grasping, always open to whatever real estate scheme Haggin hatched. But to seize the executive mansion in Sacramento, perhaps a villain was what the Democrats needed.

—PART III—
THE ART OF THE POSSIBLE

We hang the petty thieves and appoint the great ones to public office.
—Aesop

—12—

HEARST FOR GOVERNOR

(1880–1882)

I knew no more about a newspaper than the man in the moon.
—George Hearst

In January 1880, George Hearst was reported dead by the Deadwood press. To create an obituary, newspaper reporters in San Francisco began canvasing Hearst's old friends. The reporters immediately disseminated two important facts. The first was that Hearst was alive and well. The second was that he was planning to run for governor.[1]

With the election more than two years away, Hearst headed to Arizona Territory. On February 4, he checked into Tucson's Cosmopolitan Hotel with William McCaskell, a well-known mining expert, and Juan Castro, who had sold Hearst portions of Piedra Blanca and could serve as translator once they crossed into Mexico.

That Hearst was trading the relative safety of the United States for the chance to gobble up some Mexican property wasn't lost on him. If he was going to die, his will would have to be modified. On April 29, coincidentally his son's seventeenth birthday, papers were filed in San Francisco. In the event of his death, Hearst's entire fortune would now go "to my wife absolutely." There was a hitch, however. If Phoebe remarried, the boy would get it all.

"I commend my son, William R. Hearst, to my said wife, having full confidence that she will make suitable provisions for him, but in the event of the marriage of my said wife after my death, I hereby give and bequeath to my son all of my said property that may remain in the possession of my said wife at that date." Doubtless, Hearst kept the details of his new will private.[2]

With Hearst's house now in order, he and McCaskell were reported in Sonora, Mexico, in May looking over mining enterprises. On June 12, Hearst and geologist Walter P. Jenney were in Harshaw, Arizona Territory, thirteen miles north of the border. Acquiring an old Mexican property known as the Trench, Hearst began building it up. Before long, the Trench boasted a shaft reaching 106 feet and a 40-foot tunnel, though a lack of lumber forced a temporary halt to construction. Once the facility was operational, Hearst's workmen sank a four-hundred-foot shaft and installed cutting-edge steam hoisting works to reap greater profits.[3]

Hearst also purchased the Boquillas Land Grant—located about ten miles northwest of Tombstone—from the Elias family in Sonora. Hearst sold some of the land to new owners, who then formed cattle ranches and silver mines. On the portion of the land grant that Hearst felt was most promising, he started a cattle ranch, began work on a railroad, and built up the Contention Mine.[4]

On July 18, Hearst wrote Haggin: "I have done more and accomplished less, so far than I would like, but I think it will be all right yet. . . . But I assure you this is the hardest place to accomplish anything I have ever met. No telegrams or even mail." Hearst also praised the Contention Mine—"she is a beautiful mine"—and predicted that its future would be as good as any silver mine he knew.[5]

Haggin, meanwhile, had been busy. Under the auspices of Haggin, Tevis, and Hearst, he had purchased for $650,000 the lucrative Jocuistita silver mines in Sinaloa, Mexico. While in Tucson, Hearst had a chance encounter with newspaperman John M. Barrett. As noted in the memoirs of Richard E. Sloan, a *Rocky Mountain News* reporter and future governor of Arizona, Hearst and Barrett "proceeded to celebrate their newly formed acquaintanceship in the then characteristic Western manner"—that is, with whiskey. In his cups, Hearst shared with Barrett his political ambition. Barrett saw potential, encouraging Hearst to buy the fledgling *San Francisco Evening Examiner* to help realize his dreams. It was advice Hearst took to heart.[6]

Back in San Francisco, "The Black Hills Bonanza King," as some newspapermen began calling him, sold his old home and purchased an opulent Nob Hill mansion—once owned by Johnny "the Buster" Skae—at 1315 Van Ness Avenue. At Phoebe's instruction, additional rooms were built to accommodate visitors.

Some of these guests were Hearst's political friends, who suggested he use his vast wealth to found a Democratic newspaper.[7]

"There is no use in doing that. Why not buy up the old Examiner?" Hearst suggested.[8]

The *Examiner* had remained a Democratic paper under the guidance of B. F. Washington, who railed against Reconstruction, Republicans, and the power of the railroads. But when Washington died of complications related to gout in 1872, the *Examiner* lost some of its verve. Four years later, historian Benjamin E. Lloyd noted that the *Evening Examiner* was "characterized for the chasteness of its contents—nothing whatever of a sensational nature being permitted in its columns . . . it is not much sought after by the public as a dispenser of local gossip."[9]

It would not stay that way for long.

The publishing house W. T. Baggett & Company was formed, buying the *Examiner* in October 1880. William Baggett, a lawyer from Tennessee whose credentials included publishing the *San Francisco Law Journal*, would serve as editor, Hearst and his friends as owners. At least that was the theory. Although his friends liked the idea of managing the *Examiner*, they weren't all that interested in paying for it.

"I found that I had to put in all the money myself," Hearst lamented. "I knew no more about a newspaper than the man in the moon, and when I looked over the property I said, this looks very like a quartz mill to me, and it will take a great deal of money to manage it. The boys said they would attend to that, and turn it into a morning paper and it would not cost more than ten or twelve thousand dollars."[10]

Immediately, the newly christened *Daily Examiner* began to flounder. Turning the newspaper into a morning paper wasn't terribly difficult, but with the newspaper losing up to $500 a week, Hearst could not afford to run it as an eight-page paper. He scaled it down to four pages.

Within those four pages, Baggett began to cast Hearst in a different light, not just as a mining tycoon but as a man of the people. First, the *Examiner* covered Phoebe's October 23 meeting at their Nob Hill home, attended by about eighty women, to raise funds for the Homeopathic Hospital through a Spring Tide Festival.[11] Next, with General Winfield Scott Hancock, the hero of Gettysburg, running as the Democratic nominee for president against Republican James Garfield, the *Examiner* beat the drum for a parade in support of Hancock. Thousands of Democrats, predicted the *Examiner,* would march up Market Street, following the grand marshal, who had made his headquarters at 212 Sutter Street. The grand marshal? George Hearst, of course.

At 7:30 in the evening on October 29, 1880, with the election of 1880 just a few days away, Hearst led the Democratic parade. From Market Street to Kearney, Montgomery, and all the way to Van Ness and back, Hancock supporters marched while throngs of men and women lined the sidewalks. The next morning the *Examiner* shoveled praise: "The capitalists, the professional men, the small traders and the horny-handed sons of toil generally, under the Grand Marshalship of George Hearst, were there, in all the strength and dignity of American citizenship. The enthusiasm and air of assured victory which pervaded the whole of that mighty mass of intelligent men was an indication of the splendid triumph which is to be ours, on Tuesday next."[12] Hearst may have won the night, but on November 2, as assured victory became bitter defeat, the *Examiner* was forced to change its tune. Although Hancock carried the South, Garfield and the Republicans won the election, 214 electoral votes to 155. California, for the first time, had gone Democratic, winning the contest by a razor-thin 144 votes. Hearst and Baggett could take some credit for that. With the Democratic Party on the rise in California, the plan Hearst hatched in Tucson—to use the *Examiner* to launch his political career—was taking shape.

As the new year dawned, Hearst and Baggett worked in tandem to keep the good press going. On January 19, 1881, Phoebe held a gala event at their Van Ness mansion, raising awareness of the San Francisco Homeopathic Hospital, of which she had become a director. On February 27, the *Examiner* reported that Hearst had purchased the thirty-seven-thousand-acre Nipomo Ranch in Santa Maria. On April 2, Phoebe met her fellow directors at the Van Ness mansion and was elected president. Later that month, on April 20, Hearst was confirmed as a trustee of the California State Miners' Hospital and Asylum. *Examiner* reporters even covered Will's eighteenth birthday and a trip Phoebe and Will took to San Simeon and Monterey with Orrin Peck. When on May 21 the colt Jim Brown won a 1.75-mile race with the best time ever recorded, 3:06, the *Examiner* made sure readers knew it was Hearst's colt.[13]

Mining matters also kept Hearst in the headlines. Traveling again to Idaho Territory, Hearst reached Boise City on May 24. Assaying mining claims there, Hearst purchased the Belmont Mine on the Snake River, near Heath, in mid-June. The mine produced more than fifty thousand ounces of silver, and the ten-stamp mill that Hearst had erected became so iconic that it was later depicted on Idaho's state seal. Meanwhile, Joe Clark visited Tombstone, looking at the Tough Nut Lode. His reports back to Haggin were contradictory. After Haggin vacillated, letting the bond expire, Hearst realized the matter would ultimately require his personal attention.[14]

Back in San Francisco, Hearst seamlessly shifted from mining to politics. He, Phoebe, and Baggett had done a fair job of making "Hearst" a household name, but the newspaper could be a double-edged sword. The *Examiner* ran advertisements for the Southern Pacific Railroad, bringing in $300 a month. But knowing that any connection to the rapacious Southern Pacific would tar him, Hearst terminated the deal in October 1881. This was a good move, but it would take more than that to have a real chance in the upcoming gubernatorial fight. One way or the other, he would have to face off with Christopher Buckley, the Boss Tweed of San Francisco.[15]

Buckley's rise to political power was as unlikely as it was remarkable. Born of Irish immigrants in New York City on Christmas Day 1845, Buckley traveled to San Francisco in 1862. In his first years in the city he worked for factional ward bosses and sub-bosses, absorbing the political machinations of the city. Republican boss Martin Kelly observed that Buckley "developed a knack for colonizing boardinghouses and turning tricks in the rough work of the primaries." In his early thirties, Buckley opened the Alhambra Saloon on the corner of Bush and Kearny Streets. Around the same time, tragedy struck: he lost most of his vision. However, his politician's memory for voices, his acute hearing, and his Machiavellian understanding of city politics enabled him to rise to the position of ultimate Democratic powerbroker in San Francisco, despite his impairment. Modeling himself on Boss Tweed, by 1882 "the Blind Boss" had turned the Alhambra Saloon into his own private Tammany Hall. "Buckley City Hall" was how adherents and rivals referred to it. Visiting the Bay City, Rudyard Kipling noted, "Today the city of San Francisco is governed by the Irish vote . . . under the rule of a gentleman whose sight is impaired and who requires a man to lead him about the streets. He is officially called 'Boss Buckley,' and unofficially the 'Blind White Devil.'"[16]

Like Hearst, Buckley refused to defect to the Workingmen's Party of California. As the Democrats slunk back to the fold, Buckley formed the Yosemite Club. The Yosemites consisted of ward bosses, delegates, and the operators of political machinery. But Hearst, who liked to have things his own way, refused to join. Instead, Hearst formed his own Manhattan Club in opposition. In doing so, Hearst effectively divided the California Democrats into two wings: the Yosemites and the Manhattanites.[17]

Hearst and Baggett had an opportunity to discuss strategy in Santa Clara on July 18, 1881, attending the fiftieth wedding anniversary of Martin and Mary Murphy. If the cost of running the *Examiner* didn't come up, it was certainly on Hearst's mind. By this time, the newspaper had cost Hearst about $50,000.[18] Was Baggett to blame?

With problems at the paper and within the Democratic Party mounting, Hearst abandoned San Francisco. Boarding a train on August 26, he reached Salt Lake City two days later. Hearst didn't stay long, boarding another train, this time for Montana Territory. Basing himself out of Butte, Hearst made a canvas of the nearby mines. He saw nothing worth investing in, which must have disappointed several Butte miners. But Hearst was in an unforgiving mood. On September 15, 1881, he replaced Baggett with Greathouse as *Examiner* editor. Whether Baggett was fired or induced to resign unsurprisingly went unreported. Whichever the case, the *Examiner* now ran under the auspices of the Examiner Publishing Company instead of W. T. Baggett & Co.[19]

Returning to Salt Lake City in late September, Hearst stopped by the Ontario Mine. In early October, Hearst was back in San Francisco. Spending more and more time at the Bay District Track with Haggin and Lucky Baldwin, Hearst established the Hearst Stakes—a one-mile dash for two-year-old horses that had lost previous races. From his pocket, Hearst ponied up $175 in prize money. Although he was generous, cynics may have wondered if Hearst had political motives. In the Black Hills, Sam McMaster almost certainly had ulterior motives when on December 10—having finally completed his railroad—he christened the first engine to chug through the hills *George Hearst*. Thanks to McMaster, Hearst was now man *and* machine.[20]

In late December 1881, Hearst began planning a trip to Tombstone. This time it was Tevis who warned Hearst to be careful. Two months earlier, Virgil Earp, Wyatt Earp, Morgan Earp, and "Doc" Holliday had gunned down Tom McLaury, Frank McLaury, and Billy Clanton behind the O.K. Corral. All of Tombstone waited for "the Cowboys" to strike back, and Tevis didn't want Hearst caught in the crossfire.

Ignoring his business partner's advice, Hearst and John Sevenoaks boarded a southbound train, reaching Los Angeles on December 23. He arrived in Tombstone on Christmas. Three days later, at 11:30 P.M. on December 28, 1881, Cowboys shot and wounded Marshal Virgil Earp outside the Oriental Saloon. Hearst may have been out of town during the shooting, for on January 3, 1882, George W. Parsons, a Tombstone lawyer and friend of the Earps', noted in his diary Hearst's return to Tombstone on the evening stagecoach. The next day Parsons scribbled, "Met George Hearst this morning and had quite a talk. He seems to like the camp."[21]

According to Parsons, Hearst was still in the camp on January 13, 1882, during a "cold and frightfully windy day," on which Hearst was joined by former U.S. senator William M. Stewart and former Arizona Territory governor Anson Safford.[22] Bright and early on the morning of January 15, Hearst and a party of five others took a stagecoach fifteen miles east to the Dragoon Mountains. The leader of the party was John Henry Jackson, a sometimes lawman who was considered a safe alternative to the rowdy Earp brothers. As with his neutrality in the Civil War, Hearst tried his best to stay out of Tombstone's deadly feud.

After examining the Defiance Mine, Hearst, J. H. Jackson, and H. M. French saddled three horses and made for the harder-to-reach mines: Black Jack, Dragoon, Elgin, Lake Superior, and Hidden Treasure. Once back in Tombstone, the party dined at the popular Fourth Street restaurant Jakey's. The *Tombstone Epitaph* commented that Hearst seemed

> favorably impressed with the mines. . . . We trust that his favorable report upon his return to San Francisco will set the great mining operators of the Pacific Coast to thinking that, after all, Arizona is worth looking after a little. It is very natural that we should have a fellow-feeling for Mr. Hearst as he is a newspaper man, being the owner of the San Francisco Examiner. . . . He is also the probable Democratic nominee for Governor of the State at the coming election this fall, and will stand a good show for election if there is harmony in the party which, for his sake, we are sorry to say, now looks most improbable.[23]

The following day Hearst purchased a stake in the Contact Mine for an initial $5,000. He soon invested another $10,000 and expended another $6,000 to build up the mine. Satisfied with his work in Tombstone, Hearst next traveled south to Sonora. On February 19, he returned to Tombstone. Nine days later, he stopped in Los Angeles before boarding a Southern Pacific train north.[24]

It wasn't until April, back in San Francisco, that Hearst received the gift he'd been waiting for. After months of backbiting between Yosemite Democrats and Manhattan Democrats, both clubs disbanded and joined forces. The *San Francisco Examiner* jubilantly reported, "Victory is assured in the coming months."[25] But whose victory was another story. The primary election—which would be decided by 435 Democratic delegates—was slated for June 22 in Santa Clara. George Stoneman, a famous Union cavalry general, was running as an anti-monopolist and a fervent anti-railroad candidate, having worked diligently as a railroad commissioner for several years. James A. Johnson, the former lieutenant governor, was also in the mix. More of a machine politician, Johnson was seen as more palatable by the railroads and corporations, though this made him enemies among his own party. Both men would be tough to beat. Considering the race, the *Los Angeles Herald* branded Hearst a dark horse candidate.[26]

Leaving his political future in the hands of Greathouse and Judge George Flournoy—one of the sharpest political operatives in the state—Hearst returned to Tombstone. Spring 1882 was an especially violent time for the dusty Arizona town. On March 18, 1882, Morgan Earp was assassinated in Tombstone. Two days later, Wyatt Earp gunned down Cowboy Frank Stillwell, the opening shots in what became known as "The Vendetta Ride." By the time it was over, Wyatt and Doc Holliday had broken the power of the Cowboys but were persona non grata in Arizona Territory.

To avoid being shot himself, Hearst once again turned to J. H. Jackson. Under Jackson's protection, Hearst and A. E. Head traveled 175 miles into New Mexico to look at mines in the Victorio Mountains. Hearst and Head also established an expansive cattle ranch in Deming, twenty-five miles beyond the Victorio Mountains. Inhabited by grizzly bears, Mexican gray wolves, and mountain lions, this was wild country. But Texas Ranger Michael Gray thought it had potential as a cattle ranch. Hearst and Head thought so as well, purchasing a thousand acres from Gray for $12,000, ultimately rechristening the land as the Diamond Arrow Ranch.[27]

Hearst, Head, and Jackson reentered Tombstone on April 23, 1882, during the last days of the vendetta ride. Having lost faith in the Contact Mine, Hearst forfeited it and the $21,000 he had poured into it. Afterward, Hearst boarded a northbound train to Prescott.[28]

Returning to San Francisco, he found politics at a fever pitch. On May 6, 1882, President Chester A. Arthur signed the Chinese Exclusion Act, suspending Chinese immigration for a decade. As xenophobic Democrats cheered, Hearst determined it was finally time to announce his candidacy for governor, riding the anti-Chinese wave. On May 17, from the second page of the *Examiner*, Hearst declared, "My name will, with my consent, be submitted to the Democratic State Convention for the gubernatorial nomination."

Hearst went on to outline his platform. He backed the Chinese Exclusion Act in the name of protecting free labor. He asked readers to bear in mind that the railroad commissioners should act with "unrestricted authority" to supervise the railroad corporations. He styled himself a man of the laboring classes. Promised Hearst, "Should the choice of the nomination fall upon me, I shall use every honorable effort to crown its work with success, and I will not disappoint its best expectations."[29]

Hearst may have wished to paint himself as anti-Chinese, anti-railroad, and pro-labor, but his enemies had other ideas. The *Oakland Tribune* repeatedly castigated Hearst as a "Chivalry Democrat"—that is, proslavery—and opined that Hearst's only chance of winning the gubernatorial election was through bribing the California Legislature. The *Stockton Herald, San Francisco Chronicle,* and *San Francisco Evening Post* also strongly opposed Hearst, dubbing him the corporate candidate, the railroad candidate, and a monopolist. Through the *Examiner,* Greathouse fought back, publishing letters praising Hearst, supposedly written by old miners, and reprinting positive Hearst sentiment from newspapers throughout California. "George is a miner all over," the *Examiner* quoted a Nevada City man saying, "and even if he is worth fifteen or twenty million dollars (don't he wish he was?) he is the same old coon as ever."[30]

Although Hearst was certainly the most popular candidate in the territories, receiving endorsements from Salt Lake City, Tombstone, Butte, and Deadwood—whose citizens felt Hearst would look after their mining interests—California Democrats appeared to be lining up more with Stoneman.

To Hearst, it didn't entirely matter that the majority of Democrats preferred the general. Hearst didn't need to convince all of California; he just needed to convince a majority of the California Democratic Convention that they would benefit more from Hearst than Stoneman or Johnson. To that end, Hearst's cronies forged a secret alliance with Christopher Buckley, who instructed his adherents to back Hearst when the time was right.[31]

On June 22, 1882, the California Democratic Convention met in San Jose, fifty miles southeast of San Francisco. Judge Flournoy formally nominated Hearst for governor. "Common sense, genuine manhood, earnest labor, quickness of apprehension, decisiveness of purpose, independence of thought, adherence to his confidence in what is right, these made up the secret of his success," Flournoy declared. "Perhaps he did not have the early cultivation that so many men, more fortunate in their youth may have had, but he was richly endowed by nature with unflinching courage and with independence."

Niles Searls, who had been elected to the California State Senate in 1877, representing Nevada City, seconded the motion. Searls painted for the audience a picture of George Hearst, the miner—of his successes and all the help he gave those less fortunate: "In the pioneer days George Hearst came to Nevada County with small means, a pure heart, and an elegant backbone. He saved his money and amassed a fortune. He was no ordinary man. He was a prince clothed in the garb of a miner. If elected there will be no power behind the throne of George Hearst."

Hearst did not hear these concluding words. Though the convention was riveted by Searls's storytelling, Hearst had exited the hall, his eyes filled with tears. "The old, old times," Hearst reflected. "Searls makes me think of the days when I used the rocker, and of the boys that are dead and gone."[32]

When Hearst was called to speak, his name was greeted with applause. Hearst stepped forward, about to give the most important speech of his life to date.[33]

"If you expect a set speech of me, you will be sadly disappointed," Hearst opened. "I'm more of a worker than a man of words." These words were met with expected cheers and laughter. But in that laughter there was a touch of surprised confusion and a few jeers. Everyone knew George Hearst by reputation, as the prominent mining tycoon and newspaper owner. But not everyone had heard him speak. The pronounced Missouri drawl and slightly high-pitched voice were startling. Sensing this reaction may have thrown Hearst off his game.

After the ruckus died down, Hearst announced that if he received the nomination, he would do all within his power to make his administration "thoroughly Democratic." He admitted that he would "not be a sorehead and a whiner if . . . beaten." He concluded, "Whatever earnings I have made in mining operations on various parts of this coast I have invested in land and stock-raising, and necessarily had to employ a great number of . . . white men, and not Chinese. At all events, all that I have . . . is in this state and I expect to remain here until I die and be wrapped in the clay of this Golden State."[34]

Next to speak was George Stoneman. As the cheering ceased, Stoneman "offered as security for the future his record in the past." Stoneman also cautioned against a third-party movement. While inviting the delegates to examine his past, Stoneman was looking to the future. Should he defeat Hearst, he did not want Hearst and Buckley to bolt and form their own parties.

The first ballot cast had Hearst with a narrow lead: 126 votes for Hearst, 117 for Stoneman. Of the other strong candidates, Campbell P. Berry had sixty-six, James A. Johnson had sixty-five, and Clay W. Taylor had sixty-one. Leading the pack from the outset wasn't part of Hearst's plan. Worried by the jeers hurled at Hearst during his speech, Buckley's Irishmen—purposefully placed in the back so as to not draw attention—had dropped almost all pretense, coming out too strongly. Delegates representing the farming communities smelled a rat, hearing the name "Hoist" repeatedly called out in an Irish brogue.[35]

By the end of the day, the delegates had cast seven ballots but remained deadlocked. The final ballot showed 151 votes for Hearst, 136 for Stoneman, 92 for Taylor, 52 for Johnson, and 17 for Berry. Hearst had the lead, but he was 78 votes shy of the 229 needed to secure the nomination. At nine the next morning, the delegates again met in the Garden City. Once more they voted. The result was that Hearst had gained eight votes while Stoneman had lost four: 159 to 132. During the ninth ballot, Hearst extended his lead. The tenth showed him with 169 votes, but with Stoneman closing the gap with 147. It was at that point that Berry withdrew.

When the eleventh ballot was totaled, Hearst still led—but only just. Almost all of Berry's supporters had thrown their weight to Stoneman. The tally was Hearst 170, Stoneman 166. At the end of the twelfth ballot, Hearst was in for a shock. He had 174 votes while Stoneman leaped ahead with 189. The announcement produced cheering from the farmers, outrage from the Hearst supporters. A recess was quickly called. At 1:45 P.M. the Democratic Convention was once more called to order. If Hearst attempted to cut any backroom deals, they had little effect. By the end of the thirteenth ballot Stoneman had increased his lead, 204 to Hearst's 170. The fourteenth ballot decided the nomination. Stoneman had 243 votes, Hearst 170. Hats were flung in the air and Stoneman was cheered. The Southern Pacific contingent had ultimately decided the matter. Sensing weakness in Hearst, Johnson's supporters had thrown their votes to Stoneman.

Having lost the governorship in part because of his lackluster set speech, Hearst then made one of the best speeches of his life. Delivered in a conversational tone, as if to a group of friends and confidants, Hearst's speech was interspersed with good-natured laughter and comments from the delegates.

> I had a pride to occupy the high office of Governor. I think that was an honorable pride, but I found in that contest a great general, a man who had defeated many armies, and it is not very astonishing that gentleman defeated me. [Cheering drowned his words.] . . . You have placed a good man at the head of your ticket. Let me impress that upon you. True, I do not think it is necessary to impress it upon you, but I have to say something. [Laughter.] . . . I mean to say, you have got something to do to win this fight. You have got the state patronage and the patronage of the general government against

you, and I think you'll have to fight the corporations of this state. [A voice: "You bet your life."] I believe there will be more money spent against the General than all of us can raise. [A voice: "I think so myself."] To beat money requires combination and union of action. Now, gentlemen, all I have to say, because I know you are tired, is that I will be found in in the field as I told you, and will fight as bravely as if I had never been defeated. I'm not going to lose my generalship, either. [Cheers.]

. . . I know some people have told you I could not make a speech. I know you have heard that I spelled bird with a u and which with a t, and that I cannot write more English than my name. That is all right now.

You have also heard that I was worth ten million dollars and twenty. I would like to be worth five million, but at the same time I do not propose that my money shall drive me out of the Democratic party. [How they cheered him!] But I want more so that I can spend more of it for Democracy without injuring myself and my family. After having said this I want you to understand that I'm not a sorehead, and if all the Democracy of the state will turn out and do what I will do, we will carry the state by fifteen thousand.[36]

Expressing no chagrin, giving Stoneman his warmest congratulations, and pledging to support the general in the upcoming fight made good copy. Commented Sacramento's *Record-Union,* "The speeches of the defeated candidates were well received. Hearst's in particular being much better and very much more easily delivered than his speech of acceptance." The *San Francisco Bulletin* described Hearst's concession speech as "the best speech of the day." One of the delegates was heard to remark, "If Uncle George had only made that speech before the balloting, I guess he would not be a defeated candidate."[37]

With Hearst's blessing, the *Examiner* supported Stoneman against the Republican nominee, Morris M. Estee, a crafty politician and speaker of the assembly.[38] The day after the convention ended, the *Examiner* ran an advertisement supporting Stoneman for governor. The following editorial also appeared:

The San Jose Convention yesterday placed at the head of the Democratic State ticket the name of a glorious standard-bearer who will assuredly be the next Governor of the State of California. General George Stoneman has won his nomination in a way which, whilst it does him credit as a true man and an honest servant of the public, reflects honor upon the Democratic majority that supported him. . . . With that decision the EXAMINER not only does not quarrel, but is in every way satisfied.[39]

Although Hearst was being gracious, inwardly he was devastated. After sharing a train car with his father to Sacramento, possibly just after the primary loss, W. R. wrote to Phoebe:

> I left Papa last night at Sacramento without having talked very much for we sat most of the way wrapped in gloom and staring wofully [*sic*] at each other. The silence was once disturbed from a real estate broker who wanted to sell some land, but papa excused himself in rather a novel manner. He took the man gently by the arm and assisted him out of the section, remarking in a very audible undertone that if there was anything he did despi[s]e it was a *blanked* impertinent real estate broker. The broker retired in confusion and papa relapsed into silence and gloom.[40]

Phoebe helped soften the blow. "Never mind," she told her defeated husband, "some day you'll go to the Senate."[41]

—13—

PHOEBE'S PROPHECY

(1882–1886)

If a man wrote a splendid speech, I would only make a botch of it, but if I thought it out I would do well and everybody would know that it was me.
—George Hearst

Having had his teeth kicked in politically, Hearst returned to the life he loved.

On December 8, 1882, Hearst stepped off the train in dusty Tucson. Silver mines and cattle ranches were foremost on his mind. Along with A. E. Head, Hearst visited Prescott, examining samples of ore from the Burro, McCracken, and Centennial Mines.[1] Gathering no moss, Hearst left Prescott after a few days for his cattle ranch in Deming.

Hearst also took time to send two letters: one to Phoebe and the other to W. R. at Harvard. Hearst was of two minds considering his son's future. To Phoebe, Hearst wrote, "I hope the Boy will . . . take charge of the paper soon after he leaves college as it will give him more power than anything else." In his letter to W. R., Hearst encouraged the boy to take courses in Spanish and engineering, skills necessary should the boy take over the mining empire.[2]

In his return letter, W. R. teased Hearst, who accidentally signed "your loving husband" in the December 30 letter to his son. But W. R.'s main complaint was about the difficulty of his course work, particularly Latin and Greek, which he found useless.

Next year I can choose whatever studies I please and will take Spanish and whatever else you wish.

I have been spending a week's vacation in New York with Mama and have had a splendid time.

You are a daisy to promise. Don't you remember that you said you were coming to New York to spend xmas with your Billy Buster? Well, I didn't much believe it then, but I wish you would come on and see the College. I saw Will Crocker the other day. It's lucky that he went to Yale. He will do as a Yale man, but you could not find him at all at Harvard.

Well, I will write some more soon.

Your affectionate son,
W. R. Hearst[3]

On the last day of the year, Hearst returned on the Atlantic and Pacific Railroad with A. E. Head. The two Comstock friends celebrated New Year's Eve with Head's two brothers.[4]

On January 10, 1883, when George Stoneman was formally inaugurated in Sacramento, Hearst was still in Arizona Territory. But even in the desert, the newspapers were filled with California politics. In particular, the growing prospect of Hearst being the 1885 Democratic nominee for U.S. senator from California was welcome news in Arizona, for everyone knew Hearst had a vested interest in supporting ranching and mining.[5]

Nine days later, Hearst was sighted 220 miles south at the Palace Hotel in Tucson.[6] On January 23, he returned to his Deming cattle ranch, having secured water rights in the Animas Valley. Adding to his cattle barony, on February 4 Hearst purchased Tom Shipp's ranch for $40,000; the purchase included twenty-two hundred head of cattle. Hearst also secured for $100,000 various ranches—including their water rights—between Silver City and the Mexican border. It was predicted that Hearst would stock those ranches with twenty thousand head of cattle before the end of the year. Hearst was also heard to boast that his cattle ranches were his biggest bonanzas.[7]

On February 11 Hearst returned to Tombstone and to the Boquillas cattle ranch. Tombstone in 1883 was much quieter than it had been a year earlier. Wyatt Earp and Doc Holliday, having broken the power of the Cowboys, had moved on from Arizona Territory—incidentally making Hearst's cattle ranches safer and more profitable than when Cowboy leader Curly Bill Brocius was at large. Hearst too was about to move on.

While in Arizona Territory, Hearst received a telegram from Marcus Daly. The Irish prospector had traded Utah Territory for Montana Territory and from Michael Hickey had purchased a copper mine, which he felt had promise, sixty-five miles south of Butte. Hickey, who had fought for the Union in the Civil War, had named the mine Anaconda, a reference to Horace Greeley's description of Ulysses S. Grant's forces surrounding Robert E. Lee's forces "like an anaconda."

Daly had wanted Hearst and Haggin to help develop the Anaconda, but while Hearst had been roaming around Arizona, Haggin had let matters slide. To Hearst's dismay, in his telegram Daly said he had sought financial backing from another interested party. Sensing a fortune might be slipping through his fingers, Hearst acted quickly.

"I then telegraphed Daly that Haggin had neglected answering him and that I was ready to come in," Hearst noted. "[Haggin] telegraphed back that he had made arrangements with W. A. Clark for him to come in and make arrangements with the Bank for him."

William A. Clark, a robber baron by way of copper, habitually bought out foreclosed mines from strapped owners. After Hearst telegraphed Daly to buy out Clark, Daly "replied that he could get about a quarter back. I telegraphed him to try to get that quarter, so he bought this man Clarke out of his quarter." Ultimately, Hearst purchased the Anaconda Mine for $30,000.[8]

Hearst knew that he would have to oversee the operation himself, but that could wait. More pressing were the failures of the *Examiner*. Although Clarence Greathouse was a friend, under his supervision the *Examiner* was still the quartz mill Hearst had originally assessed it as: hemorrhaging money and failing to exert political influence. What's more, the Hearst family detected a level of indolence in Greathouse. While goading his father to spend more time buying ranches than cultivating his racing stable, W. R. Hearst wrote, "I'm afraid you are getting like Mr. Greathouse and are putting off till next week what ought to have been done the day before yesterday." To help right the ship, in March 1882, Hearst replaced Greathouse with Dr. C. D. Cleveland.[9]

On April 19, 1883, W. R. sent his father another letter from Harvard, asking Hearst to help a classmate, one year ahead of him: "Jack Follansbee whose father you must have known in early days and whose mother Mama is well acquainted with is obliged to leave college and go into business. . . . I think it is through the financial embarrassment of his uncle Jim Keen who is supporting Jack." Describing Follansbee as "honest" and having "sound sense" and "pluck," W. R. entreated,

"Do please get him a fine position with a fine salary. Could you not send him down to Victoria where Mr. Head is?"[10]

Two weeks later, on May 2, 1883, Hearst was spotted rubbing shoulders with John Mackey, the superintendent of Haggin's ranch, and Lucky Baldwin at the Oakland Trotting Park. Hearst cheered on his horse, Duke of Monday, who won the race. Three weeks later, Hearst got back to business, leaving for Salt Lake City and the Ontario Mine. With everything running well, Hearst finally boarded a train for Butte, arriving on June 12, 1883.[11]

After traveling sixty-five miles south to the Anaconda Mine, Hearst found that Daly's miners, after sinking a shaft at a depth of two hundred to three hundred feet, had struck a vein of almost pure copper, the likes of which the world had never seen. The copper vein—and Hearst's presence—created a sensation. "Mr. George Hearst . . . is now in Butte looking after his investments in the Anaconda and contiguous properties," commented the *Butte Miner*. "The Anaconda is liable to be the best of his many investments."[12]

The newspapermen were not wrong. Hearst hired a mill and continued sinking. Thirty feet later they struck a bed of pure copper. Continuing to delve, they found that the bed was thirty to forty feet wide and descended more than a thousand feet. In other words, it was the greatest copper strike on the planet.

In a flash, Hearst began developing a water ditch, labor-saving machinery, and a railroad to connect the Anaconda to Butte. He also bought more claims and spread out. Soon Hearst could brag that nine hundred men were employed at the Anaconda, bringing up thousands of tons of pure copper. Naturally, Hearst was the principal owner.[13]

By mid-July, Hearst was in Hailey, Idaho Territory, examining more mines. Hearst stayed for several weeks, finally offering $375,000 for the Mayflower Mine. Rebuffed, Hearst refused to up the ante.[14]

By August 1883, Hearst was back in San Francisco. Celebrating their Montana bonanza, on August 4 George and Phoebe hosted a dinner party at their Van Ness residence. Family, friends, and politicians all turned out. Among their relatives were W. R., on break from Harvard, and Cousin Joe. Friends included Clarence Greathouse and W. R.'s tall, black-haired college chum Jack Follansbee. Hearst, who enjoyed shooting pool with Follansbee, was charmed and hired Follansbee to help manage the Deming ranch. A. E. Head's wife, Rebecca, and daughter Anna were also in attendance. Among the politicians were Governor Thomas Crittenden, from the Hearsts' home state of Missouri, and Governor Eli Murray of Utah Territory. Quietly, Hearst was gaining political strength.

One man who missed Phoebe's soiree was A. E. Head. Having just partnered with Hearst in buying up a cattle ranch just north of Santa Fe, Head also played a part in Hearst's newest venture: the purchase of the 670,000-acre Rancho Jose de Babicora in Chihuahua, Mexico. All told, Hearst's cattle barony now involved a nine-hundred-mile stretch from Babicora to Santa Fe, with Deming in the middle. Head and Follansbee would be kept busy.[15]

Despite his newfound cattle empire, mining remained Hearst's true calling. On the last day of August, Hearst left for the Mariposa mines. A week later he was spotted near Mount Raymond, south of Yosemite Valley, examining mining outfits. On September 13 the *Nevada State Journal* reported that Hearst had incorporated the General Shields Mining Company in Eureka.[16] Phoebe was equally busy during this time. Charitably inclined and ever forward-minded, in early October she made a sizable donation to the Golden Gate Kindergarten Association, establishing the Hearst Free Kindergarten, No. 1, at 512 Union Street. As the new year loomed, Hearst was back in San Francisco.

In December, C. D. Cleveland retired from the *Examiner*. Despite his reservations, Hearst once again turned to Greathouse, who returned to his position as editor. This was good timing for Greathouse, for Hearst was once again feeling political.[17]

On December 21, Hearst met with Winfield Scott Hancock. Although the Union general had lost the election of 1880 to James Garfield, he was still leader of the Democratic Party. To have Hancock's blessing would give Hearst the measure of gravitas he desired. To this end, in a speech before Hancock and dozens of prominent Democrats at the Bohemian Club, Hearst praised Hancock's efforts to save the South from carpetbaggers after the war. Two days later, Hearst hosted Hancock in his home. Notables joining them were Joe Clark, J. B. Haggin, Clarence Greathouse, Jasper McDonald, and Judge George Flournoy.[18]

Almost immediately afterward—with Flournoy, Greathouse, and Buckley plotting how best to send Hearst to Washington—Hearst set out for Arizona Territory, dishing to Jack Follansbee details of his dinner with Hancock.

A quick study, Follansbee excelled at managing the ranch, but he oftentimes grew lonesome traveling between Arizona Territory and Sonora. Through letters, Follansbee struck up a correspondence with Phoebe, who knew through her husband how lonely life in the West could be. Maternal Phoebe would often send care packages to Deming to keep Follansbee in good cheer. On January 14, 1884, Follansbee wrote Phoebe from Deming, "I was delighted to hear that Mr. Hearst's dinner to General Hancock was such a success, there must have been a great unanimity of ideas on political questions." Four days later Follansbee wrote to Phoebe, "Head told me this morning that he would want me to go with him to Chihuahua tomorrow evening, for how long, and all that, I do not as yet know."[19]

Although Hearst was enjoying his new station as a cattle baron, reflecting on 1883, it was clear that the mining empire was still the Hearsts' bread and butter. In 1883 the Anaconda Mine had brought in $1.7 million, and that had been in crude ore. With the new machinery, Hearst expected to yield great profits. Additionally, the dividends paid to Hearst, Haggin, and Tevis in silver and gold from February alone were astronomical: $144,909 from the Ontario Mine, $96,356 from the Homestake Mine, and $77,809 from the lesser Black Hills mines. As of February 1884, the Homestake had yielded $4.5 million.[20]

Not content to rest on his laurels, in early March 1884 Hearst established with Joe Clark the North Peer Gold and Silver Mining Company in Quijotoa, Arizona Territory. At the end of March he and Henry Janin were seen seventy-five miles east at Tucson's Porter Hotel.[21] Hearst was back in San Francisco in April, preparing to make a big speech before a crowd of Democratic representatives.

With the Republicans probably pitting railroad baron and former governor Leland Stanford against him, Hearst amended his strategy from the one he employed while running for governor. Instead of focusing on the Chinese, Hearst made his central platform denouncing the railroads and calling for reform.

On April 18, 1884, Hearst delivered the closing speech in San Francisco's Union Hall:

> The platform adopted in the San Jose Convention a year and a half ago is still fresh in my memory. . . . The railroads have been built for the party who built them. The railroad in this State has been built at a cost of $30,000 per mile. The railroad company asks us to pay not $24,000 or $30,000, but $48,000 and $50,000 on the bonds of this road and also on the stock. If the corporations are able to build all their roads without hindrance, if they get the right of way over public domain and can charge for freight whatever they demand, they can water their stock to sixty or one hundred thousand dollars per mile, and if they have lined with railroads every valley where a road will pay and they are allowed to charge whatever the freight will bear, it will enslave every producer in this country.

Although Hearst's *San Francisco Examiner* described cheering from the audience, the Republican *Record-Union*—dubbing Hearst a "bloated capitalist"—took a sharper angle: "Mr. Hearst can neither think nor talk. It was painful, as well as funny, to see this amiable old man floundering about helplessly, all tangled in his broken sentences and little scraps of ideas. A sterile mind, a squeaky voice and awkward manners are surely a poor equipment for a United States Senator."[22]

A week after the Union Hall speech, the *Fresno Bee* made further sport of him in an article by "Twaddler," the nom de plume of Arthur McEwen. After sailing from Scotland, McEwen had made his name as one of the sharpest journalists on the West Coast, becoming friendly with both Mark Twain and Ambrose Bierce. For the *Fresno Bee* article, McEwen created a drunken argument between McEwen's alter ego, Persiflage, and Hearst, whom McEwen called Senator, as though his election were a foregone conclusion.

> Deep in their cups, Senator Hearst said to Persiflage, "I am in favor of maintaining the dignity of labor."
>
> "Dignity of labor be hanged," Persiflage cried. "That's cant, that's rot, and you know it. . . . You vote catchers go around telling the poor devils who toil with their hands for a living their doing something to be proud of, when you know devilish well that they're doing nothing of the sort."
>
> "Tut, tut . . . you're old enough to know better than to talk like that," Senator Hearst scolded.
>
> "Don't twist me with my years, sir. . . . I'm going to give you as a toast one of the best things that my friend Bierce ever said. It was in the old *Town Crier* of the *News Letter*. It is 'The Workingman, whom we all honor—and avoid.'"
>
> "I won't drink it!" exclaimed Senator Hearst, indignantly.
>
> "Well, begad, I will for you," Persiflage said, recovering his good humor and reaching for the glass, which he drained as well as his own, to the great delight of the cultivated company.[23]

Both the excoriating attack by the *Record-Union* and McEwen's playful satire in the *Fresno Bee* painted Hearst as a figure of fun. It all made for good copy. Under such a carnival atmosphere, both the Republican and Democratic newspapers were poised to strike when it was announced that Hearst's next speech would be on May 20 in San Francisco's B'nai B'rith Hall. This time, however, before a crowd of more than four hundred prominent Democrats, Hearst spoke about a subject on which he was an absolute authority—mining in gold rush California. With nowhere to go, the tempest returned to the teapot. Even the antagonistic *San Francisco Chronicle* recognized that Hearst had crushed the speech: "George Hearst drew a vivid picture of mining in early days, his speech being one of the successes of the evening."[24]

"I never could make a speech and let anybody else write it out for me," Hearst reflected. "If a man wrote a splendid speech, I would only make a botch of it, but if I thought it out I would do well and everybody would know that it was me."[25]

Deciding not to push his luck, Hearst made certain he was nowhere near a lectern when the Democratic Convention convened in Stockton on June 11. Instead, Hearst was nearly a thousand miles away in Arizona Territory. After inspecting the Great American Mine in the Swisshelm Mountains, he returned to Tucson on June 18. Later that night he left for Deming, rendezvousing with A. E. Head before visiting their New Mexico property and traveling farther east. On July 10, Hearst was spotted in San Antonio.[26] Sixteen days later, Hearst reunited with Niles Searls in Nevada City while attending a Democratic meeting with Judge Flournoy.

After sharing in the excitement of ratifying Grover Cleveland for President, Hearst returned to San Francisco. In October 1884, Hearst sold the home at 1315 Van Ness, including the furniture, to Captain R. R. Thompson for $200,000, moving slightly down the street to a smaller residence at 1501 Van Ness. One rumor swirled that the *Examiner* had finally busted him, another that he was so certain he'd win the election and move to Washington that he had made the move down the street only temporarily. Others speculated that he had no need of so large a place. One thing for certain was that the *Examiner* hadn't busted him. It was losing money, but Hearst could stand it.[27]

No one was more delighted to hear the house had sold than Hearst's son, whose vivid imagination began construction of a great mansion atop a mountain on their Piedra Blanca ranch, overlooking San Simeon Bay. To Phoebe, W. R. wrote, "And since the house is sold, Vive le ranch! . . . And on the ranch in such a house nestled between two hills, protected from the wind, commanding a view of the sea &c., why existence would be perfect. And garden of Eden couldn't hold a candle to it."[28]

On October 21, 1884, Hearst and Joe Clark joined Mayor Washington M. Bartlett and a crowd of other Democrats at Metropolitan Hall, three-quarters of a mile down Van Ness from Hearst's new home. Senator Jim Farley and former governor William Irwin both made speeches in support of Grover Cleveland's bid for president, which were greeted with applause.[29]

On November 4, 1884, America went to the polls to determine whether Democrat Grover Cleveland or Republican James G. Blaine would become the twenty-second president. The following evening—with New York, Indiana, Connecticut, New Jersey, and Wisconsin too close to call and Colorado, Nevada, Oregon, and California not yet reporting—the outcome was undecided. Deeply invested, Hearst and Flournoy were seen up late at Democratic headquarters on November 5, poring over the electoral map.[30]

On the evening of November 6, Hearst had relocated to the *Examiner* building when the news was boomed across the country: despite California voting for Blaine, Cleveland had won the presidency with 219 electoral votes. The place went wild. Hats were thrown into the air and cheering erupted. Outside, a triumphant throng of thousands of San Franciscan Democrats marched down Market Street. Fireworks filled the sky and a band played "Hail to the Chief." When the marchers saw Hearst within the *Examiner* building, they happily cheered him as well.[31]

With Phoebe and Will on the East Coast—Will at Harvard and Phoebe bouncing between Cambridge and New York City—Hearst felt their absence keenly.[32] On December 21, 1884, he penned a particularly lonely letter to Phoebe, admitting to being

> quite lonsam at all times. . . . What is a home without a wife and baby? . . .
> At all events I want to see the Boy very much. So anxious for him to get
> through. The *Examiner* is about the hardest thing of all to no what to do
> with or how to do it? . . . Can you find out about the newspaper men? . . a
> man that understands the printing business from the bottom up and all the
> way through, so as to be able to take full charge of the paper. . . . We know
> such a man is hard to get. . . . Perhaps Will can attend to it?[33]

Along with finding a newspaperman to run the *Examiner*, Hearst soon needed to find a superintendent to run the Homestake Mine, for on December 23. Samuel McMaster—whose health had been deteriorating for years—died in San Francisco. Thomas J. Grier, who had worked for McMaster as a telegrapher and accountant, moved up to the top spot. But Hearst wasn't satisfied that all was running well. Before the year was out, he'd have to see for himself.[34]

On January 8, 1885, Hearst delivered another speech about the Pacific Coast mining industry at B'nai B'rith Hall, this time as part of a banquet to honor the election of Cleveland. Beyond various speeches, business was discussed, in particular the paltry display of California fruit reportedly exhibited at the World's Fair in New Orleans. A committee of eleven was appointed to make the display more grand. Its ranks included Stanford and Hearst.[35]

On January 21, a Democratic caucus met in Sacramento to discuss who would be the nominee for senator. Present were Flournoy, who was backing Hearst with everything he had, and Buckley, flanked by adherents. Nothing definitive was put forth, but the next night, on January 22, they reached a consensus. Hearst was unanimously nominated for the U.S. Senate.[36]

As gratifying as the nomination must have been for Hearst, there was a snag. Although President-elect Cleveland was preparing to move into the Executive Mansion, and Governor Stoneman was muddling through California affairs in Sacramento, the Democratic Party was struggling in the California Legislature. There were simply too many Republicans for Hearst to defeat Stanford. When, on January 28, the joint legislature voted in Sacramento for the state's U.S. senator, Niles Searls received one vote and Jim Farley received two votes. The real fight was between Hearst and Stanford, but even that wasn't much of a contest. Hearst received thirty-seven votes, Stanford seventy-eight. Leland Stanford would be the next U. S. senator.[37]

Despite Phoebe's prophecy, once again Hearst had been defeated.

Never one to brood on his failures from home, Hearst did what he always did in times of hardship, heading into the wilds. Two days after Stanford won the election, Hearst traveled to his cattle ranch in Deming. On March 20, he was in Washington, D.C., where, along with several other California Democrats, including California representative Brigadier General William S. Rosecrans, Hearst paid a call on President Cleveland at the White House.

Cleveland cut an imposing figure. Nearly six feet tall and just shy of three hundred pounds, Cleveland had a bulldog jaw, a large mustache, and piercing blue eyes. "Ugly Honest" was his nickname. A bachelor, forty-eight-year-old Cleveland was secretly courting twenty-year-old Frances Folsom, who would become his wife the following year and ultimately a good friend of Phoebe's. She knew what it was like to marry an older man.

Hearst and Cleveland took to each other. On April 3, Hearst and Rosecrans returned to the White House to speak with Cleveland. Later that day, Cleveland requested a private audience, and the fast friends spent two hours closeted together. The press could not pry the contents of that meeting out of Hearst. Perhaps appreciating Hearst's discretion, Cleveland asked Hearst to visit him again, with former San Francisco mayor Frank McCoppin, on April 15. The three discussed California politics at length.[38]

Things were also looking up for W. R., who had found his knack running the *Harvard Lampoon*. In the spring of 1885, W. R. implored his mother to show "Papa" a letter he had written demonstrating his achievements at the *Lampoon* and to "tell him just to wait till Gene and I get hold of the old Examiner and we'll boom her in the same way—she needs it!"[39]

While in the nation's capital in 1885, Will had written directly to his father:

> Dear Father: I have just finished and dispatched a letter to the Editor of the Examiner in which I recommended Eugene Lent to his favorable notice, and commented on the illustrations, if you may call them such, which have lately disfigured the paper. . . .
>
> I have begun to have a strange fondness for our little paper—a tenderness like unto that which a mother feels for a puny or deformed offspring, and I should hate to see it die now after it had battled so long and so nobly for existence; in fact, to tell the truth, I am possessed of the weakness which at some time or other of their lives pervades most men; I am convinced that I could run a newspaper successfully.
>
> Now if you should make over to me the Examiner—with enough money to carry out my schemes—I'll tell you what I would do!
>
> In the first place I would change the general appearance of the paper and make seven wide columns where we now have nine narrow ones, then I would have the type spaced more, and these two changes would give the pages a much cleaner and neater appearance.
>
> Secondly, it would be well to make the paper as far as possible original, to clip only when absolutely necessary and to imitate only some such leading journal as the New York World which is undoubtedly the best paper of that class to which the Examiner belongs—that class which appeals to the people and which depends for its success upon enterprise, energy and a certain startling originality and not upon the wisdom of its political opinions or the lofty style of its editorials. And to accomplish this we must have—as the World has—active, intelligent and energetic young men; we must have men who come out west in the hopeful buoyancy of youth for the purposes of making their fortunes and not a worthless scum that has been carried there by the eddies of repeated failures.
>
> Thirdly, we must advertise the paper from Oregon to New Mexico and must also increase our number of advertisements if we have to lower our rates to do it, thus we can put on the first page that our circulation is such and our advertisements so and so and constantly increasing.
>
> And now having spoken of the three great essential points let us turn to details.

The illustrations are a detail, though a very important one. Illustrations embellish a page, illustrations attract the eye and stimulate the imagination of the masses and materially aid the comprehension of an unaccustomed reader and thus are of particular importance to that class of people which the Examiner claims to address. Such illustrations, however, as have heretofore appeared in the paper nauseate rather than stimulate the imagination and certainly do anything but embellish a page.

Another detail of questionable importance is that we actually or apparently establish some connection between ourselves and the New York World, and obtain a certain prestige in bearing some relation to that paper. We might contract to have important private telegrams forwarded or something of that sort, but understand that the principal advantage we are to derive is from the attention that such a connection would excite and from the advertisement we could make of it. Whether the World would consent to such an arrangement for any reasonable sum is very doubtful, for its net profit is over one thousand dollars a day and no doubt it would consider the Examiner is beneath its notice. Just think, over one thousand dollars a day and four years ago it belonged to Jay Gould and was losing money rapidly.

And now to close with a suggestion of great consequence, namely, that all these changes be made not by degrees but at once so that the improvement will be very marked and noticeable and will attract universal attention and comment.

There is little to be said about my studies. . . . Congress is as stupid as it is possible to conceive of. . . .

Well, good-by. I have given up all hope of having you write to me. . . . By the way, I heard you had bought 2,000 acres of land the other day and I hope some of it was the land adjoining our ranch that I begged you to buy in my last letter.

Your affectionate son,
W. R. Hearst[40]

Hearst didn't immediately rush back to California, opting to vacation in New York instead, renting a palatial Fifth Avenue residence. While Hearst enjoyed New York City, on June 25, business partners C. P. Duane and Lucky Baldwin saw the San Francisco Street Committee supervisors grant them a franchise to construct a trolley line from D Street to Eddy and Powell.[41]

In a widely disseminated story, Hearst also purportedly spoke off the cuff to a New York City reporter:

> I reckon I am going to leave this place if the "strikers" don't let up on me. They are after me all the time. One feller wanted $1,000 to-day, and if I should tell you who it was you would recognize his as one of the biggest "N. G's." Pauper alley ever produced. Reckon they think I ain't on to 'em. Why, I know 'em from the ground up. I know what they want when they approach me, and some of them I give a hundred or two to get shut of 'em. Why, I left California to get rid of just such a lot of dead-beats. They used to run to the house, corral me in the street, and write me letters for money—fellers that I hardly know. Then the ministers, priests, and scout of the Y.M.C.A. laid siege to me. I tell you, a man has got to give up, or go into the mountains and hide away.[42]

In late July, Hearst headed to the mountains, boarding a westbound train with Follansbee and W. R. By now it was obvious to Hearst, and especially to Phoebe, that if they didn't keep a close eye on W. R., the boy might run wild. It wasn't as if he had been idle in college, having racked up a number of successes.

W. R. had joined Harvard's Hasty Pudding Club, taking the role of Pretzel in the burlesque *Joan of Arc*. Will was also known to pluck the banjo, strum the ukulele, and amaze his Harvard friends with vaudeville routines. The legendary black entertainer Billy Emerson was a particular favorite of W. R.'s. Young Hearst practiced Emerson's steps until he could perform them in his sleep.[43]

Like his father, W. R.'s appearance was striking. He was six foot three—when not slouching—blue-eyed, blond-haired, and a flashy dresser. Phoebe's first biographer, who knew W. R. as a young man, described him as "tall, slender, good-looking, very blond, with a pink and white complexion and a little golden mustache, boyish . . . and still a bit under the influence of the impish high spirits of youth." He was also charming to people who knew him and generally kind to strangers, having a generous spirit and being prone to largesse. Above all, W. R. delighted in doing the unexpected, shocking his audience, treating life as a circus. At the same time, W. R. could be painfully shy outside his owns social circles, with a high-pitched, cooing voice and unusually long fingers.[44]

Notably, W. R. was instrumental in expanding the *Harvard Lampoon* from four to six pages. After using a cigar to burn five small marks on his arm as an initiation rite, W. R. went on to act as a combination business manager/managing editor at the "Lampy" with Gene Lent. The experience W. R. had at the *Lampoon* kindled in him a passion that would turn into a forest fire. After being given an introduction to the *Boston Globe*'s proprietor, Charles H. Taylor, W. R. made the *Globe*'s pressrooms a second home.[45]

Unfortunately, W. R. also excelled as an inventive prankster.

As a member of the Med Fac fraternity, W. R. vandalized school property, threw custard pies at chorus girls in the Howard Athenaeum, and secreted a jackass into the room of one of his professors with a note that read, "Now there are two of you." W. R. also kept to a grueling schedule of Welsh rarebit dinners, all-night poker sessions, beer parties, cafés, cabarets, and musical comedies. Additionally, W. R. kept a pet alligator and a young waitress. The alligator was named Champagne Charley and the waitress was named Tessie Powers. Keeping Tessie as a sweetheart was as scandalous as keeping Charley as a pet, for at the time it was conventional for men of society to either marry well-born young ladies or discreetly visit prostitutes. But W. R. didn't care at all for Victorian convention, as the world would come to see. He had a style all his own, an electrifying playfulness in a stuffed shirt congregation.[46]

Years later, Will wrote to Gene Lent:

> Dear Gene:
>
> Of what use is a biography which does not record our rides back to Cambridge from Boston on the top of a hack, and our friendly and forceful distribution of oranges to policemen on route, and the dire consequences. "Them was the good old days."
>
> What has happened since is of little importance.
>
> Give me back those *Lampoon* days. When good fellows got together with a stein on the table—although it didn't say on the table very long.[47]

If that weren't bad enough, W. R.'s grades were suffering, and there was real danger he would fail out of the Ivy League school. All this scandalized Phoebe, who thought George needed to take more of a hand. Taking the boy with him to the Black Hills was a step in the right direction.

In early August they reached Lead.[48] Several years had passed since Hearst had last visited the Black Hills. In that time the cities of Lead and Deadwood had grown prosperous through Homestake gold. The Hearst store in Lead, the largest store in the city, paid a monthly dividend of $2,000. Although some diehards still remembered the killing of Alex Frankenberg by Hearst's guards, time had cast Hearst in a different light. "George . . . is entirely at home in an old flannel shirt," noted the *Black Hills Daily Times*, "and all the baggage he ever carries is a clean collar and a comb. George knows a mine by instinct, and is about as shrewd an examiner as they find."[49]

On August 7, Hearst traveled northwest to assay the Carbonate City mines. Six days later, Hearst and Superintendent Thomas Grier looked over Homestake water ditches, and Hearst examined a number of mines on Bald Mountain, a few miles east of Lead. As for the Homestake Mine, Hearst was pleased. To a friend he stated that "enough ore is in sight in the mine to ensure continuous work as at present for the next twenty years." All in all, Hearst stayed in the Black Hills for more than two weeks before leaving for California on August 23. On September 22, 1885, he finally returned to San Francisco. Having traveled from coast to coast that year, Hearst idled for some time, renting A. E. Head's Nob Hill home at 1105 Taylor Street.[50]

Opening a letter from Phoebe, written from New York's Hotel Brunswick on October 22, 1885, he learned that W. R. was up to his old tricks again:

> [W. R.] insisted today upon drawing money as usual and I can do very little unless you help me. If he continues to spend too much money and neglect study it will not be my fault and you can take the blame upon yourself. I will not be held responsible when you go on giving him the means to do just as he pleases. . . . I, of course, want him to have a moderate amount of spending money, but if he is to have $250, per month, I can tell you that he will not study much.[51]

Phoebe's tone was lighter in a November 19, 1885, letter sent from Baltimore. She liked Baltimore "very much," but it was the District of Columbia she and Will had their eyes on: "[W. R.] is delighted with Washington and thinks that it is the place to live and hopes you that you may come and buy a house."[52]

Washington was as charmed with Phoebe as she was with it. While in the capital, she attended a reception at the White House. As a guest, Phoebe brought along Eleanor Calhoun, a beautiful and cultivated charmer who—with Phoebe's financial support—was studying to be a Shakespearean actress. Although Phoebe didn't yet realize it, Eleanor had her eye on W. R. "Whatever she saw in me," W. R. reflected, "I do not know."[53]

Meanwhile, W. R. let his studies slide and was placed on probation. While he weighed whether he wanted to continue at Harvard, and Phoebe made good her plan to live in Washington, D.C.—renting a house at 401 Taylor Street later that month—George stayed put. But wanderlust soon struck. On January 7, 1886, Hearst was spotted in Merced, and on January 11 it was reported that he had purchased the Welch ranch six miles south of Sunol for $50,000.[54]

At this point in his life, buying land was old hat to Hearst, but on March 8, 1886, something unexpected launched Hearst's life in a different direction: U.S. senator John F. Miller, a Republican, died of a heart attack. Governor Stoneman was to appoint Miller's successor, and Hearst naturally came to mind. After all, Hearst had kept his pledge to "not be a sorehead" during Stoneman's gubernatorial campaign, actively championing Stoneman and unleashing the *Examiner* against the railroads. Additionally, Hearst still enjoyed the shadowy patronage of "Blind Boss" Chris Buckley. And, for better or for worse, Hearst had the support of the people. Stoneman's decision was made even easier when Hearst received a complimentary vote from the Democrats in the state legislature.

On March 23, 1886, George Hearst was appointed to the United States Senate.[55]

—14—

FIVE BARRELS OF BAD WHISKEY

(1886)

This is my ranch, and if these here folks don't like my shirt they can go home.
—George Hearst

Hearst was more than twenty-four hundred miles from Washington, D.C., on a business trip in Mexico City, when word reached him that he'd been appointed senator. He didn't reach the capital till the second week of April. On the morning of April 9, in the Capitol Building, Leland Stanford escorted Hearst to the desk of John Sherman of Ohio, brother to William T. Sherman and president pro tempore of the Senate. Sherman administered the oath of office, and Hearst—the newest member of the Forty-Ninth Congress—took his seat in the Democratic side, at the extreme right of the aisle.[1]

Immediately afterward, the Senate began debating whether women's suffrage should be allowed in Washington, D.C. Hearst voted with his Democratic colleagues against women's suffrage. The next day, Hearst again toed the Democratic line, voting against Washington receiving statehood. As the newest U.S. senator, Hearst had no intention of stepping out of line. But outside the Capitol Building, Hearst's true colors showed—he gained infamy for his "western style" barroom manner.

For the first few weeks after he was appointed senator, Hearst frequently visited the watering holes of Washington, D.C., often placing a $20 gold piece on the bar and inviting all the patrons to drink with him. This became so common-place that military men would send scouts to follow the senator after the Senate adjourned. Soon the bars Senator Hearst frequented were packed, along with the men's wineskins.[2]

Although Hearst was enjoying the spoils of victory, by the end of April 1886 he was informed that his western style was harming his reputation. "Senator Hearst is evidently a very simple-minded man," the *Santa Cruz Sentinel* opined on April 17. "He is a politician without prevarication, and a Democrat in whom there is no guile."[3]

With the honeymoon period over almost as soon as it began, Hearst's next misstep came when he was forced to choose between the president and his party. Because President Cleveland had bucked the spoils system by announcing that he would not replace a Republican who was performing his job admirably with a Democrat simply out of party loyalty, he was out of favor with fellow Democrats. Caught in the middle, Hearst cast his lot with Cleveland's enemies.

Shunned by the White House and finding little warmth for him in the Senate, Hearst cast about for an adviser. From the *Examiner,* he selected thirty-one-year-old Edward Waterman Townsend, as skilled a politician as anyone on the staff. Born in Cleveland, Ohio, "Ned" Townsend had worked at the *Virginia City Chronicle* in the early 1870s before trading that paper for the *San Francisco Call.* After joining the Bohemian Club and marrying Annie Lake, daughter of Delos W. Lake—one of Hearst's lawyer's during the Great Mining Suit—Townsend quickly rose as an up-and-comer in the Hearst circle.[4]

Club member Arthur McEwen wrote of Townsend:

There was no man in the Bohemian who showed a more conscientious concern for his apparel. He had a delicate taste in wines, and at the table he inspired the respect of the oldest and best among us. Damme, if I haven't seen him turn pale with disgust and anger at the sight of a duck cooked fifteen minutes, when his order had been fourteen. His conversation, though frequently touched with a levity due to his journalistic associations, was ever that, on the whole, of an elegant man of the world.[5]

Ostensibly, Townsend began serving in April 1886 as Senator Hearst's private secretary. As the *Oakland Tribune* noted, "Townsend sticks closer to Hearst than a sick kitten to a hot brick."[6]

While Townsend worked as Hearst's private secretary, one of his colleagues at the *Examiner,* A. M. "Andy" Lawrence, was summoned to the White House.

The man doing the summoning was Daniel S. Lamont, President Cleveland's private secretary. Lamont's list of credentials included having been chief clerk in the New York State Department, secretary of the Democratic State Committee of New York, and the man whispering in Samuel Tilden's ear while Tilden simultaneously governed New York and ran for president in 1876.[7]

After Lamont introduced Lawrence to Cleveland, the president asked, "Why doesn't Senator Hearst come visit me?"

Lawrence answered, "That is as much your fault as his, Mr. President."

Cleveland mulled Lawrence's answer in silence. Finally Cleveland said, "Will you tell Senator Hearst for me that I wish he would call on me?"

The next morning Lawrence visited Hearst, relaying the message. Hearst pulled on his beard. Friends and rivals with whom Hearst played poker may have picked up that this was a tell, indicating that he was deep in thought. "Well," said Hearst, "if the President wants to see me, I suppose I will have to go, but I don't think he has treated our friends right."

"Tell him so," Lawrence advised.

"I don't want to quarrel with the President," Hearst replied.

At five o'clock that evening, Hearst visited the White House. The president and the senator renewed their friendship, getting along splendidly. To Lawrence, Lamont wrote that never in his life had he seen a friendlier, more winning personality than that of George Hearst. Their friendship restored, Hearst called on Cleveland in the White House on April 20 and April 28, and the Cleveland administration began to confer with Hearst on appointments on the Pacific Coast. Visiting Cleveland at the same time was Maryland senator Arthur P. Gorman, a leader of the Bourbon Democrats, with whom Hearst became friendly. With Townsend, Lawrence, and Gorman by his side, Hearst's first month as a U.S. senator wasn't half bad.[8]

The news from Harvard, however, was all bad. In May 1886, W. R. was expelled. As his collegiate coup de grace, young Hearst sent each of his professors a decorative chamber pot—or "thunder mug"—with the professor's name engraved on the bottom. The philosopher William James was one such professor.[9]

To his horrified mother, Will wrote, "I assured the gentlemen of the Faculty of Harvard College that I didn't regret so much having lost my degree as having given them an opportunity to refuse it to me."[10]

Following his expulsion from Harvard, W. R. began working as an apprentice at Joseph Pulitzer's *New York World*, under the guidance of Ballard Smith.

Instead of studying rhetoric, history, chemistry, and philosophy, W. R. studied sensational journalism.[11]

George Hearst could have used some of his son's pizzazz just then. The true test of whether he could play the part of senator occurred on May 27, when Hearst was tasked with eulogizing the late senator Miller in the Capitol Building. Up until this point, Hearst's speech making had been up and down. Having blown the gubernatorial nomination with his opening speech in San Jose, Hearst had immediately knocked it out of the park with his concession speech, helping to keep his political chances alive. While running for senator in 1884, Hearst had nosedived with his April 18 oration in San Francisco's Union Hall, only to rebound with two well-received Pacific Coast mining speeches in San Francisco's B'nai B'rith Hall. If that pattern continued—that Hearst fell flat before finding his footing—spectators were in for a rare treat.

"Mr. President," Hearst began, addressing Sherman. "The Senators who have preceded me have spoken of Senator Miller as a soldier and statesman. It now becomes my privilege to speak of him as a citizen, in which capacity he also served his country. He and his associates were the recipients of one of the most important franchises in the gift of the government."

Although Hearst was reportedly shaky as he began the oration, the introduction itself was typical. But it soon went off the rails. While praising Miller's management, Hearst went on to say that "a system was created which enabled the helpless and ignorant Indians . . . to save . . . in the banks of San Francisco, $100,000, which amount might have gone into the coffers of the company for the simple consideration of five barrels of bad whiskey."

By now the galleries were craning for a good view of Hearst, hoping to see him break down entirely. But Hearst, sweating profusely—which some took to indicate that he was intoxicated—kept at it.

"This instance alone is sufficient to show the purity and integrity of the man's life," Hearst continued before lapsing into purple prose that might have sounded harmonious had Townsend delivered it but that sent many into gleeful gales of laughter. "Such an example should be written on the mile posts of the highway, chiseled on the cliffs along the trails of the Rocky Mountains, graven in the granite of the Sierras, hewn on the tall pines of the Pacific slope, and commemorated in the flowers of the dead senator's adopted state."

The laughter soon spread throughout the country. The *Pittsburg Daily Post* delighted in describing how Hearst nearly fainted into his chair as he read the last words. The *Rural Vermonter* added, "The galleries were convulsed, and, all in all, it was one of the most remarkable senatorial performances in the history of the republic." The *Oakland Tribune* commented, "Senator Hearst's eulogy was a brief but extraordinary composition of commercial business, Indians, barrels of whiskey, mountain scenery, and respectful adjournment—in honor of the deceased. Senators were speechless, but they found their tongues afterwards and used them freely."

The Associated Press had the largest impact. Not only had Hearst delivered the speech in a state of "extreme intoxication," but afterward a copy of Hearst's speech had supposedly been found, rife with misspellings. "There have been some curious characters in the Senate," the dispatch concluded, "but Hearst is unique."[12]

Smelling blood in the water, in mid-June the *New York Times* wrote a long exposé on the new senator, categorizing Hearst as a "Western backwoodsman. Over 6 feet in height, straight as an arrow, long, swinging arms, big feet and hands, a somewhat awkward gait, a pleasant, ever-smiling face, a drawling, but musical voice, and a pronounced accent of the Southerner of the slave days."

The *Times* went on to describe Hearst as an embarrassment to Phoebe. Specifically, the *Times* highlighted an instance when George arrived at his Van Ness Avenue mansion in San Francisco while Phoebe held a soiree. George had forgotten about his wife's social gathering, the implication being that he'd been drinking. Spying George with his shirtfront stained by tobacco, Phoebe attempted to usher him upstairs before her guests caught sight of him. Hearst went upstairs, but not before spoiling the atmosphere: "Thrusting his hands in his breeches pockets—a habit of his—and drawing himself erect, he said in a voice loud enough for the company to hear: 'This is my ranch, and if these here folks don't like my shirt they can go home; it's time for folks to be in bed, anyhow, and I'm gwine thar,' and he steadied himself up the stairs to his apartment."[13]

With his personal reputation suffering, Hearst did his best to blend in with the other Democrats. In his political positions he was somewhat successful, largely paralleling the California Democratic platform: ostensibly anti-Chinese, anti-monopolistic, and supportive of hydraulic mining, tariff reform, and an enlarged navy. But he could no more blend in than a drunken crocodile at a Sunday picnic.[14]

Although Hearst mostly kept quiet in the Senate, when he did speak he was prone to reveal his ignorance. In one instance, clearly without realizing what he was doing, Hearst was the only Democrat to vote against going into executive session. Another time, Hearst addressed Sherman as "Senator" instead of "Mr. President." As his colleagues laughed at the grievous faux pas, Hearst became red-faced with embarrassment.[15]

As spring turned to summer, Hearst lurched from one political disaster to another. On July 16, he broke party lines to vote against the Rivers and Harbors Appropriation Bill, designed to protect California rivers, creating consternation and confusion throughout California. The next day the Senate voted on whether to consider a controversial bill that would define butter and impose a tax on oleomargarine. Although Hearst was in attendance, he was one of thirty-five senators who abstained from voting. The bill passed 28–13, and the Butter Wars were now on.[16]

Oleomargarine was first created in 1869 in France as an inexpensive alternative to butter. As it spread across the world, oleomargarine threatened to drive down the price of butter. By 1886 dairymen had finally pushed the federal government to vote on oleomargarine, which was reviled by ranchers and celebrated by those who refused to kowtow to the price of butter set by cattlemen. The dairymen wanted oleomargarine clearly labeled and—if they could not prohibit it outright— sharply taxed. Caught between supporting his own dairy interests (which would appear self-serving) or supporting oleomargarine, Hearst attempted to be on every side of the issue.

On July 19 Hearst voted to amend H.R. 8328, to make it unlawful to sell oleomargarine in the District of Columbia unless the package was marked "oleomargarine." The bill did not pass, but Hearst's vote pleased the dairymen. On July 20, Hearst voted to again amend H.R. 8328, to drive the tax manufacturers would pay for oleomargarine down from five cents a pound to two cents a pound, making the manufacturing of oleomargarine less expensive. It was this last vote Hearst was remembered for. "Oleomargarine Hearst" was born.

On July 20, Hearst also received dire news from California. Governor Stoneman had called for an extra session of the California Legislature. In his proclamation, Stoneman insisted that only the business of water rights, immigrant troubles, and reorganization of the state supreme court should be transacted, but rumor had it that the Republican-controlled legislature had other ideas. On the night of July 20, Hearst was reportedly anxious and in communication with his friends in California. But they could give him no assurance that in the extra session, the California Legislature might declare Hearst's appointment unlawful, triggering a special election.

On the afternoon of July 28, the Republican caucus met in Sacramento. To Hearst's dismay, it resolved to declare his appointment unconstitutional. The special election was to be held on August 3, 1886. That morning, the Republican caucus announced that A. P. Williams—a schoolteacher from Maine who had become founder and president of the San Francisco Board of Trade and the chairman of the Republican State Central Committee—would be its nominee. Later that day the vote took place. A. P. Williams received almost three times as many votes: seventy for Williams, twenty-four for Hearst. Politically humiliated—his stint as senator lasting less than five months—Hearst was removed from office.[17]

Returning to California, Hearst desperately sought redemption.

—15—

GERONIMO

(1886–1887)

I have made up my mind after all my experience that the members of the
Senate are the survival of the fittest.
—George Hearst

In announcing the results, the *Examiner* referred to the special election as a
"Senatorial scheme." Immediately afterward, the *Examiner* dropped the issue.
In the unflattering position of serving as senator for less than five months before
being ignominiously tossed from office, Hearst searched for a path to return him
to the Senate.[1]

Three major votes stood in Hearst's way. The first would take place on November 7, when the people would vote for a new California Legislature. The second vote
would take place in January, when Democratic members of the legislature would
vote for their gubernatorial candidate. The third vote would take place shortly
thereafter—the entire legislature would vote on whom to send to Washington
as the junior senator from California. If the legislature remained Republican,
that man would be Henry Vrooman, a former blacksmith from Michigan who
had risen to become the district attorney of Alameda. If the legislature became
Democratic, it could conceivably choose Hearst as its candidate. But with Hearst
having embarrassed himself so thoroughly in Washington, becoming a national
joke, the odds seemed slim.

The Charleston Earthquake unexpectedly shook things up.

On August 31, 1886, a magnitude 7.0 earthquake rocked the Carolinas. The powerful quake was felt as far away as Milwaukee, New Orleans, and Cuba. It damaged thousands of buildings and killed more than sixty people. Furthermore, it activated one of San Francisco's leading patronesses, Phoebe Hearst, who recognized a unique opportunity to repair the South Carolina port city and her husband's political career in one fell swoop.

To this purpose, Phoebe began imagining a charity event to aid Charleston. Pooling her resources, she brought together Ned Townsend and her son's friend Ernest Thayer, who had graduated magna cum laude from Harvard and while there had written the hilarious burlesque *Joan of Arc, or the Old Maid of New Orleans*, in which Phoebe had caught W. R. portraying the comic character Pretzel. If Thayer could write another burlesque, Phoebe and Ned would have it performed at San Francisco's Grand Opera House, with the proceeds benefiting Charleston.

Fortunately, Thayer had a subject in mind.

Holed up in a canyon in the Peloncillo Mountains of Arizona Territory in early September, Geronimo and his band of Chiricahua Apaches were tired of running. By the time General Nelson Miles and the Fourth U.S. Cavalry rode into Skeleton Canyon on September 4, the infamous warrior knew it was over. After capitulating, the Indians were placed in train cars destined for Florida's Fort Marion and Fort Pickens. While papers throughout the United States and Mexico boomed the news, Thayer got to work, reinventing Geronimo's capture as a fun-filled romp.[2]

Meanwhile, Hearst kept busy on two other fronts: capitalizing on Geronimo's capture and supporting the Democratic legislative nominees.

Hearst quickly realized that with Geronimo removed from the equation, Mexican land adjacent to Babicora Ranch in Chihuahua would be worth good money again. Acting quickly, Hearst's agents expanded Babicora Ranch by purchasing for twenty to forty cents an acre an additional 330,000 acres. Hearst's Chihuahua property now totaled an immense million acres. It was soon worth several millions.[3]

Rumors also began to circulate that Hearst had written a check for $100,000 to the Democratic State Central Committee to help fund Democratic campaigns. This money was put to good use. Democratic managers thought it possible to carry the Nineteenth and Twentieth Assembly Districts, generally Republican, and sent money to Butte, Plumas, and Sierra. In Oakland, Hearst's money was said to have gone toward the Fourth Ward. Additionally, sums of $50 and $100 went to legislative districts in Sacramento County that had not before seen financial support.[4]

In early October, help also arrived from Washington in the form of Hearst's friend Senator Arthur Gorman of Maryland, with instructions from Cleveland to help the Democrats. On October 6, after making a speech extolling President Cleveland, Gorman met with hundreds of prominent Democrats at the Palace Hotel. Among them were George Hearst, Mayor Washington M. Bartlett, James G. Fair, George Flournoy, and A. B. "Boyd" Henderson of the *Examiner*. Along with rallying Democrats to his side, Gorman also came with Washington money to help fund Democratic campaigns. Republicans began to worry that if the Democrats were successful, Hearst might just be their nominee. "Every vote for a Democratic legislative candidate is a vote to reseat George Hearst in the United States Senate," commented Sacramento's *Record-Union*, "and to give him a new opportunity to assail the dairy interests of the land and the integrity of river navigation."[5]

Working in concert, throughout early October Republicans sought to embarrass Hearst and the Democratic Party by reminding the people of his senatorial record of supporting the unpopular oleomargarine bill and rivers appropriation bill. Calls of "Bull butter Hearst" and "Steer clear of him" filled newspaper columns. They also painted him as an ignoramus and a buffoon. "Senator Gorman will intrigue with the Democrats of California," the *Oakland Tribune* noted acerbically, "if he can bore a hole for an idea to get through George Hearst's head."[6]

On October 16, Republicans hit upon a new strategy. The *Santa Cruz Sentinel* dug up a facsimile of the 1865 vote by the California Legislature on the Thirteenth and Fourteenth Amendments, reminding California that Hearst had voted to keep slavery legal. "What do the 'boys in blue,' who spent their early manhood on the field of battle during the great struggle, think of this aspirant to the United States Senatorship?" the *Sentinel* asked. Soon newspapers throughout the state took up the cry. Hearst's vote against admitting Washington Territory as a state was also added to his list of faults.[7]

Although on October 19, the *Record-Union* referred to him as a "muttonhead," Hearst showed his chops the following day by investing in the West Coast Telephone Company with former governor George Perkins and his business manager, Irwin C. Stump. As for politics, no one knew whether Hearst's moves were making a difference. Each party announced it anticipated a sweeping victory for its side.[8]

On Thursday, November 4, George and Phoebe attended the wedding reception of Joseph Donahue Grant and Lizzie Hull at the Grant residence on Bush Street. Mixing with the Stanfords and the Crockers, the guests had politics on their minds. Two days later California voted. That evening the results were tallied. It was a Democratic blowout. Phoebe, hosting a reception at their Taylor Street home that afternoon, must have been ecstatic. On November 9, Hearst was seen in a Democratic Committee room, smiling agreeably as the boys called him "Uncle George" and "our next United States Senator."[9]

More smiles would be had four days later, on the night of the play.

At 8:30 P.M. on November 13, carriages crowded Mission Street outside the Grand Opera House. Prominent theatergoers included Theresa Fair and Mary Flood, U.S. congressman Charles Felton, former mayor Frank McCoppin, Harvard professor Josiah Whitney, and the editor of the *Argonaut,* Frank Pixley. Naturally, James Haggin and Lloyd Tevis escorted their wives, Eliza Sanders Haggin and Susan Sanders Tevis. Humorous souvenir programs were available for twenty-five cents. Ordinary seats ran $2 a ticket, while box seats fetched $200. Naturally, Hearst and Phoebe sat in a box.

After everyone settled in, attorney Eugene Deuprey delivered Judge Timothy Rearden's prologue. After praising Phoebe, Deuprey lampooned Geronimo's capture in verse:

> They caught Geronimo—you may have heard—
> He was a gamesome and precarious bird;
> You've heard, too, that they sent him south:
>   In sooth,
> That's hardly, as we'll show, the solid truth;
> An open secret! He is here tonight
> On exhibition—as a cheerful sight!
> We hope he will amuse: If not, the cause
> Wherein we labor merits your applause.

As the audience clapped appreciatively, the green curtain lifted and Geronimo was revealed. With him was a bulldog done up with war paint and feathers. The audience was soon acquainted with Reddypen, Strong Man, General Smiles (a parody of General Miles), John Smith, Geronimo's daughter Gushing Water, and Quack-Quack the Medicine Man. Thayer himself played Strong Man. Hasty Pudding actors all, the cast brought a touch of Harvard to San Francisco through a plot that pivoted from Geronimo's capture and "imprisonment" in San Francisco to his daughter's nuptials. A chorus composed of a dozen men dressed as braves and a dozen women dressed as Louis XIV courtiers added to the excitement.

An early scene catching Thayer's sharp humor set the tone:

GERONIMO: How many?

BRAVE: Two.

GERONIMO: Color of hair?

BRAVE: One glossy brown.

GERONIMO: The other?

BRAVE: Red.

GERONIMO: Thank Heaven! That hue was wanting in my crazy quilt.

Backstage, Ned Townsend seemed everywhere at once, making certain the show was a success. But it was Willis Barton, playing Gushing Water, who brought down the house through his lovemaking scene with John Smith. As the players took their bows, Phoebe tossed the young man a bouquet of roses.[10]

Everyone seemed to enjoy the burlesque. Both Republicans and Democrats noticed that Hearst, whose plucky wife had been the driving force behind the charity event, had demonstrated that he could be as at ease in an opera seat as in a mineshaft.[11]

Three days later Hearst was spotted at the Bay District Race Track with Haggin, Lucky Baldwin, and Christopher Buckley. Doubtless, Hearst and the Blind Boss had a lot to discuss. Indeed, the race for the U.S. Senate had narrowed. As Hearst gained prominence, three other Democrats quietly began securing political backing. These men were John P. Irish, J. W. Hellman, and Samuel M. Wilson. Irish, a fiery speaker who could trounce Hearst in any debate, led an anti-Hearst Democratic minority that condemned mistreatment and xenophobia aimed at Japanese and Chinese immigrants. Hellman, who like his friend George Stoneman owned a large vineyard in Los Angeles, was well connected and could boast of his business acumen. Wilson appeared the most dangerous. A self-educated Ohioan, he had never received a college diploma but nevertheless had served as district attorney of Galena.[12]

With other Democratic candidates in the field, even Democratic newspapers turned on Hearst, while the Republican papers sharpened their claws. The *Folsom Telegraph* thanked Hearst for political support during the recent election but preferred Irish. The *Los Angeles Herald* dismissed Hearst and backed Hellman. Questioned the Democratic *Petaluma Courier*, "If wealth and the spending of it to influence the late election is not George Hearst's chief qualification and recommendation, then, in the name of all that it good, what is it?" The *Fresno Republican* condemned Hearst as "a disgrace" and "the butt of ridicule." While the *Los Angeles Times* dubbed him "Brainless George Hearst," the cantankerous

Los Angeles Times described Hearst as "an old ignoramus, as unlettered as the backside of a tombstone" and an "illiterate Money Bags."[13]

Despite the bad press, Hearst exuded confidence, renting a house in Washington. Senator Gorman left California in the last week of November, but Hearst had faith in his backers in San Francisco. On November 27, Hearst was spotted at the Bay District Track with Buckley and Cousin Joe. Two days later George and Phoebe enjoyed the wedding reception of Sugar King William G. Irwin at the Palace Hotel, mixing with Alice and Jasper MacDonald, Senator John P. Jones, and Governor Stoneman.[14]

Conspicuously absent from the San Francisco social scene that fall were W. R. and Eleanor Calhoun. The two had spent the summer in each other's company; W. R. had wooed her with flowers and gifts. This culminated on June 18, 1886, when W. R. proposed to her in the Hotel Del Monte in Monterey. Whether Eleanor saw the man in him or merely the millions of dollars, she was eager to tie the knot. If she knew about Tessie it did not bother her. Phoebe knew about both of them and didn't like it. She had been willing to sponsor Eleanor in San Francisco, but she wanted more for a daughter-in-law than an aspiring actress. That W. R. wouldn't heed Phoebe's advice cut her to the quick. To Orrin Peck she complained, "You well know all that I have been to him, the devotion lavished upon him. You also know he is selfish, indifferent and undemonstrative as his father. Both have their good qualities, but the other sides of their natures are most trying. . . . I feel that it will ruin my boy's life to marry such a designing woman."[15]

Seeking to quash the romance, Phoebe swore the two to secrecy, sent Eleanor on a European holiday, and convinced her husband to send their son to Mexico. To entice W. R., and possibly give him a purpose in life other than dallying with young ladies and criticizing *Examiner* mismanagement, Hearst gave the boy one hundred thousand acres of Babicora Ranch in Chihuahua, allowing him to hire Jack Follansbee to manage it. They found there was work to be done.

The ranch house—known as Babicora House—had been erected north of the Babicora Plain, fertile with springs, lake beds, and tule grass, where thousands of cattle grazed before being driven north to Deming. Without a fence, the cattle typically wandered into the mountains, seeking the pine forests to protect them from storms. Babicora Ranch was also only forty-five miles from Louis Terrazas's San Miguel Ranch, and this created chaos when the cattle, which were without branding, invariably mixed. W. R. thought it a grand property, despite its drawbacks. To Phoebe, he wrote, "I really don't see what is to prevent us from owning all of Mexico and running it to suit ourselves."[16]

To his father, W. R. wrote that between him, Follansbee, and Hearst's Mexico manager, J. A. Verger, "there is no reason that we should not soon be as rich as Crocker or anybody. . . . Stir yourself daddy pop. First get elected by all means and then between December and the time you take your seat we can raise enough money to work all our remaining things in a way that will allow us to sit back and watch the coffers swell."[17]

Leaving Follansbee in charge of his slice of the property, W. R. boarded a northbound train, arriving in San Francisco on December 7. To Phoebe's chagrin, he announced that he had no intention of breaking off the engagement with Eleanor. Hearst fled the family drama for Sacramento a week later, creating a flutter of excitement when he arrived on the evening of December 14. The next day he attended the Citrus Fair, showing his support for southern California produce. Meanwhile, in San Diego, the second phase of Phoebe's Charleston charity plan came to fruition. There, in Armory Hall, more than two hundred dolls were displayed. Their sale would aid San Diego's St. Paul's Cathedral and Charleston. The most prominent patronesses commissioning the dolls included Frances Cleveland, Jane Stanford, and Phoebe Hearst. Phoebe's doll, named California and representing the state seal, was particularly eye-catching.[18]

Hearst returned to San Francisco on December 17 in the company of newly elected state senator T. J. Clunie. While Hearst politicked, Phoebe continued to demonstrate her compassionate nature, organizing her kindergarten pupils to raise $725.88 for the children of those who had drowned in a flood at Sabine Pass, Texas. At Christmas, Phoebe and George hosted a festive dinner party. Beneath their Christmas tree were dozens of presents for the children to unwrap. Still, hostile newspapers continued to skewer Hearst as "Money Bags," and the Democratic opposition began to coalesce around Sam Wilson as their savior. Needing a diversion, Hearst and Phoebe spent the evening of December 29 at Pioneer Hall with the Haggins and Tevises, absorbing the chamber music of Henry Heyman.[19]

Staying true to Hearst, on New Year's Day San Francisco's popular satirical magazine the *Wasp* gave Hearst a ringing endorsement. In a color cartoon, it showed Hearst standing tall and heroic—an homage to Ulysses returning to chase off Penelope's would-be suitors—with a nocked arrow pointed at the fleeing forms of Irish, Hellman, and Wilson. "George Hearst . . . stands head and shoulders above all competitors," the writer declared. "We believe the Democratic party has wisely concluded to give him the vacant seat . . . and that it has done this because he draws the lustiest bow that is drawn in the contest."[20]

On the night of January 2, 1887, Democratic assemblymen and state senators rattled into the Sacramento depot. Although they formed a caucus, led by Clunie, they did not vote on a senatorial candidate. To Republicans who favored anyone but Hearst, the delay engendered hope. Further injuring Hearst was a circular enclosed in an envelope marked "Secret and Private" and disseminated to the California Legislature. It contained clippings from eastern newspapers antagonistic to Hearst. With the tide rising against him, Hearst, who had been holed up in Haggin's expansive horse-breeding Rancho Del Paso, journeyed seven miles southwest of the ranch to downtown Sacramento. On January 7, he and Townsend crossed the American River and made his headquarters the Golden Eagle Hotel. His rooms were immediately thronged with visitors. At 11 P.M. the Jefferson and Democracy Clubs appeared and asked for Hearst's presence in the Assembly hall. Hearst obliged, giving a short speech.[21]

For the next several days, the Democrats refused to vote on the senatorial question. Hearst continued to glad-hand and dole out cigars, but his managers grew increasingly anxious. After all, they had pinned their hopes to Hearst before and seen it all come crumbling down. "Boss Buckley," commented the *San Francisco Chronicle*, "evidently shares the nervousness of the Hearst leaders. He was out at a late hour to-night [January 10], making his headquarters in the corridors of the capitol." When on January 13 it was finally agreed that the vote would be held the next day, no one could be quite sure what would happen.[22]

As the caucus met, several prominent Democrats filled the anterooms outside the chamber. They included Buckley, Townsend, and the newly elected governor, Washington M. Bartlett. Hearst, on the other hand, waited in the Golden Eagle Hotel. If multiple votes had to be taken, as they had in San Jose, it would never do for Hearst to be waiting in the wings like an eager schoolboy. This time, Hearst did not have to wait long.

From outside the chamber, Townsend was elated and relieved to hear the cheer of "Hurrah for Hearst!" emanate from beyond the heavy doors. When the multitude of men who had gathered in the lobby heard this, the cry of "Hearst!" was instantly taken up. As the heavy doors were flung open, the crowd surged forward to congratulate the outcoming senators and assemblyman on their vote and to learn the details. Meanwhile, Clunie and Townsend raced the other direction, down the stairway and out the glass door, wishing to be the first ones to congratulate Hearst. That honor went to the fleet-footed state senator John Boggs, who found Hearst in his apartments in the Golden Eagle. Boggs shared the news: Hearst had been nominated on the first ballot, with fifty-four of sixty-five men voting to return him to the Senate. Wilson had received only five votes. Ironically, Boggs had cast one of them.

As the crowd surged into the Golden Eagle, bottles of champagne popped open and Boggs proposed a toast to Hearst: "While I have been opposed to him, I know that he is an honest man. He is now my Senator, as he is everyone else's Senator, the choice of his party, and the choice of the people of California."[23]

Five day later, on January 19, 1887, the two houses of the legislature met at noon in a joint convention in Sacramento. There, 118 votes were cast to choose California's next senator. Chancellor Hartson, a Republican who had worked for the Internal Revenue Service, received one vote; Henry Vrooman gained fifty-two votes; George Hearst received sixty-five votes. George Hearst would be a senator once more.

Around ten o'clock that night, a mass of Democratic state senators, assembly-men, and supporters found Senator-elect Hearst in the Golden Eagle. After cheer-ing Hearst, they brought him to a crowded reception at the Capitol Hotel. Wine was served. Other refreshments were eaten. Senator Jones made a witty speech, and Hearst—who may have been having the best night of his life—followed it up with a short but heartfelt one. "Gentlemen, I can only thank you all, and to thank the Democracy of this State for the honor which they conferred upon me to-day."[24]

No one thing ever wins an election. It was quietly rumored that Hearst had personally coughed up $500,000 while bribing his own Democratic colleagues at $10,000 dollars a vote. [25] The *San Francisco Examiner* had also silenced its campaign against the railroad monopolies, and Hearst had successfully cut a deal with Senator Stanford, who claimed to have no dog in the fight. Additionally, a certain blind bartender applied pressure to the Democratic legislators, inducing them to toe the line. In his memoirs, Buckley wrote that after the election, "I was then at the zenith of my power."[26] Phoebe's charitable inclinations and manage-rial skills, particularly in putting on *The Capture of Geronimo* with the help of Ernest Thayer and Ned Townsend, also helped demonstrate that Hearst could be refined as well as generous. Each event factored into Hearst being elected in his own right to the U.S. Senate.

To Townsend, Senator-elect Hearst was especially grateful. So he offered Townsend a promotion at the *Examiner*. It was not the position of editor in chief, however. That position was going elsewhere.

—16—

SUNSET

(1887–1888)

I said to myself, I'll scratch my name on that list if it takes every damn
cent I've got, and I've scratched it.
—George Hearst

Uncle George had bought himself a slice of the good life. Worth $15 million at
the outset of 1887, increasing every week by $60,000, Hearst was at the top of
his world. For the last two years of Cleveland's first term, Hearst would live it
up. Whiskey, cigars, horse racing, Washington receptions, and trips across his
empire would fill his days. Hearst could do just about anything he wanted—and
he wanted everything.[1]

W. R. Hearst proved a chip off the old block. Although W. R. was closer to his
mother, like both his parents he had an iron will, a mind capable of seeing minute
details and the broader picture, and a vaulting ambition. Just then W. R.'s twin
ambitions were to take over the *Examiner* and marry Eleanor Calhoun, despite
Phoebe's objections.

From England, Eleanor helped their cause by slipping word of the engagement
to a *New York Post* reporter. Talk of the impending nuptials broke in New York
on February 3 and by February 4 it was national news. The following day hordes
of reporters mobbed Hearst, hoping for a reaction. Although he tried begging off

with a cold, Hearst was heard to mutter that "the disparity in age and experience makes the union undesirable."[2]

To Orrin Peck, Phoebe wrote, "I am so distressed about Will that I don't really know how I can live if he marries Eleanor Calhoun. She is determined to marry him and it seems as if he must be in the toils of the Devil fish. . . . We are trying to delay matters. . . . I am so heartbroken."[3]

In mid-February, the Washington newspapers reported that the marriage would take place in early spring. Without much time to act, Phoebe made the most of it. On February 18, when the steamer *Wisconsin* arrived in New York with Eleanor on board, Phoebe and W. R. were there to greet her. Despite the opposition to the marriage, the trio traveled to Phoebe's rented house in Washington, D.C. Using all of her wiles, Phoebe managed to put an end to the engagement.

"We must be firm and kind and help him get out of this," Phoebe wrote George, telling him that "he will be all right. He worried a great deal for two or three days, but he eats and sleeps well, and has too much strength of character to be seriously affected by this."[4]

His plans to marry Eleanor thwarted, W. R. doubled down on his other ambition: running the *Examiner*. With Clarence Greathouse having left the paper the previous year—appointed by Cleveland to serve as consul general in Japan—the *Examiner* clearly needed fresh blood. Although Hearst couldn't shake the feeling that the paper was a quartz mill and would never pay, he ultimately agreed.[5]

"There's one thing about my boy Bill," Hearst commented. "I've been watching him, and I notice that when he wants cake, he wants cake; and he wants it now. And I notice that after a while he gets his cake."[6]

In February 1887, Will wrote to his father that he was

> anxious to begin work on the *Examiner*. I have all my pipes laid, and it only remains to turn on the gas. One year from the day I take hold of the thing the circulation will have increased ten thousand. . . . We must be alarmingly enterprising, and we must be startlingly original. We must be honest and fearless. We must have greater variety than we have ever had. . . . There are some things that I intend to do new and striking which will constitute a revolution in the sleepy journalism of the Pacific slope and will focus the eyes of all that section on the *Examiner*. I am not going to write you what these are, for the letter might get lost, or you might leak. You would be telling people

about the big things that Billy Buster was proposing to bring out in the paper, and the first thing I knew somebody else would have it.[7]

On Friday, March 4, 1887, a light rain was falling in San Francisco, blown in by northwesterly winds. Across the city, subscribers to the *San Francisco Examiner* picked up their rain-spattered Friday morning papers and noticed something different—something never seen before but that would change the history of publishing and the world. The words "W. R. Hearst, Proprietor" appeared on the second page.[8]

While his boy began his whirlwind campaign to sensationalize the news, Hearst quietly returned to Washington. On March 4, the same day W. R. took over the *Examiner,* Hearst was officially made senator again. Four days later he strode into the White House, reuniting with President Cleveland. Having made certain promises during his senatorial campaign, Hearst had favors to ask. Specifically, Hearst wanted William T. Coleman, Adam Grant, and T. J. Clunie appointed Post Office commissioners and for them to select the site of the new San Francisco Post Office.[9]

Cleveland thought other men more suitable. With Hearst once again embarrassed, rival newspapers and political opportunists pounced on the story. The *Weekly Nevada State Journal* commented that Hearst seemed "disgusted" by how the commissioners were appointed. The *San Francisco Chronicle* chortled that "Senator Hearst is quite indignant about the manner in which he has been snubbed" and that Hearst seemed to miss Townsend. Eldney Lacey, a prominent mugwump with Republican leanings, griped to the *Los Angeles Herald,* "What's the matter with Hearst anyway? . . . Is it possible that a Democratic United States Senator hasn't influence enough with a Democratic administration to name who shall occupy a small-sized Post Office? If I was Hearst I would give the administration a black eye for this refusal."[10]

Shaking off the bad press, Hearst retreated to New York City, headquartering himself in the Hoffman House. He returned in time for Phoebe's latest reception, held on April 12, 1887.

From 4 to 7. P.M. guests were dazzled by the hydrangeas, marguerites, lilies, azaleas, maiden hair ferns, Jacqueminot roses, and pink and white tulips that festooned every table and mantel. Refreshments and seasonal delicacies were served in the dining room while an orchestra played. Alice, visiting from San Francisco, was on hand to help Phoebe receive her guests. Notable attendees included John

Sherman, Margaret Sherman, General William S. Rosecrans, Anna Rosecrans, Secretary of War William Endicott, and Ellen Peabody Endicott. Hearst could be especially proud of the wine cellar, worth showing off. Secured inside was a stash of whiskey, cognac, liqueurs, champagne, and wine, which Tom Ochiltree had delivered on behest of Senator Stanford.[11]

A success, Phoebe quickly became a fixture of Washington's high society.

Hearst, of course, was more at home at a racetrack, a mining camp, or a bar stool than dressed in a swallowtail suit, sipping terrapin soup at a Washington reception. Shortly after his wife's first Washington dinner party, Hearst stole away to New York City. At the Union League Club, over coffee and cheese, Hearst discussed free trade, interlacing his arguments with his own unique vernacular. But in July 1887, Hearst's penchant for drink and free and easy speech once again landed him in trouble.

While Hearst lifted elbows at Chamberlin's, one of Washington's toniest bars, a private conversation about the election was overheard. "I didn't care how much it cost," Hearst said, "for I was bound to git there. . . . I said to myself, I'll scratch my name on that list if it takes every d— cent I've got, and I've scratched it." Afterward, newspapermen trumpeted the story across the country. Allegations of bribery followed.[12]

Rumors of corruption weren't enough to run him out of office, but it may have rankled Hearst to realize just how much he missed Townsend. But Hearst wasn't about to summon back his right-hand man, then serving as the *Examiner's* business manager, for Townsend and W. R. were hard at work. Revolutionizing the entire newspaper industry was no easy task.

W. R. receives most of the credit for transforming the *Examiner* from a second-rate newspaper with a lackluster circulation of fifteen thousand to one of the most sensational newspapers on the coast. With headlines trumpeting fires, murders, earthquakes, floods, shipwrecks, and train wrecks, circulation increased at an unbelievable rate. Sensationalism had come to California, courtesy of young Hearst.

Championing the people (the subscribers), the *Examiner* locked in the pro-labor and anti-immigrant demographic. The air and sea were also W. R.'s domain. W. R. paid to have a couple married in a balloon over the city, with "THE EXAMINER" emblazoned on the balloon and a follow-up story appearing in the next issue. On another outing, W. R. himself floated above San Francisco, camera in hand. Ever more generous, the *Examiner* gave out free boat rides in exchange for coupons clipped from paper. The news in San Francisco was suddenly exciting.[13]

Bold headlines from a typical *Examiner* front page during this time—March 31, 1887—included these:

ASSASSINS. Uneasy Lies the Head That Wears the Crown of All the Russias.
  HUMAN BLOODHOUNDS ARE HUNTING HIM TO DEATH.
NEMESIS. The Hidden Crimes of William Kissane Summon Him to Justice.
  THE STORY OF HIS LONG PENT-UP GUILT.
RAILROAD RULES. The Commission Under the Interstate Law in Washington.
  AN IMMEDIATE ORGANIZATION TO BE HAD.
AN OCEAN OF HORROR. The Sealing Steam Eagle Lost in the North Atlantic.
  TWO HUNDRED VICTIMS.
VERONA'S LUCK. The Alleged Kinswoman of E. J. Tuttle Testifies in Los
  Angeles. SENSATIONAL SCENES OVER THE DIVULGED DETAILS.
ANOTHER MURDER. A Mongolian Restaurant-Keeper & in the Forehead.
  THE ASSASSIN ARRESTED[14]

Believing that publishing without promoting was "like winking at a girl in the dark," W. R. also gave the *Examiner* a new moniker—"Monarch of the Dailies"—which the paper heralded in its spacious masthead as "THE LARGEST, BRIGHTEST AND BEST NEWSPAPER ON THE PACIFIC COAST."[15] It was hard to argue that it wasn't.

Few people who glanced at the first page of the *Examiner* could stop themselves from reading the rest. Everything seemed to have that "gee-whiz emotion," as Arthur McEwen phrased it. Arthur James Pegler, another Hearst reporter, famously noted, "A Hearst newspaper is like a screaming woman running down the street with her throat cut."[16] In other words, it was offensive, impossible, mesmerizing, and out of control.

With the *Examiner* suddenly the hottest thing on the Pacific Coast, Hearst had to see it for himself. "I shall be return to New York in time for the fall races," Hearst announced. When he checked out of the Hoffman House, the porters were amazed that a man of his wealth had only a trunk and a valise as luggage. Wasting little time, Hearst rattled into the St. Louis Depot on April 26, 1887. He spent the night in El Paso on April 29, dined at Los Angeles's Depot Hotel on May 1, and on May 2 was back in San Francisco.[17]

Looking in on his son's business, he saw that the *Examiner* still wasn't paying but was making an impact. Ambrose Bierce, the acid-tongued Civil War veteran, was now on the payroll, as was McEwen, the Scot who had worked at Virginia City newspapers and the author of the "Twaddler" piece that had poked fun at Hearst three years before, during Hearst's senatorial campaign against Stanford.

Hearst and McEwen took a liking to each other. McEwen acknowledged that Hearst was not "a bully or a slave driver" like Collis Huntington and that he understood human nature.[18]

Hearst also understood, having seen the great cities of the East, that San Francisco needed to be revitalized. He just didn't know how to articulate it. At a San Francisco meeting in late May, Hearst spoke about the need for improvements: beautiful streets, clean sewers, and big hotels with fresh paint. "We must make this city the Paris of America," Hearst declared.

"Any city can be a Paris so easily with big hotels and fresh paint?" questioned a wit for the *Buffalo Commercial*. "Hearst is a treasure."[19]

Hearst did not let these little gaffes bother him. Swept up in the horse racing craze, Hearst spent some of July importing racing stock from Australia and purchased Stanford's filly Gorgo. Like Haggin, Hearst planned to race his own stable of horses at the greatest racetracks in the country. He even selected his own colors for the jockeys to wear: orange-yellow and green caps and orange-yellow shirts with green sleeves.[20]

While in San Francisco, Hearst also met with the California Board of Forestry, where he lamented the wanton damage done to trees by mountain goats and fires. Hearst supported the creation of stations staffed by officers trained in fighting fires and preventing destruction. "The most important thing for us to do is to protect the trees we have already," Hearst said in closing. "There are plenty of them for a long time to come, even if they did not reproduce themselves, but we must take care of them."[21]

Apparently, Hearst also needed to take care of his empire. After traveling through Zion to Park City, Hearst spent a week with Robert Chambers overlooking the Ontario Mine. From there he traveled northeast to Salt Lake City on the way to Montana, where Haggin had joined Marcus Daly. Hearst spent a couple weeks in the mining region around Ramshorn, seventy-five miles as the crow flies from the Anaconda. In Butte he dined with Daly and his wife, Margaret. On August 20, Hearst was enjoying his after-breakfast cigar in front of the St. Nicholas Hotel when a reporter for the *Inter Ocean* found him. Hearst was polite enough. He supported Cleveland for president in next year's election, believed Montana Territory would gain statehood before long, and laughed heartily when caught dodging financial details of Anaconda copper. Without knowing it, Hearst may have also given some insight as to why he was in Butte rather than Washington.

"The west is making its influence felt more and more at Washington, but the country west of the Mississippi has not got much consideration in Washington yet," Hearst stated. "A man from west of the Mississippi is a pretty small man in Washington."

In other words, Hearst was still treated as a cowpoke in the capital.[22]

On August 30, 1887, Hearst left Butte for Salt Lake City. On September 8 he was spotted on a train car passing through Reno on his way back to California. Four days later California governor Washington M. Bartlett died of Bright's disease. Later that day Robert Waterman, a Republican who had served as California's lieutenant governor, was elevated to the top position. Hearst split his time between San Francisco and Sacramento, adapting to the new political climate, before heading to the Stockton Fair, slated for September 29. Joining Hearst were Stanford and Waterman. Naturally, Hearst made a conspicuous figure at the racetrack at the fair. He even spent $420 at the fair's livestock auction, buying three cows for one of his ranches.[23]

In mid-October Hearst and Phoebe donated money toward the building of a new synagogue in San Francisco. On November 13 Hearst passed through Los Angeles on his way to Mexico, spent some time at Babicora Ranch, and reached El Paso on November 24. Although he was en route to Washington over Thanksgiving, back in California he had forty turkeys distributed to families too hard-pressed to buy one. Hearst could certainly afford to be generous. In early December, Hearst, Haggin, and Tevis sold the profitable Custer Mine for $125,000. By December 4 Hearst had returned to Washington.[24]

While Hearst had been busy crisscrossing the United States, Phoebe had been making plans of her own. Having brought from California her Japanese art collection, Phoebe was ready for the Washington social season. For Christmas, she hosted guests new to the capital. On January 5, 1888, George and Phoebe attended Frances Cleveland's dinner reception at the White House, officially kicking off the year's festivities. Phoebe's white satin gown with gold brocade evened out her husband's rough edges. The following evening Phoebe held her own reception, complete with live music, and when rain clouds threatened to spoil the mood, she bested them with two awnings spanning from the carriageway to her front door. On January 17 Phoebe hosted another reception, where seventy-five guests supped at her dinner table.[25]

On the night of February 16 Phoebe played host to W. R. and Arthur McEwen, who had taken a four-day train cross-country. The Clevelands had also gotten wind of W. R.'s arrival and sent a card to the Hearst mansion, inviting them to another White House reception. This time it was McEwen, not Hearst, who filled the role of country bumpkin. While slipping on doeskin gaiters, McEwen was heard to complain, "Damned Comstock bunion!" McEwen also dandified himself in a dress coat and white necktie before cramming into Hearst's carriage.

At the reception, McEwen reunited with General Philip Sheridan, whom he had met on a train in Virginia City, and Bill Stewart, who returned to the Senate on the same day as Hearst. Stewart was flabbergasted to see the Comstock pen-pusher strutting about the White House with a lady on his arm.

"Why—why—Mr. McEwen—What are you doing here?" Stewart stammered.

"Same as you are, Senator," McEwen replied in Scottish brogue, "enjoying myself."

Stewart, Hearst knew, was working on a bill that would divide Idaho Territory's 53 million acres between Nevada and Washington, vastly increasing the size of both states. Although Hearst knew Stewart would expect his help when the time came, Hearst kept his own council on the matter. Appointed to the Pacific Railroad Committee that February, Hearst suspected Stanford would also seek his help before too long.[26]

In the meantime, horses rather than horsepower dominated Hearst's thoughts. Hearst attended the races at Coney Island while his trainer, Matt Allen, sent his stable from San Francisco to New York. Hearst was too late to enter the Kentucky Derby, but with luck his horses would make a good showing at the New Jersey and New York tracks. Estimating that the stable would cost him $50,000 a year, Hearst certainly hoped he would win a few races.

The expenditure made for some lively exchanges between Hearst and W. R., who thought the money would be better spent at the *Examiner*. But Hearst wouldn't be budged. Speaking to a New York correspondent, Hearst related, "My son is opposed to me going into horse racing, but I tell him . . . I have worked hard all my life, and I think I am entitled to a little enjoyment."[27]

Having reinvented himself as a senatorial turfman, Hearst finally made one of the social transformations Phoebe had been requesting for years: he stopped dressing like a bum. Hoffman House patrons noticed the change right away. Gone was the old black slouch. In its place was a shiny silk hat. His claw-hammer coats were of the finest material. Even his beard was kept carefully trimmed. But at heart he was still George Hearst.[28]

Hearing of Hancock's, a hole-in-the-wall establishment on Pennsylvania Avenue that served simple fare, Hearst concluded that it would be a welcome change of pace from the rich dinners he'd had since returning to Washington. Running into Kentucky senator James Beck, Hearst said to him, "Beck, there is a place down here on the avenue where they say you can get a good dinner. Not one of the new-fangled kind with terrapin and all that, but the plain old jowl and 'greens' of our early days. Let's go down and try it."

Gathering like-minded senators, the party sat down at Hancock's at eight o'clock. The interior was wild. Sabers and pistols hung from the walls and dangled from heavy oak beams. A glass case held Zachary Taylor's tall white hat, which "Old Rough and Ready" had worn at the Battle of Lake Okeechobee. Andrew Jackson's umbrella hung nearby. But the bill of fare was simple enough: bacon, cornbread, jowl and greens, fried chicken in gravy. Hearst food. A large pitcher of beer was set on the table, which suited the company fine. For Hearst, it brought back nostalgia for the early days in California. Enjoying every bite, Hearst insisted it was the best meal he'd eaten since the gold rush. They stayed until eleven, whereupon Hearst paid for the table. Rather than the $12 meals he'd been accustomed to buying, the bill came to less than $1 a head.[29]

On March 17, Phoebe had another reception, this one attended by one of Hearst's old friends from the Comstock, Mark Twain, who had just come from a performance he'd given at the Congregation Church, which Phoebe and Frances Cleveland had attended. Although the celebrity author was always a hit, Chief Justice Morrison Waite caught a chill after leaving Phoebe's reception, dying six days later. More than Mark Twain, attendees recalled that the last time they saw Waite alive was at Senator Hearst's. Hearst may have caught the same germ, for he became sick shortly thereafter and spent most of the rest of March convalescing. Hearst recovered in time for his next big reception, on April 11, smoking after-dinner cigars with his guests in the drawing room.[30]

One week later, Hearst boarded a Washington train, heading for Mexico. On April 23, he was in El Paso. In Chihuahua, Hearst met Alexander Robey Shepherd and was made the guest of honor at a magnificent party. Shepherd, a legendary westerner who had been appointed governor of Washington, D.C., by President Grant in 1873 and had since made a fortune in Chihuahua silver, accompanied Hearst on his journey south to Mexico City. There they were received by President Porfirio Díaz. While in Mexico, Hearst purchased 2 million acres in Terra Caliente for the purpose of growing coffee, sugar, and tobacco. He also obtained a concession for the building of a railroad to the Pacific Ocean, coincidentally passing through his newly acquired holdings.[31]

Returning to Washington in late May, Hearst was pleased that his stable was doing well. On April 24 his horse Surinam had won the Pacific Derby, and with it $4,750. A photograph he'd sat for while smoking a cigar had also been mass produced and created a stir. Some were aghast that the senator would besmirch his honor by posing with a cigar in his mouth; others argued that without the cigar, the image would not be true to life. Throughout June and July, Hearst spent more and more time at the track. Of all his horses, Gorgo did the best, winning twice at Monmouth Park. Hearst also bought one of Haggin's horses, King Thomas, for $40,000—the largest amount anyone had offered for a horse since Richard III.[32]

Hearst was back in Washington on July 18 when Senator Stewart finally made his move. On the Senate floor, Stewart argued that because Idaho Territory was mostly wasteland, it would never be able to sustain itself as a state; therefore, its 53 million acres should be divided between Washington and Nevada.

Stewart might have buffaloed the dudes, but he hadn't buffaloed the junior senator from California. From the Golden Chariot Mine in Flint to the Custer Mine in Bonanza City to the Belmont Mine in Heath, Hearst knew Idaho Territory like the back of his hand. Stewart had just roused a grizzly bear. The *Congressional Record* illustrates the mauling.

"Will the Senator allow me to ask him a question?" Hearst asked.

"Certainly," Stewart responded.

"Are you perfectly familiar with the valleys of Idaho?"

"I've been through them," Stewart stated.

"What part of the country?"

"I have followed the Snake River down to below the line and through those valleys. I have been in the Panhandle down to Lewiston. I have seen a large portion of the valley."

"Does the Senator not know that around Lewiston is one of the finest agricultural countries in the United States?" Hearst questioned.

"Certainly."

"Leaving there and going up Snake River there is fine land, and when you get through the cañon there is a valley there about 600 miles long and 40 miles wide that would hold two or three million people. It has the finest land in all the world. Besides, there are many valleys running up into the mountains, which are fine agricultural lands, and that eastern portion does not need irrigation, as the Senator well knows."

"I should like to ask the Senator if there is any waste land in Idaho?"

"There is very little waste land in Idaho," Hearst responded. "It abounds in rivers with large rich valleys, and the tops of the mountains are covered with the finest kind of timber.... The Territory abounds in rivers such as Snake River, Clear Water, Pelonse, Pen d'Oreille, and Kootenai.... The mountains, where there are mountains, are terrible mountains, but there is not better country for mining that I know of in the United States. But that is the very toughest portion of Idaho. I think it would make one of the grandest states in the Union."

The two old friends sparred for several more minutes before Stewart said in closing, "I do not think it will ever sustain a population to compare favorably with the other Western states known as agricultural states. I think it will necessarily have a small population."

But it was Hearst who got the last word. "If the Senator will allow me, I will state that I have been all over the territories west of the Rocky Mountains as much, perhaps, as any other man, and I think Idaho has more agricultural land in it than all the other Territories there."[33]

After his scheme fell apart, Stewart said to Hearst, "George, I thought you were with me."

"With you on almost anything, Bill," Hearst replied, "but this time I don't think you're right." Hearst proved correct about Idaho's agricultural potential. After one resourceful prospector discovered he could grow hearty Idaho potatoes on the snowbanks of the Caribou Mountains, enterprising young men began looking anew at Idaho Territory. Perhaps it had sustainability for statehood after all.[34]

On August 11, 1888, Phoebe was aboard a Northern Pacific Railroad car at Livingston, Montana, sixty miles north of Mammoth Hot Springs in Yellowstone National Park. She was traveling with Alice and Jasper McDonald, as well as Marcus Daly's wife, daughter, and sister. Fulfilling a promise to Will, Phoebe scribbled a letter to her husband concerning their son:

> Will expected to start east yesterday, and if he did will soon see you. He was anxious for me to assure you that he feels very sorry for his having spent so much money, and has stopped. A different plan will be adopted *next* time. The account astonished him and he thinks you will feel distressed. He appreciates all your kindness and I have never known him to express so much. I am glad he can go east now even though it is for a short time. He can explain so much more fully than I can write. There is a great deal that I do not like to trust to paper.
>
> In regards to the Examiner, Townsend says they *need* not draw more than five thousand per month, and after Dec, nothing. When Will said they would need to draw thirty thousand dollars *extra* money for the campaign, they had not made the careful estimate now reported. Will is very anxious to cut down but of course not to the extent of injuring the paper. I know you are glad to have me feel

contented about Will, and I do. . . . He has been kind, thoughtful and considerate, and has shown me so much affection that I scarcely know how to express my happiness. I feel ten years younger. Tenderness and love is more to a mother than all else.[35]

Three days later, on August 14, Hearst was joined at the Hoffman House by W. R., Townsend, and another of the *Examiner's* reporters, Henry Derby "Petey" Bigelow. By then Hearst had the numbers, courtesy of Phoebe's letter. Yes, W. R. had boosted circulation from fifteen thousand to forty thousand. But the boy had also run the *Examiner* at a loss, to the tune of $184,513, not including W. R.'s own expenses, a mere $47,939. Fortunately for W. R., Hearst had bigger fish to fry. Benjamin Harrison had emerged from the Republican Convention in Chicago as the Republican candidate for President. To defeat Harrison, the Democrats would need to carry California. The boys at the *Examiner* thought they could help with that. A newspaper editor instructing his staff of reporters and cartoonists to demonize one candidate while glorifying another wasn't exactly new, but young Hearst was fine-tuning the process. Yellow journalism would soon be born.

At the end of August, Jack Follansbee joined Hearst and W. R. at the Hoffman House. With Hearst owning eighty thousand head of cattle between his various ranches, Follansbee could make a good report.[36]

Hearst was at Long Island's Sheepshead Bay Race Track on September 2, watching Gorgo practicing the mile-and-an-eighth track. The filly ran so beautifully that Hearst tipped Lucky Baldwin, Joe Clark, and James Haggin that he had a sure thing. Two days later, at the Siren Stakes, Baldwin stabled his own horse, Los Angeles, and bet heavily on Gorgo. But Haggin was game for a good race, placing his money on his pride and joy, Yum Yum. Of the four horses competing for the Siren Stakes, Yum Yum was favored to win.

Out of the gate it was Gorgo, Lilyship, Peg Woffington, and Yum Yum trailing. Gorgo looked to be leaving the others behind, but Haggin's horse came back with a fury. Leaving Lilyship and Peg Woffington in the dust, Yum Yum was close on Gorgo's heels as the racehorses rounded the last turn. But Gorgo picked up speed, winning by two lengths. Finally, Hearst had beaten Haggin at this own game. That night Hearst sent a long congratulatory cable to Stanford for selling him the filly.[37]

On September 17, Hearst was back in the Senate. In Hearst's absence, the Senate had passed H.R. 11336, an amendment to the Chinese Exclusion Act of 1882. More xenophobic than ever, the proposed law forbade Chinese Americans abroad from returning to the United States. Republican Senators who thought the amendment too draconian had asked for H.R. 11336 to be reconsidered. Hearst joined with fellow Democrats and voted nay. With President Cleveland planning to sign the amendment into law on October 1, twenty to thirty thousand Chinese Americans were about to be stranded.

Phoebe also had her hands full.

Having helped organize the Century Club of San Francisco, composed of about two hundred reform-minded women, on September 22, 1888, Phoebe was elected its president. The Century Club promoted "the improvement of womankind," and under President Phoebe A. Hearst, it took on Blind Boss Buckley, Hearst's old confidante, to improve schools. For years the Irish saloonkeeper and his cronies had treated public education as they might a stray dog, feeding it the occasional scrap and hoping it would go away. The result was that by fall 1888—having seen schools shuttered and salaries slashed—stellar teachers were either dismissed or had quit to find more lucrative employment. Schools that remained open were dilapidated and in desperate need of repair.[38]

Phoebe determined that the best course of action was to defeat Buckley at the ballot box, convincing six female reform candidates to run for the San Francisco School Board in 1888. Three of the candidates were Century Club members: Nellie Weaver, a nationally recognized lecturer on education; Amelia Truesdell, a public school teacher; and Sarah Dix Hamlin, a Greek and Latin scholar who had previously run for the school board. Phoebe also contributed the lion's share of the capital to form the Committee of One Hundred, an organization founded on supporting female candidates. Furthermore, Phoebe let it be known that she would pay any remaining debts incurred by the six candidates during the election.

Hearst returned to San Francisco just in time to see his wife and the Blind Boss lock horns. Rather than choosing between Phoebe and Buckley, Hearst elected to stay out of it. Tariff reform, faith in Cleveland, and Chinese exclusion were his main talking points. School reform was not.

On September 28, Hearst presided over a Democratic rally at Metropolitan Hall, booming Cleveland. On October 4, he left for Palermo in the company of R. C. Chambers and his business manager, Irwin C. Stump. Ostensibly, Hearst's senatorial object was to look over the San Joaquin Land and Water Company's works on the Stanislaus River. But if he also happened to check in on his orange groves and the new house he was having built in Palermo, it was no one's business but his.

On October 15, while eating breakfast in Stockton, Hearst spoke frankly about Cleveland's chances against Harrison in the next month's election. New York and

New Jersey would go Cleveland's way, as would California. "I have not the slightest doubt," Hearst boasted. Hearst was back in San Francisco on October 22.[39]

Meanwhile, bolstered by Phoebe's liberal progressivism, supporters of school reform went house to house in their canvas, printing a circular to trumpet their cause:

> Good people of all parties and creeds deplore the fact that our public schools have fallen under political control. When places on the School Board though unsalaried, are sought with the most eager persistence; when it is freely charged that teachers' positions have been bought and sold; when the interests of the children of the city are used as pawns in the political game, to forward political ends of petty politicians, and teachers kept trembling in dependence on the turns and tricks of the game for their chances of security of place, or promotion in their work—it is time for reform. . . .
>
> We appeal to voters, without regard to politics or creed, to rally to its support.

Knowing where its bread was buttered, the *Examiner* reprinted the circular on October 31 and supported Phoebe against Buckley.[40]

On November 6, 1888, voters across the country went to the polls. The result was a surprise. President Cleveland won the popular vote: 5,534,488 to 5,448,992. However, Harrison won the electoral vote, 233 to 168, and with it the presidency. Along with losing his home state of New York, Cleveland also lost California by seven thousand votes. To the Hearsts' credit, this was six thousand fewer votes than Cleveland had lost by in 1884, and San Francisco had given Cleveland a plurality of thirty-five hundred votes. But it was New York that made the difference. Had New York gone to Cleveland, he would have won the election 204 to 197. Harrison carried New York by less than 15,000 votes out of 1,286,303 cast—winning by 1.09 percent of the vote. Accusations of ballot fraud were rampant.[41]

Phoebe's reform candidates also lost. Despite Phoebe's financial support, her hand at the wheel of the Century Club, and the backing of the *Examiner,* Buckleyism proved too deep-rooted. But Phoebe did not give up on the Century Club. She shifted their focus toward developing women's skills in money management and debates, arenas typically dominated by men. As a result, membership increased and the club's coffers grew.[42]

Celebrating the Republican victory, on November 21 Stanford held a magnificent reception at his San Francisco mansion. Never one to let politics interfere with a good party, Hearst attended, able to reminisce with John O. Earle about their early days in Virginia City. In early December Hearst was at the Bay District Track, buying colts and likely fending off questions. Just then it wasn't so much about missing the mark so wide with the election; it was about W. R. Demonstrating the impulsivity of youth, W. R. had checked out of the Hoffman House on November 23, telling the porters, cashiers, and clerks to keep his destination secret. They did for almost two weeks, finally revealing that W. R. had absconded across the Atlantic Ocean on *La Champagne* with his old college flame Tessie Powers. By December 6 it was national news.[43]

It was said Hearst did not bear the boy any ill will for pulling up stakes. After all, Hearst could be impulsive as well. He proved that in the last days of 1888, purchasing from Eli F. Sheppard the Madrone Vineyard, between the Napa foothills and Sonoma Creek, for $80,000. The property included a four-hundred-acre tract where Mataro, Zinfandel, Medoc, Girarde, and Semillon vines grew plentiful. There was also a winery, a distillery, wagons, horses, and a sprawling mansion. Built by William Tecumseh Sherman and for a time the general's home, and later the home of "Fighting" Joe Hooker, the mansion held a cellar with eighty thousand gallons of wine and brandy.[44]

That may have been more liquor than even Hearst could drink. But he could sure try.

—17—

NIGHTFALL

(1889–1891)

I have got the nerve and can stand anything until death calls for me,
and then I must weaken, and not until then.
—George Hearst

Hearst had no intention of slowing down.

Hopping off the Southern Pacific in Los Angeles at 8 A.M. on February 7, 1889, Hearst selected for breakfast the Century Club, occupying second-story rooms above the Tally-Ho Stables. At 11 A.M. Hearst was at the Commercial Street Depot, where Jack Follansbee and more than three dozen businessmen greeted the senator before whisking him away in a special railcar. Once in San Pedro, Hearst and company climbed a sandy bluff and looked out over the Pacific Ocean. The sky had cleared of clouds. Hearst could see all the way to Dead Man's Island.

Hearst's purpose in Los Angeles County was to add San Pedro to an appropriations bill in support of California rivers, harbors, and forests. From the deck of *Warrior*, Dr. J. P. Widney pointed out where a pier and a seawall could be constructed. Hearst was sold. "I have always believed in this harbor," he told the delegation, "but since I have looked the ground over more thoroughly and seen the vast strides this country is making, I am more than ever convinced that we can demand this appropriation as our right."

The next destination was Santa Monica, where Hearst met with Senator Jones. Hearst was back in Los Angeles at 7 P.M., catching a musical at the Grand Theater. At nine o'clock the next morning Hearst boarded a train for Pasadena and Lucky Baldwin's famous ranch. That night he left Los Angeles, rolling into El Paso on February 10. In the morning he caught a train north to Santa Fe before heading east. On February 16, Hearst sauntered into the Capitol Building, having traveled thirty-five hundred miles in nine days.[1]

Three days later Hearst was on hand when Phoebe threw her first reception of the year, a colonial ball honoring George Washington's birthday. Phoebe charmed in her Catherine De Medici gown, Cousin Joe kept the guests entertained, and thirty guests participated in the cotillion. Everyone agreed that the ball was one of the hits of the season. Everyone but Hearst. Uncomfortable among the glitterati, Hearst caught hold of a newspaperman and said, "Get a few good fellows together, and we'll go to some quiet room together and enjoy a bottle of wine and some cigars together."

After a couple whispered conversations, Hearst led three guests through the mansion and down to the wine cellar. There, one of Hearst's black servants set them up with a table and chairs. Wine was poured and cigars were lit. "Now," said Hearst, sighing with relief, "we can have a good time without being interrupted by those idiots up-stairs. I can't see the fun in my wife's rackets."[2]

But Hearst couldn't avoid the social scene. On February 27 the Hearsts stopped by the Endicotts' reception, and the following week they attended President Harrison's inaugural ball. At 1 P.M. on March 6 Hearst was in the Senate for the executive session. The newest Democratic senator was Virginia's John Barbour. This meant that Hearst could move one seat toward the middle, closer to the action.[3]

Hearst stuck around the capital throughout March. From Phoebe he received a box of Indian River oranges and a letter dated March 15, 1889: "My dear husband . . . I suppose the Senate is very busy confirming Harrison appointments. I hope they will soon finish and you can do as you please." Phoebe also expressed her desire that Hearst buy the thirty-room Fairchild mansion at 1400 New Hampshire Avenue. Knowing her husband's mind, she mentioned that it would "increase in value" and that "changes" to the property could be made.

This time Hearst was way ahead of her. He'd been looking for a Washington property large enough for his horses, and the Fairchild mansion certainly fit the bill. Just a mile from the White House, part of Washington's elite Dupont Circle, the high-colonial residence came with a nearby lot where his horses could be stabled. On March 10, 1889, Hearst and Charles Fairchild settled on a price of

$56,000. Phoebe returned to Washington ecstatic, brimming with reconstruction plans. In late March, Hearst spent an additional $35,000 by buying up a 421-acre ranch adjacent to his ranch in Sunol, California.[4]

As Senate business wrapped up in early April, Hearst began making plans to revisit Mexico. The $100,000 bond he had placed on a Chihuahua mine would soon expire, and Hearst had business in Mexico City. In late April, Hearst said good-bye to Washington and, taking Head, Chambers, and Follansbee with him, headed south.[5]

Because the railroads did not yet run all the way from El Paso to Mexico City, the Americans took a rough road through the foothills of the Sierra Madre. There the party journeyed through fertile lands that reminded Hearst of Napa, Sonoma, and Santa Clara Valley. The hot weather cooled once they reached a spot between three thousand and four thousand feet. Hearst marveled at the immense tracts of arable land, void of farmers. Sheep were plentiful, but Hearst noted that the only cattle and horses they came across were "scrawny little things that could not be exported."

Once they reached Mexico City, Hearst was treated as a visiting dignitary. He also checked in on the railroads. Noticing they had greatly expanded, Hearst was pleased to see that enterprise and trade had subsequently improved. But after a few days Hearst began to feel unwell. He thought he might have caught yellow fever but wasn't sure. Whatever the case, it was time to skedaddle. Traveling north, the gringos took the Mexican Central some 575 miles over mesas and tableland before running out of track. By the time they reached the old silver mining town of Parral, two hundred miles later, the fever had set in. Hearst announced he could go no farther without medical assistance.[6]

Unfortunately, Parral was no kind of town to hole up in. Centuries before, in the days when Madrid ruled Mexico, cosmopolitan Parral had been the greatest producer of silver in the Spanish Empire, with the jefes living in beautifully decorated stone mansions. But the town had since fallen on hard times. It was now known for its unpaved streets and cockfighting, with a population of about ten thousand. Those citizens who didn't work the silver mines scratched out a meager living through ranching and farming. Legend had it that on February 18, 1886, "Dirty" Dave Rudabaugh—who'd been hunted by Wyatt Earp and rode with Billy the Kid—was shot to death and decapitated outside a Parral cantina.[7]

"We put up at the hotel, a one-story adobe building," Hearst recalled. "In a large room were a lot of bunks, into one of which I crawled." Hearst also gave instructions to Head, Chambers, and Follansbee for two telegraphs to be sent.

One went to W. R. in San Francisco. The other went to a doctor 190 miles away. The message in both was clear. If Hearst didn't get help soon, Parral would be the end of the line.[8]

In the meantime, the locals sent for their own physician. Eventually a little Spanish doctor appeared. The native medicines the Spaniard gave Hearst seemed to work, for the fever finally broke. But the town's water almost made him relapse. Fortunately, he had just the fix. "The water was vile, but fortunately we had some French wine to mix it with, which made it palatable."[9]

On May 26, the party finally reached El Paso. While convalescing, Hearst debated whether to return to San Francisco or Washington. He ultimately chose San Francisco and the boy, but he made certain to be back on Coney Island on July 2 for the Realization Stakes. Having had a bad racing year, Hearst declined to enter the race but instead cheer on Haggin, whose stallion Salvator won the contest. That same day Hearst gave power of attorney regarding some Victoria Gold Mining stock to a New York lawyer, H. B. Parsons, with whom Phoebe and Tevis were friendly. Hearst still enjoyed playing the market, but by now he was wise enough to let someone else handle the nitty-gritty.[10]

On July 17, 1889, Hearst was back in Washington, working with Stanford and the Treasury Department on gaining appropriations for Sacramento and Los Angeles. After checking in on a two-story stable being constructed near his new home, Hearst traveled to New Jersey and New York, taking in the races. Meanwhile, letters poured in from Phoebe in Europe: St. Petersburg, Moscow, Copenhagen, Vienna, Munich, Berlin. "I find Berlin wonderfully changed and improved since Will and I were here in 73," Phoebe wrote in August. "The population has increased enormously." Phoebe was also impressed by the German method of university instruction.[11]

With Phoebe on the other side of the planet, Hearst may have had a few wild nights. On September 11, 1889, a New York gossip columnist wrote, "At the Hoffman I notice Senator Hearst, or as he called by some, 'George,' and by others 'Lum-aTum.' He was out 'slumming' the other night with some of the boys, and no doubt saw a great deal of the lights and shades of life in Gotham."[12]

In bowery slang, *lum-tum* meant "naughty." Carousing with the boys wasn't anything new for Hearst. Veiled insinuations that he had been "naughty" were. If the story leaked back to Phoebe—who kept abreast of her husband's exploits through newspaper clippings—she didn't cause a public scene or write any scathing letters, accusing her husband of having an extramarital affair. But Phoebe did compose a suggestive poem on 1400 New Hampshire Avenue letterhead:

Write on the sands when the tide is low
Seek the spot where the waters flow
Whisper a name when the storm is heard
Pause that echo may catch the word
If what you write on the sand should last
If echo is heard in the tempest blast
Then believe & not till then
There's truth in the vows of men

Throw a rose on the stream at morn
Watch at eve for the flowers return
Drop in the ocean a golden grain
Hope will shine on the shore again
If the rose you again behold
If you gaze on your grain of gold
Then believe & not till then
There's truth *in the vows of men*[13]

Senatorial work soon took Hearst from the East Coast. On October 3 Hearst passed through Pittsburgh en route to Chicago. Two days later he met in the Windy City with his fellow committee members on the Pacific Railroad, attempting to reach a settlement between the Union Pacific Railroad and the U.S. Treasury. Although California's robber barons had become some of the wealthiest men on the planet through the railroads, the Union Pacific had not returned a dime of the $55 million the Treasury had loaned the corporation in 1862. "Our desire is to be reasonable with the companies," Hearst explained to the press, "or at least mine is." Hearst went on to say that he wanted to find a way for the railroad to pay its debt in twenty to fifty years. This talk of delay was music to Stanford's ears.[14]

On October 25, Hearst and Stanford shared a train from San Diego to Los Angeles, accompanied by several senators and Governor Waterman. In Los Angeles Hearst and Waterman caught a production of *Little Lord Fauntleroy*, starring Wallie Eddinger, at the Grand Theater. After the performance Hearst joked to Eddinger that he hoped he would grow up to be as good a man as he was a boy.[15]

On November 9, Hearst was in San Francisco's St. George's Hall, celebrating Congressman-elect T. J. Clunie's victory. Three days later, Hearst and Clunie were lounging at Haggin's ranch, drinking wine and talking horses. On November 14, W. R. steamed into Sacramento on his vessel *Pride of the Bay*, whereupon Hearst, Clunie, and a small party of men from the Sacramento Transportation

Department borrowed the boat to survey the Sacramento River. Hearst, who had traveled the river several times, pointed out differences between the water levels and damage done by debris from hydraulic mining. Considering the commerce the river brought, Hearst felt confident that he could acquire sizable appropriations from the U.S. Senate.[16]

At the end of November, Hearst and Clunie boarded a train east. On December 1, they took rooms at Welcker's Hotel in Washington, joined by Phoebe and Clunie's wife, Florence. The following day they rented a shared office next to Hearst's home, where they drafted appropriation bills to send to the Senate. Finally, Hearst had a hardworking partner on Capitol Hill with whom he saw eye to eye. Ten days later Hearst and Clunie attended the first meeting of the Northwestern Congressional Association, chaired by Senator Bill Stewart. The next day, Friday the 13th, Hearst and Clunie spoke with the Treasury Department about the appropriations bill they were drafting. Ill luck: that same day a defective fuse incinerated Hearst's new house in Palermo. The insurance covered $6,000 of the $10,000 lost.[17]

Hearst's run of bad luck continued three days later. In Welcker's Hotel, where he stayed while his Washington house was being modified, he was robbed by his own valet, Harry Redcliffe. Before climbing into bed, Hearst had tossed his trousers over the back of a chair. While Hearst was soundly snoring, Redcliffe went through his trouser pockets and lifted $210 dollars. Awaking to find his money missing, Hearst alerted the police and put his champagne cocktail on his tab. The next day Redcliffe was arrested, having been implicated in similar thefts at the hotel.[18]

Shortly after Christmas, Hearst determined that it was time to put his stamp on the East Coast mining industry. This time it was West Virginia coal that fired his engines. On December 31, 1889, Hearst, Clunie, and railroad man L. Kessler arrived in Charleston, West Virginia, 350 miles west of Washington, D.C. Guided by West Virginia state senator John Carr, the four men took the Kanawha River ten miles west, inspecting government improvements. But at St. Albans, the mission became more personal. Mounting horses, the four men rode south into coal country.

"We found the coal veins all right. . . . The owners began to expatiate on their virtues as soon as they arrived. . . . The samples were fine, the price was low," recalled Clunie, "and I expected to see Hearst snap at the offer." But Hearst was silent.

"What's the matter, senator?" Clunie asked.

"Well," replied Hearst, "I don't like to buy a pig in a poke, and we had better crawl up and see that coal for ourselves before we discuss the price." Sixty-nine-year-old Hearst and thirty-seven-year-old Clunie climbed a three-thousand-foot hill to out-of-the way coal veins, whereupon Hearst performed a series of experiments, lighting the coal on fire. One piece of coal burned only a moment before going out; Hearst dismissed it as worthless. At a different vein, however, another piece of coal was set afire. Hearst "watched as a mother does her first-born." This one burned for ten minutes. Satisfied, Hearst bought the coal vein.[19]

On January 28, 1890, Hearst was feeling triumphant. The Senate Committee of Appropriations had agreed to report favorably on Hearst's $1 million appropriations bill for the new San Francisco Post Office. Afterward, Hearst and Stanford attended President Harrison's White House reception.[20]

On February 13, 1890, the newspapers got wind that Hearst, Clunie, Senator John Kenna of West Virginia, and Senator Zebulon Vance of North Carolina had formed a railroad syndicate. Hearst would be its president. The railway would run one hundred miles from Charleston through coal country.[21]

A few days later Hearst and Phoebe finally moved into their Dupont Circle mansion, despite construction still being under way. Even unfinished, the house was gorgeous. The walls of the library were finished with mahogany and lined with blue India velvet, while the walls of the smoking room were covered with California redwood. It was there Hearst enjoyed his after-dinner cigars.

But it was not all cigars and brandy. Hearst found the time to draft a letter to Dr. G. M. Dixon, chairman of the Executive Committee of the River Improvement Convention, which Dixon received on March 3. Hearst argued in the letter that a California commission should be appointed to examine the Sacramento and its tributaries. On the confluence of mining and California rivers, Hearst noted, "Hydraulic mining has ceased for the purpose of saving the navigable streams of the State for the benefit of the whole country. . . . After this sacrifice it is clearly the duty of the Government to see that the rivers are restored to their former usefulness."[22]

With the Rivers and Harbors Bill gaining strength, Hearst left Washington, attending a dinner with once and future president Cleveland in New York on March 8.[23]

Hearst was back in the marble halls of the Senate on March 22, once again lending his support to the California appropriations bill. No one expected him to speak, of course. Hearst hadn't made a speech in the Senate since his eulogy of Senator Miller had made him a national laughingstock. But after Senators

Spooner, Platt, Vandever, and Stanford lobbied for the appropriations bill, Hearst shocked everyone by rising. Hearst provoked good-natured laughter by referring to himself as "the silent man of the Senate." He also spoke of the character of Californians, that they did not ask for $300,000 when they needed only $100,000, but they expected to get every dollar they asked for. He also described the current San Francisco Post Office as "a sort of shed that had to be propped up." When Hearst reached the five-minute allotment for speaking, by unanimous consent the Senate allowed him to continue his remarks. Hearst declined the privilege, closing, "Well, go ahead and pass the bill; I will have plenty of time to talk on the other bills that are coming." As Hearst took his seat, senators from both sides of the aisle thanked him for his words. He sought solace in the cloakroom, where colleagues crowded about him and shook his hand till he grew embarrassed.[24]

Despite Hearst's political horizons having broadened, his business manager, Irwin Stump, still worried about his financial appetite. On March 22, 1890, Stump wrote Hearst a letter, counseling the senator against any further "adventures."

> My Dear Senator,
>
> Will returned yesterday all well, and we had a full talk over his matters as well as yours, and that you may understand how your money goes I send you herewith a Statement showing amount drawn during the months of January and February, and for this month the disburse-ments will be equally as large, as Parson's drafts came in the early part of this month for $41,000 for money drawn by you in New York and Verger draws for 15,000 balance due on the Mexican Bonds pur-chased. From the foregoing you will observe that you are spending money at the rate of near one million dollars per year, more than your income and while money matters are so tight with Mr. Haggin, it does seem to me that you cannot afford to embarrass yourself by going into new speculations. For God's sake you have enough already without straining matters to obtain more. Besides all this you know that the "Examiner" will require a great deal of money in a short time or *it must stop.* There is one of two things, you must go slow in your expenditures or you must commence selling property to keep up.
>
> Mind you I have no reason to complain—except to protect you, and to that extent I deem it my duty to speak plainly for your own good. Do not allow the pursuasive [sic] eloquence of your friends to lead you into new adventures no matter how promising they may

be. The house in Washington must be furnished—the Brew Mine must be completed and paid for. The racing stable expenses will go on until you dispose of it—the Examiner property must be protected. The Ranch properties must be maintained—Verger adventure must be carried to completion—your Washington expenses must be provided for—the Equipment of the Mexican Mine (Wilson) must be attended to. All these properties need our fostering care for another year, when the pressure will be over and until that time your income will be required for these properties—leaving nothing for outside adventures—no matter how seductive or promising.

What I have said must be my excuse for telegraphing as I did yesterday.

Sincerely your friend,
Irwin C. Stump

Stump also provided the "Expenditures of Geo Hearst during Jan & Feb. 1890":

San Mateo Marsh Lands	121.10
Ranch Piedra Blanco	9,697.88
P. E. Hearst	24,021.50
W. R. Hearst	5,079.70
Alameda Co. Lands	2,409.04
Bills Receivable	145.
Fresno Co. Lands	1,96.80 [*sic*]
Ida Neal	1,291.36
Examiner Pub. Co.	39,227.39
Racing Stable	10,445.
Mexican Land (Follansbee)	2,983.35
J. A. Verger	1,200.
Texas Land (Cleveland)	217.80
Brewer Mine	8,500.
Tulare Co. Land (R. P. Hammond)	355.36
(W. H. Hammond)	95.20
Palermo L & W. Co., Stock	4,166.
Madrone Vineyard	2,584.66
Palermo Orchard	9,371.74
Petty Expenses (N.Y. & S.F.)	4,088.05

Chrome Mine	30.95
Washington Residence	19,123.38
S. F. Real Estate Taxes	1,481.44
	149,161.43[25]

If Hearst's "adventures" continued to cost him $150,000 every two months, he would pay nearly $1 million a year. No wonder Stump was worried. On any given day, Uncle George could invest a fortune in a mine, a railroad, an orchard, a vineyard, a newspaper, a political career, a ranch, a mansion, a charity, a stable of horses, a herd of cattle. Even Hearst's bread and butter could cost him a fortune when mines dried up and towns were deserted. In his memoirs, Hearst noted that the heaviest loss he and his partners ever suffered happened in Bodie District, sixty miles northwest of Yosemite Valley. "We first made a little money and then we went on until it did not pay for hoisting," Hearst lamented. All told, they lost $900,000 in Bodie.[26]

But Hearst wasn't worried. What Stump didn't fully comprehend was that even if Hearst lost a million dollars a year, he was still making a profit. His adventures in Utah Territory, the Black Hills, and Montana Territory were making millions. All told, he employed five thousand men from Mexico to Washington, D.C., all working in his interest. As extravagantly as his family lived, they simply couldn't go broke.[27]

By mid-1890, the Hearst family had become a national fixture. On the West Coast, W. R. had fulfilled his promise to his father, making the *Examiner* profitable with a circulation of fifty-seven thousand copies read a day, far exceeding the *Chronicle* and *Call*. In Washington, Phoebe's charities, receptions, and cultured manner made her a force, while her support in San Francisco for school reform and women's suffrage lit the path from the antiquated beliefs of the nineteenth century to modern thought. And more than ever, Hearst was affecting policy.

Robert Underwood Johnson, an associate editor of the *Century*, utilized Hearst's sudden popularity while lobbying for the creation of Yosemite National Park. "Next to Muir himself, who knows the region by heart, there was no better authority on the subject than . . . Senator George Hearst," reflected Johnson. "I remember how emphatically he spoke to me in favour of such a reserve in 1890, in Washington."

"Reserve the Tuolomne?" Hearst broke out. "Why I'd favor reserving the whole of the Sierra top from Shasta down. It includes very little agricultural land, the region has been pretty thoroughly prospected and, of course, mining and other private rights would not be interfered with."

Johnson later commented, "It may be imagined that in urging the Yosemite National Park scheme I did not fail to make use of the pronouncement of the shrewd and far-sighted Californian."[28]

On June 6 Hearst displayed his newfound oratory confidence, arguing before the Commerce Committee on immediately pushing through the Rivers and Harbors Bill. A delay of two years would cost the U.S. government several million dollars, Hearst claimed. Even the antagonistic *San Francisco Call* commended Hearst, whose "splendid talk" before the committee "made a favorable impression on them."[29]

Along with proving himself politically, Hearst was genial and a natural peacemaker. On June 12, 1890, after a fight erupted on the Senate floor between Senators Stewart and Regan, Hearst induced the two elderly combatants to shake hands. That night Hearst had a guest from San Francisco, Christopher Buckley. Clunie, who had been a Buckley disciple prior to becoming Hearst's partner, stopped by as well to converse with the Blind Boss.[30]

Hearst was in New York on the night of June 24 to attend a dinner for Buckley at Delmonico's. Hearst never made it. Instead, sick with cholera, he suffered through the evening in his rooms at the Hoffman House. Hearst was still fighting off the cholera at the Hoffman House on July 2 when his prized colt, Tournament, won the Realization Stakes at Sheepshead Bay. Cousin Joe was on hand to collect the senator's $45,000 prize. On July 19, Hearst was back in Washington, successfully lobbying the Senate to increase spending on Santa Monica's soldiers' home by $27,000. Two days later Hearst and Clunie secured an order for a government snag boat to begin clearing the Sacramento River of debris. On September 8, the Senate passed the Rivers and Harbors Appropriation Bill, which included the component Hearst had introduced: preserving and protecting California's giant sequoias. Riding this momentum, Hearst also went up against Stanford on September 12, arguing that lands patented by the railroads that proved to possess mineral wealth must be open to the public to mine.[31]

On October 1, 1890, President Harrison established with a signature what John Muir and, to a lesser extent, George Hearst had been advocating for years, the creation of Yosemite National Park. Hearst wasn't there for the Washington celebration, however, relaxing at New York's Hotel Brunswick and the Morris Park Racecourse. Still in New York on October 9, Hearst dined that evening at the Astor House with President Cleveland, Senator Arthur Gorman, and William T. Sherman.

Hearst and Sherman could swap stories about the Madrone Vineyard. Sherman had liked to read under the shade of a massive tree on the property. Hearst's vines had all been killed by an infestation of phylloxera, grape-eating microscopic aphids, prompting Hearst to have the vineyard replanted with three vines from North Carolina—Sauvignon, Semillon, and Muscat—which were grafted onto phylloxera-resistant rootstock. Hearst likely didn't mention to the famous Union general that he'd just cut a check for $1,000 to the Confederate Soldier's Home in Missouri.[32]

A week later, Hearst splashed much more money around in San Francisco, having caught a cross-country train to visit the boy. At W. R.'s behest, Hearst purchased the Nucleus Building on Third and Market Streets as the new Examiner Building. Hearst also composed a forty-page memoir. At times rambling, it was pure Hearst. Concerning religion, Hearst expressed himself in deistic terms: "When I was young I had very strong religious views, and was brought up to a thoroughly orthodox way; but after leaving home my ideas got broader, and on studying these things for myself, without any influence from parents, or ministers, I came to the conclusion that I knew just about as much about it as anybody, and I knew nothing."

On his own death, Hearst reflected, "I came into this world without my consent, and I expect I will go away from here without my consent[,] and while I believe that there is something in the great future, I do not know what it is. I believe that the Great Being which made me has got some place prepared; but how, or where, I know not."[33]

On October 21, Hearst acted as chairman of the Young Men's Democratic League at Metropolitan Hall, once again booming Cleveland for president. In late October Hearst was named president of the Saratoga Racing Association. Returning to New York City, Hearst's plans of overseeing the Saratoga Race Track were disrupted when he fell ill.

Hearst had become accustomed to random bouts of sickness. In the previous eighteen months he'd caught yellow fever and cholera and beaten them both. But this time seemed different. Hearst met with Dr. Charles S. Ward and in the second week of December felt healthy enough to travel the 250 miles to Washington, arriving on December 14. But Hearst wasn't well by any stretch.[34]

Dr. Nathan S. Lincoln was quickly called to the Hearst residence. The trouble was located in his stomach and bowels, but Lincoln couldn't provide a proper diagnosis or a cure. For more than a week, Phoebe played nursemaid, her husband barely eating. On December 22, with Lincoln still unsure how to treat Hearst, they summoned Ward from New York City, hoping Hearst's initial doctor could shed some light. No dice. Although the doctors saw slight improvement, they told

Phoebe her husband wouldn't be able to sit at the table for Christmas dinner. For two more days Phoebe hovered over Hearst, until on Christmas Eve, in exhaustion, she called for a nurse. The next day she sent a telegram to San Francisco. If W. R. wanted to see his father alive, there was no time to lose.[35]

On Christmas Day, W. R. boarded a Central Pacific railcar, heading to Washington. By the time young Hearst arrived there seemed to be some improvement in his father's condition. The Peck family—W. R.'s friend Orrin, his sister Janet, and their mother, Helen—were also staying at the Hearst residence before traveling to Europe. Jack Follansbee paid his respects as well. Stanford frequently dropped by. Their company did wonders for Hearst's spirit. On January 1, 1891, the front page of the *Examiner* reported that Hearst's health "continues to improve" and that if the weather lightened, he might be soon up and about.[36]

Hearst's physicians knew better. On January 11, Lincoln and Ward finally agreed what was ailing Hearst, as evidenced by a growing tumor: stomach cancer. The disease stemmed from smoking, as well as a diet low in fruits and vegetables and high in salted and smoked foods. The symptoms included vomiting, nausea, and loss of appetite. There was no cure.[37]

Over the next week, Hearst grew weaker as the tumor grew larger. On January 24, Ward and Lincoln privately predicted that Hearst had but two days to live. Though the doctors attempted to keep the worst from him, Hearst saw through the charade. He smiled deprecatingly at them, lit a cigar, and chatted amiably with Follansbee and W. R.[38]

As the nation realized Hearst was dying, newspapers trumpeted the story. They also printed what Hearst was now said to be worth: $20 million. But more tender letters also arrived. On January 26 Janet Peck received a letter from Boston written by Phoebe's dear friend Clara Anthony. "Poor Mr. Hearst is entering the eternal mysteries," Anthony wrote. "A telegram this morning announces that he can live but a few days, as a great change has come, and he knows his fate. I feel very badly about it—and for dear Mrs. Hearst, who has so much to pass through before the rest."[39]

Hearst lingered in pain for the next month, growing steadily weaker. At 9 P.M. on Saturday, February 28, 1891, Hearst lay in bed. Crowding the room were several nurses, Jack Follansbee, and W. R. One of Hearst's hands was held by Ward. Hearst's other hand held Phoebe's. At 9:10 P.M. Hearst appeared to drift off to sleep. He never woke up.[40]

EPILOGUE

Resurrection

> I made up my mind that I came into this world without my consent, and I
> expect I will go away from here without my consent and while I believe that
> there is something in the great future, I do not know what it is.
> —George Hearst

The Senate was burning the midnight oil when Senator Stanford burst in with the news. George Hearst was dead. Although intending to meet all night, the Senate adjourned. President Harrison was also notified, as were newspaper editors throughout the country.

Later that morning, nearly every cosmopolitan paper printed an obituary, including a brief sketch of his life. Governor Henry Markham made a speech and sent a telegram from Sacramento to Phoebe: "It is with deep regret that I learn of your husband's death. He was a true Californian, ever alive to the interests of the people." On March 2, A. E. Head sent a letter to Phoebe from New Orleans. "Dear dear friend," Head began, "the heavy blow has fallen at last. . . . In this night-time of your life my heart goes out to you in kindest sympathy. The sadness of it *all* I understand."[1]

At noon on March 5, a service was held at the Hearst mansion. Hearst had been placed in a casket bedecked with flowers in the music room. The curtains were closed but a little sepulchral light filtered in nonetheless. Phoebe and W. R. hosted as much as they could. Notables included Follansbee, Stewart, Stanford, Clunie, Ochiltree, and Lincoln. The president and First Lady also attended, donating a huge wreath of lilies and yellow roses. With the room filled beyond capacity, those who could not find a seat crowded together, while others paid their respects from the adjoining room or outside the house.

"I am the resurrection and the life," commenced the Reverend George Douglass.[2]

Those well acquainted with Hearst knew the senator would have preferred being in the casket than suffering through the sermon. But the next step was fitting. Two days later Hearst's body was placed upon a catafalque in a train car dyed titian red with W. R., Phoebe, Clunie, and Follansbee aboard. One last time, Hearst was heading to San Francisco.

On March 15, Hearst's funeral took place at Grace Episcopal Church during a drizzling rain. Of Hearst's friends and business partners, R. C. Chambers, Ned Townsend, Jack Follansbee, Irwin Stump, Niles Searls, T. J. Clunie, Jasper McDonald, and Arthur McEwen were on hand. Family included Phoebe, W. R., Joe Clark, and Randolph and Drusilla Apperson. The body was carried two miles to Laurel Hill Cemetery, with Governor Markham and Mayor George Sanderson serving as honorary pallbearers, and placed in a vault. Phoebe and W. R. were the last to leave.[3]

Although Hearst's body had been entombed, his memory was about to undergo some radical alterations. First came the eulogies in the Senate and House in 1892 and 1894. Published in book form by the Government Printing Office in 1894, the words of Senator Stanford, Senator Stewart, and several others made out Hearst to be the greatest American since Paul Bunyan. Hearst, as it turned out, was manly, honorable, courageous, charitable, and industrious. Naturally, no one mentioned that Hearst had been accused of bribing jurors during the murder trial in Deadwood and the Great Mining Suit in Pioche, well before he was accused of bribing his way into the Senate. Nor did anyone broach Hearst's dependence on alcohol or the rumors of infidelity. The senators and congressman also missed Hearst's defining characteristic. Emblematic of the Gilded Age, Hearst was pathologically competitive.

Throughout his life, Hearst strove to increase his holdings in all areas, taking huge risks to do so. As a young man, he determined mining rather than farming was the best way to make money, and he gambled away his easy life as a Missouri slaver and landowner for a chance at California gold. Similarly, when the Comstock Lode was discovered, Hearst traded his paying gold mine for funds to invest in

Virginia City silver. When he returned to Missouri, he was able to show off his wealth, attracting the attentions of Phoebe, winning out over her other suitors.

Although not quite indicating an oedipal complex, it is noteworthy that, shortly after his mother died, Hearst married the woman who had been named after his mother: Phoebe *Elizabeth* Apperson, named after *Elizabeth* Collins. What's more, Phoebe and Elizabeth had similar body types and were both managing women. Although Hearst admired his father, his competition drove him to best his father financially—which Hearst certainly did, time and time again.

After making a killing at the Comstock Lode, Hearst could have lived quietly and let that money last the rest of his life. He was a man of simple tastes—happy with worn clothes and unpretentious dinners—so the fact that he desired more and more wealth was indicative of his fiercely competitive nature rather than a desire for extravagance. Throughout his career, Hearst proved among the most industrious miners in the country. He made and lost fortunes, employing lawyers and engaging in devious schemes when the opportunity arose (a characteristic expected in red-blooded males of the era), but it was through real estate and the stock market—competitive fields in which Hearst was a novice—that he got himself into hot water.

Rebuilding his fortune through the Ontario Mine, Hearst had more than enough money to retire in style, but his ravenous desire to attain greater wealth and status pushed him to further ventures. It's in the Black Hills where we see Hearst as the true apex predator. Dogged by lawsuits and mining operators who treated him as an invader, Hearst tirelessly worked to get the better of them. Even in his reports to Haggin we can see the sparks of Hearst's rivalry. Clearly the junior partner in the triumvirate (Tevis at the top, then Haggin, and Hearst bringing up the rear), how Hearst must have relished writing Haggin, "You must wake up Tevis to the importance of protecting our interest here, for while the quartz is not very rich, the amount of quartz that will pay a profit is enormous." Shutting down the Homestake Mine to give the false impression that it was a bust, directing lawyers on strategy, and personally hunting down the original demarcations of the mine, Hearst demonstrated for good and all that in the great game of paydirt, he was second to none.

That Hearst helped stitch the country together, further industrializing mining communities and creating the need for railroads, was incidental to his purpose but not insignificant. A force of nature, Hearst arrived like a storm hitting. With him came the advent of urban and economic growth. At the same time his coming could signify violent upheaval, and though the potential for a financial boom was high, Hearst chiefly looked after his own interests. Although Deadwood, Butte, Park City, Tombstone, and countless other mining towns ultimately benefited from Hearst, the treasures he pulled from the earth primarily fattened his own coffers.

At the same time, Hearst was more than a shark, single-mindedly feeding on prey. That he freely gave to charities, old mining friends, and hard-luck cases speaks to his generous nature and grizzled experience. Hearst had seen too much of the world—from Mexico City to New York City and virtually everywhere in between—to fail to recognize how much luck played a part. "I struck it rich. They didn't," Hearst explained to a secretary who thought him mad for grubstaking old friends. "They might have been lucky. So I ought to divide."[4]

One area in which his belief in himself overleaped his abilities was in the political arena. As a political pit fighter, Hearst wasn't bad. Interested in politics as a young man in Missouri, Hearst again sought to emulate and then outshine his father's "public spirit." As a natural leader in the mining camps, he developed the confidence and navigational skills necessary to become a California assemblyman in 1865 and 1866. He put his money where his mouth was, buying the *San Francisco Examiner* to help propel him to office. Shades of his father, who visited all the civic parades in Franklin County, Hearst donned the hat of grand marshal during the election of 1880, leading the San Francisco parade in support of Hancock. Two years later, Hearst's run for governor had been a close thing. His grace in losing helped propel him to the Senate. That he'd been flattened by a tidal wave of bad press, factoring into his removal from office after five rough months, was unsurprising. After all, westerner David Crockett had also been made to look the fool by the national papers after becoming a congressman. But Hearst's competitive edge forced him to fight back. Stubborn as a mule, instead of crawling into a bottle he marshaled his resources. That this cowpoke from Missouri regained his seat in the Senate demonstrates his tenacious nature. But it is in his politics that one sees the grand irony of the George Hearst story.

As with many extraordinarily successful self-made men, hubris ultimately affected Hearst. He couldn't see that his political beliefs were largely mired in the past, at odds with his career of catapulting the American West toward an industrial future. Whereas Phoebe championed causes that would gain traction in decades to come—women's rights and education reform—Hearst never quite shook the same stodgy politics of antebellum Franklin County. In his votes against emancipation, Chinese immigration, and women's suffrage, Hearst added his weight toward anchoring the United States in place when it was ready to rocket forward. Such torpid beliefs stemming from such an active mind are understandable when one considers that Hearst's focus had mainly been in acquiring political capital, not in spending it. He would leave that part of the Hearst saga to his wife and son.

In 1896 Phoebe put a half million dollars of the Hearst fortune to use, commissioning the erection of a mausoleum in Cypress Lawn, Colma, nine miles south of Hearst's resting place in Laurel Hill Cemetery. Shortly thereafter Hearst's bones made their last move. In 1897 Phoebe also commissioned James Paxton Voorhees to sculpt a bust of Senator Hearst, now located in the Hearst Castle Visitor Center.[5]

While Hearst's memory became marbled, and his acquisitive nature faded further from public conscience, another transformation took place. As the wizardry of Thomas Edison and Nikola Tesla electrified the country, the public hungered for the memory of an earlier age. Newspaper columnists, drumming up nostalgia for the Old West and playing fast and loose with the facts, enjoyed writing tall tales of frontiersmen, riverboat captains, and westerners of all stripes. In prospecting stories, adding Hearst into the narrative became commonplace. After all, Hearst was the most famous miner in American history. He had made his mark on countless old mining towns, as well as San Francisco, New York City, and Washington, D.C. He was known from coast to coast, a wild and vibrant patch in the American crazy quilt—silver, copper, and gold, and stained with whiskey. And after his death, Hearst's mythos continued to grow.

Six years after his death, Hearst was larger than life. In the summer of 1897, Henry Stull of New York's *Spirit of the Times* conjured a tall tale of Hearst and a dozen other prospectors getting lost in the wilds of Idaho Territory. That fall, another widely published article depicted Hearst hunting for hidden treasure near a dead prospector's shack in Loafer's Hollow, California, tearing up the cabin in his desperation to find the gold. On December 25, 1898, the *New York Times* gave a Christmas present to its readers, a Mark Twain/George Hearst yarn.

"In those days," purportedly recalls Virginia City miner William F. Bailley, "when Mark Twain . . . and Old Man George Hearst, the great prospector and Mark Twain's partner, were the ruling spirits of C Street, there used to be some hot old times. There was a great rivalry between Hearst and Mark Twain whenever any social function came off, and it was a hard race between them to see which would dress the best."[6]

By the turn of the century, Hearst had passed into legend. He was the famous husband to Phoebe Apperson Hearst, the influential philanthropist and educator, and the father of William Randolph Hearst, the most sensational newspaperman on the planet. To his own credit he filled the bill as the quintessential American prospector, full of piss and vinegar and with a nose for gold.

When in 1902 construction began on the Hearst Memorial Mining Building at University of California–Berkeley, where Phoebe Hearst was serving as the school's first female regent, on hand to write up the article for the *Examiner* was none other than Jack London. "Not only will the Hearst Memorial Building be the finest of its class, but it will be the greatest of its kind," London declared. When it was completed in 1907, the building featured a mold—a type of bust built into one of the walls—of George Hearst. Along with the mold appeared the following words: "This building stands as a memorial to George Hearst, a plain man and good miner. The stature and mould of his life bespoke the pioneers who gave their strength to riskful search in the hard places of the Earth. He had warm heart toward his fellow men and his hand was ready to kindly deed. Taking his wealth from the hills he filched from no man's store and lessened no man's opportunity."

When Cora Older and Fremont Older published their glowing biography of Hearst in 1933, they closed the book with those words. It was also in this spirit that they had written it. Ignored was Hearst's capitalistic nature. But history has a way of coming full circle. At the dawn of the twenty-first century the HBO series *Deadwood* returned Hearst to the American consciousness. In *Deadwood* Gerald McRaney portrayed Hearst as a vicious sociopath, employing a small army to terrorize the town in order to gain control of the largest gold mine in the hills. The real George Hearst wasn't so bloodthirsty. He let his lawyers fight his battles, used newspapermen to color public opinion, and kept his cards close to his vest.

The best portrayal of George Hearst can be seen at Hearst Castle, the great mansion his son built on his beloved Piedra Blanca Ranch. In his son's bedroom is a framed photograph of Hearst smoking a cigar, the one that had caused such a stir on the East Coast. He's taking it easy. He's happy. There's a touch of defiance in his eyes. He'll smoke that cigar if it kills him. Fittingly, he's looking west.

NOTES

Abbreviations

Bartlett Letters	Dwight Bartlett Letters, Huntington Research Library
George Hearst Autobiography	George Hearst Letters and Autobiography, 1877–1890, Bancroft Library, University of California–Berkeley
Hearst Papers	George and Phoebe Hearst Papers, Bancroft Library
Hearst Letters	George Hearst Letters, Huntington Research Library
Paul Papers	Almarin Brooks Paul Papers, Huntington Research Library
Peck Papers	Peck Family Papers, Huntington Research Library

Chapter 1

1. Judith Robinson, *The Hearsts: An American Dynasty* (San Francisco: Telegraph Hill Press, 1991), 29, 30; Oliver Carlson and Ernest Sutherland Bates, *Lord of San Simeon* (New York: Viking Press, 1936), 3–4; George Hearst Autobiography, 1.

2. *St. Clair Chronicle*, 21 October 1965; Carlson and Bates, *Lord of San Simeon*, 4.

3. Edmond. D. Coblentz, ed., *William Randolph Hearst: A Portrait in His Own Words* (New York: Simon and Shuster, 1952), 7; George Hearst Autobiography, 2.

4. George Hearst Autobiography, 1.

5. Robinson, *The Hearsts*, 30; George Hearst Autobiography, 1.

6. *Topeka State Journal*, 6 June 1890; George Hearst Autobiography, 7.

7. George Hearst Autobiography, 7; "Senator George Hearst," *Wasp*, 10 April 1886; Robinson, *The Hearsts*, 30, 34.

8. James W. Erwin, *The Homefront in Civil War Missouri* (Charleston, S.C.: History Press, 2014), 19, 20.

9. *Topeka State Journal*, 6 June 1890; George Hearst Autobiography, 7.

10. "Meramec Caverns History," wall text, Meramec Caverns, Stanton, Mo.

11. George Hearst Autobiography, 3.

12. George Hearst Autobiography, 2, 4, 5.

13. George Hearst Autobiography, 3; Robinson, *The Hearsts*, 30, 31; "Benjamin Rowe of Ontario," American Colonial Origins, 2005–2015, http://www.amcolan.info/rowe /index.

14. Robinson, *The Hearsts*, 31.

15. George Hearst Autobiography, 1, 3. W. V. N. Bay, "A Brief Sketch of the Life of the Hon. George Hearst," 12, Hearst Papers; *St. Clair Chronicle*, 21 October 1965.

16. Erwin, *Homefront in Civil War Missouri*, 15

17. George Hearst Autobiography, 1, 5; *Notables of the West*, vol. 2 (New York: International News Service, 1915), 33.

18. George Hearst Autobiography, 6; Robinson, *The Hearsts*, 25.

19. George Hearst Autobiography, 2.

20. George Hearst Autobiography, 7.

21. George Hearst Autobiography, 3, 7.

22. Robinson, *The Hearsts*, 33; *Franklin County Tribune*, 24 November 1899; Bay, "A Brief Sketch," 2. Bay noted that the Hearst "farm was within 3 or 4 miles of the Virginia Led mine."

23. Jim Winnerman, "French Missouri Still Spoken Here," *Wild West* 29, no. 3 (October 2016): 20–21; Stephanie Lecci, "Paw Paw French: Two 20-Somethings Bet St. Louis Can Save a Vanishing Dialect," *St. Louis Public Radio*, 13 July 2015.

24. George Hearst Autobiography, 7–8.

25. George Hearst Autobiography, 4, 6, 7–8; Fremont Older and Cora Older, *George Hearst: California Pioneer* (Los Angeles: Westernlore, 1966), 29; W. A. Swanberg, *Citizen Hearst* (New York: Scriber, 1961), 4.

26. *Record Union*, 18 October 1884; *New York Times*, 25 June 1886; *Arizona Weekly Citizen*, 21 May 1882; *St. Clair Chronicle*, 21 October 1965.

27. Bay, "A Brief Sketch," 2, 14–15.

28. *Palmyra Weekly Whig*, 23 August 1849.

29. Older and Older, *George Hearst*, 48; Robinson, *The Hearsts*, 40.

30. Robinson, *The Hearsts*, 24; Alexandra M. Nickliss, *Phoebe Apperson Hearst: A Life of Power and Politics* (Lincoln: University of Nebraska Press, 2018); Winifred Black Bonfils, *The Life and Personality of Phoebe Apperson Hearst* (San Francisco: John Henry Nash, 1928).

31. Older and Older, *George Hearst*, 46; *St. Joseph Herald*, 12 May 1895; George Hearst Autobiography, 17; Robinson, *The Hearsts*, 49.

32. Victoria Kastner, *Hearst Ranch: Family, Life, and Legacy* (New York: Abrams, 2013), 22; Robinson, *The Hearsts*, 34; George Hearst Autobiography, 1.

33. *Democratic Banner*, 30 August 1847; *Palmyra Weekly Whig*, 17 February 1848; Bay, "A Brief Sketch," 5; *Democratic Banner*, 30 August 1847; *Palmyra Weekly Whig*, 17 February 1848; George Hearst Autobiography, 7.

34. George Hearst Autobiography, 36.

35. *St. Clair Chronicle*, 21 October 1965; Robinson, *The Hearsts*, 34.

36. J. S. Holliday, *The World Rushed In: The California Gold Rush Experience* (New York: Touchtone, 1981), 25–33.

37. Holliday, *The World Rushed In*, 31–32.

38. Holliday, *The World Rushed In*, 38.

39. Wall placard, visitor center, Point Reyes National Seashore, Point Reyes Station, Calif.

40. Holliday, *The World Rushed In*, 38.

41. *Palmyra Weekly Whig*, 26 October 1848.

42. Holliday, *The World Rushed In*, 48.

43. *Palmyra Weekly Whig*, 16 May 1850.

44. George Hearst Autobiography, 10, 40.

45. Robinson, *The Hearsts*, 35.

46. George Hearst Autobiography, 7.

Chapter 2

1. George Hearst Autobiography, 10.

2. Kastner, *Hearst Ranch*, 22; George Hearst Autobiography, 11; Older and Older, *George Hearst*, 48; *San Francisco Chronicle*, 6 January 1900.

3. Robinson, *The Hearsts*, 36.

4. George Hearst Autobiography 12; "The Dred Scott Case," wall text, Old Courthouse, Gateway Arch National Park, St. Louis.

5. George Hearst Autobiography, 12; "The Dred Scott Case," wall text; Older and Older, *George Hearst*, 46.

6. George Hearst Autobiography, 10–11; *St. Clair Chronicle*, 21 October 1965.

7. George Hearst Autobiography, 11.

8. Church of Jesus Christ of Latter-Day Saints, *Deseret Weekly: Pioneer Publication of the Rocky Mountain Region*, vol. 46 (Salt Lake City: Deseret News, 1893): 409.

9. Church of Jesus Christ of Latter-Day Saints, *Deseret Weekly*, 409. Afterward, Ochiltree noted Hearst's recorded words: "Tom Ochiltree, you are a blank blank liar!"

10. George Hearst Autobiography, 11–12; John Gorenfeld and Will Gorenfeld, "Dishonorably Discharged," *Wild West* 21, no. 1 (June 2018): 60–61.

11. George Hearst Autobiography, 11–12.

12. George Hearst Autobiography, 12.

13. *Palmyra Weekly Whig*, 25 July 1850.

14. The *El Dorado Visitor's Guide* states that Hangtown was named for the frequent hangings that took place there. In 1854 Hangtown's elders decided that the name was too ominous and changed it to Placerville.

15. George Hearst Autobiography, 12; Holliday, *The World Rushed In*, 38.

16. George Hearst Autobiography, 13.

17. George Hearst Autobiography, 9, 10, 33–34.

18. *Anaconda Standard*, 18 November 1923; George Hearst Autobiography, 38; Susan Lee Johnson, *Roaring Camp: The Social World of the California Gold Rush* (New York: W. W. Norton, 2000), 31, 62.

19. George Hearst Autobiography, 38–39.

20. *Nevada City Herald*, 19 January 1889.

21. *Arizona Daily Star*, 1 February 1883.

22. *San Francisco Chronicle*, 25 August 1907; Paul Papers.

23. William Stewart, *Memorial Addresses on the Life and Character of George Hearst*, edited by United States Congress (Washington, D.C.: Government Printing Office, 1894), 26–27; Bay, "A Brief Sketch," 4.

24. *San Francisco Chronicle*, 25 August 1907, 13 October 1907.

25. Carlson and Bates, *Lord of San Simeon*, 7; Older and Older, *George Hearst*, 87–89.

26. *San Francisco Chronicle*, 13 October 1907.

27. *San Francisco Chronicle*, 25 August 1907; Eagle Rock Gold Mine tour, Julian, Calif., April 21, 2018.

28. George Hearst Autobiography, 10.

29. George Hearst Autobiography, 14; Robinson, *The Hearsts*, 38.

30. Older and Older, *George Hearst*, 92–93.

31. *Los Angeles Times*, 1 March 1891.

32. Robinson, *The Hearsts*, 38.

33. *Topeka State Journal*, 6 June 1890; George Hearst Autobiography, 14.

34. Older and Older, *George Hearst*, 93; *San Francisco Chronicle*, 25 August 1907.

35. Edwin F. Bean, *Bean's History and Directory of Nevada County* (Nevada City: Daily Gazette Book and Job Office, 1867), 115; Robinson, *The Hearsts*, 39.

36. George Hearst Autobiography, 36.

37. Robinson, *The Hearsts*, 41.

Chapter 3

1. Dan De Quille, *The Big Bonanza* (New York: Alfred A. Knopf, 1967), 10.

2. De Quille, *Big Bonanza*, 10; *San Francisco Chronicle*, 25 August 1907; Henry Theodore Hittell, *History of California*, vol. 3 (San Francisco: N. J. Stone, 1898).

3. Bartlett Letters.

4. De Quille, *Big Bonanza*, 10; *San Francisco Chronicle*, 1 September 1907.

5. George Hearst Autobiography, 14.

6. George Hearst Autobiography, 10.

7. *Anaconda Standard*, 25 September 1890; George Hearst Autobiography, 14.

8. *Anaconda Standard*, 25 September 1890.

9. George Hearst Autobiography, 15; *Anaconda Standard*, 25 September 1890.

10. *Anaconda Standard*, 25 September 1890.

11. George Hearst Autobiography, 15.

12. *San Francisco Chronicle*, 1 September 1907; Paul Papers.

13. Even the main players don't agree on the history. Hearst gives the date June 1, 1859. Others suggest that the Comstock Lode was discovered on June 12, 1859.

14. *San Francisco Chronicle*, 25 August 1907.

15. *Nevada State Journal*, 26 November 1907.

16. Gregory Crouch, *The Bonanza King: John Mackay and the Battle over the Greatest Riches in the American West* (New York: Scribner, 2018), 77.

17. George Hearst Autobiography, 14–16.

18. Older and Older, *George Hearst*, 105.

19. George Hearst Autobiography, 14–16; Rodman Wilson Paul, *Mining Frontiers of the Far West: 1848–1860* (Albuquerque: University of New Mexico Press, 1974), 63.

20. *Reno Gazette-Journal*, 7 March 1891; Sierra Nevada Silver Mining Company Papers, Huntington Research Library; *New York Times*, 27 February, 1860.

21. *Anaconda Standard*, 25 September 1890.

22. Joe Clark to George Hearst (GH), March 16, 1860, Hearst Letters.

23. Ron Powers, *Mark Twain: A Life* (New York: Free Press, 2005), 105.

24. Robinson, *The Hearsts*, 45.

25. William M. Lent to GH, April 5, 1860, Hearst Letters

26. John O. Earle to GH, April 28, 1860, Hearst Letters.

27. Crouch, *Bonanza King*, 94–96; Paul Papers.

28. Robinson, *The Hearsts*, 43; George Hearst Autobiography, 17.

29. Crouch, *Bonanza King*, 77; wall text, The Way It Was Museum, Virginia City, Nev.; Robinson, *The Hearsts*, 45; *New York Times*, 14 August 1860.

Chapter 4

1. *St. Clair Chronicle*, 21 October 1965; Erwin, *Homefront*, 17.

2. Erwin, *Homefront*, 17.

3. *St. Clair Chronicle*, 21 October 1965.

4. *St. Joseph Herald*, 12 May 1895.

5. Robinson, *The Hearsts*, 47.

6. "The Dred Scott Case," wall text.

7. James M. McPherson, *Battle Cry of Freedom* (New York: Ballantine Books, 1988), 66.

8. "Meramec Caverns History," wall text.

9. *St. Joseph Herald*, 12 May 1895.

10. *Rolla Herald*, 10 January 1895.

11. Robinson, *The Hearsts*, 27.

12. Robinson, *The Hearsts*, 49.

13. *Rolla Herald*, 10 January 1895; *History of Franklin, Jefferson, Washington, Crawford and Gasconade*, part 2 (Chicago: Goodspeed, 1888), 1038.

14. J. B. Dickinson to GH, May 1861, Hearst Papers; *St. Clair Chronicle*, 21 October 1965; Austine McDonnell Hearst, *The Horses of San Simeon* (San Simeon: San Simeon Press, 1985), 83.

15. Stephen W. Sears, "Badly Whipped He Will Be," *America's Civil War* 30, no. 4 (September 2017): 20.

16. "Meramec Caverns History," wall text.

17. George C. Rable, "Damn Yankees," *Civil War Monitor* 6, no. 2 (July 2016): 39.

18. Melissa A. Winn, "I Thought I Had Received My Death Stroke," *Civil War Times* 57, no. 6 (December 2018): 58.

19. Robinson, *The Hearsts*, 47–48.

20. Harold Holzer, "Stop the Presses," *Civil War Times* 53, no. 3 (December 2014): 33.

21. Sean McLachlan, "Grudge Match at the O.K. Corral," *America's Civil War* 29, no. 1 (March 2014): 49–50.

22. Andrew E. Masich, "Desert Warriors," *America's Civil War* 30, no. 4 (July 2017): 46.

23. Chuck Lyons, "The Great Western Flood," *Wild West* 28, no. 6 (April 2016): 36–41.

24. William M. Lent to GH, October 7, 1862, Hearst Papers.

25. William Hearst to GH, Hearst Papers.

26. Robinson, *The Hearsts*, 46.

27. Early biographers maintain the lighthearted fiction that Phoebe was unaware that Hearst was rich. That makes for a heartwarming story, but it clearly wasn't so.

28. Robinson, *The Hearsts*, 51–52; Nickliss, *Phoebe Apperson Hearst*, 34; *Sullivan Tri-County News*, 1 August 1963; Miscellanea, Hearst Letters.

29. *Sullivan Tri-County News*, 1 August 1963; Miscellanea, Hearst Letters; Swanberg, *Citizen Hearst*, 6.

Chapter 5

1. Robinson, *The Hearsts*, 53, 54.

2. *San Francisco Call*, 23 January 1904.

3. Henry G. Langley, *The San Francisco Directory for the Year 1864* (San Francisco: Commercial Steam Press, 1864), 57.

4. Swanberg, *Citizen Hearst*, 8.

5. William A. Bullough, *The Blind Boss and His City: Christopher Augustine Buckley and Nineteenth-Century San Francisco* (Berkeley: University of California Press, 1979). 35. George Hearst Autobiography, 25; *St. Joseph Herald*, 12 May 1895.

6. Molly Flagg Knudtsen, *Under the Mountain* (Reno: University of Nevada Press, 1982), 70; Lander Silver Ledge Company, Hearst Papers.

7. *Santa Cruz Weekly*, 19 December 1863; Linda Karen Miller, *Images of Early Las Vegas* (Charleston, S.C.: Arcadia Publishing, 2013), 46.

8. Mark Twain, "Sam Clemens's Old Days," *New York Sun*, 16 October 1898.

9. Powers, *Mark Twain*, 123; Older and Older, *George Hearst*, 131.

10. *New York Sun*, 16 October 1898.

11. *Knoxville Journal*, 8 June 1925.

12. The story of Horace Greeley's wild ride was repeated throughout the West. In 1872, Mark Twain commented in *Roughing It* that in 1861, while he and his brother were traveling by stage from Missouri to Virginia, they heard it from a stagecoach driver in Julesburg, Colorado, at a crossroads by a Denver man who had just boarded the

stagecoach, at Fort Bridger from a cavalry sergeant, and outside Salt Lake City from a Mormon preacher. Twain laments that they would have heard it again from a poor wanderer on the Carson River just west of Ragtown, Nevada, had he not warned the man "to proceed at your peril."

13. *Santa Cruz Weekly*, 19 December 1863.
14. *San Francisco Chronicle*, 2 March 1873; Langley, *San Francisco Directory*, 57.
15. *St. Clair Chronicle*, 21 October 1965; Phoebe Apperson Hearst (PAH) to Eliza Pike, June 25, 1864, Hearst Papers.
16. Austin Clark to GH, July 28, 1864, Hearst Papers; newspaper clippings, July 12, 1864, September 9, 1864, Paul Papers.
17. GH to PAH, April 24, 1864, Hearst Papers.
18. Deborah Coleen Cook, "Vestiges of Amador—A Hearst in Drytown? A California Icon and Amador Mines," *Ledger and Dispatch: Amador & Calaveras Objective Regional News*, 28 January 2018; Hearst Papers.
19. Cook, "Vestiges of Amador."
20. Older and Older, *George Hearst*, 133.
21. *San Francisco Evening Examiner*, 12 June 1865.
22. Kastner, *Hearst Ranch*, 38; Hearst, *Horses of San Simeon*, 106.
23. PAH to Eliza Pike, July 2, 1865, Hearst Papers.
24. *San Francisco Examiner*, 5 September 1865.
25. *San Francisco Chronicle*, 6 September 1865.
26. *San Francisco Examiner*, 12 September 1865.
27. *Buffalo Daily Courier*, 16 October 1865.
28. Cook, "Vestiges of Amador."
29. Bonfils, *Life and Personality of Phoebe Apperson Hearst*, 26–27.
30. Bay View Park Hotel missive, June 12, 1866, Hearst Papers; PAH to Eliza Pike, November 18, 1866, Hearst Papers.
31. Robinson, *The Hearsts*, 77.

Chapter 6

1. Langley, *San Francisco Directory*, 57; Merle W. Wells, *Gold Camps and Silver Cities: Nineteenth Century Mining in Central and Southern Idaho* (Moscow: Idaho State Historical Society, 1983); *Oakland Tribune*, 17 September 1881; GH to PAH, August 29, 1867, Hearst Papers.
2. His two-story house on D Street served as the superintendent's house for the Gould & Curry Mine until it burned down in 1875. When it was rebuilt, John Mackay purchased it for himself. Today it stands as the Mackay Mansion Museum, with a framed photograph of George Hearst on the piano.
3. Bonfils, *Life and Personality of Phoebe Apperson Hearst*, 30.
4. PAH to Eliza Pike, September 15, 1867, Hearst Papers.
5. PAH to Eliza Pike, November 20, 1867. Hearst Papers.
6. Swanberg, *Citizen Hearst*, 10; Kenneth Whyte, *The Uncrowned King: The Sensational Rise of William Randolph Hearst* (Berkeley: Counterpoint, 2009).

7. *San Francisco Examiner*, 20 March 1868.

8. *San Francisco Examiner*, 2 May 1868; GH to PAH, July 28, 1868, Hearst Papers; Eliot Lord, *Comstock Mining and Miners 1883* (San Diego: Howell-North Books, 1980), 101. In 1859, Alexander Baldwin served with William M. Stewart as counsel for the plaintiff, the Ophir Company, against David S. Terry and James Hardy in what was commonly called the Middle Lead Case, concerning nebulous boundaries between mining claims. The result was a hung jury.

9. *San Francisco Examiner*, 18 August 1868; *San Francisco Chronicle*, 1 December 1868; Wells, *Gold Camps and Silver Cities*, 45; George Hearst Autobiography, 17.

10. PAH to GH, 1868, Hearst Papers.

11. Robinson, *The Hearsts*, 107.

12. *San Francisco Chronicle*, 27 February 1869; Robinson, *The Hearsts*, 96, 113, 116. Elbert remained a problem. In December 1884, Phoebe wrote a letter to Hearst from Deming, New Mexico—175 miles northwest of Tombstone—while journeying to New York to visit Will. She reluctantly related that Elbert believed he owned two of Hearst's horses and that he should be paid $300 if Hearst wanted to keep them. "I only tell you this because I promised him I would," Phoebe wrote, half-apologetically.

13. George Hearst Autobiography, 17.

14. Older and Older, *George Hearst*, 138; Kastner, *Hearst Ranch*, 82.

15. Carlson and Bates, *Lord of San Simeon*, 11.

16. Robinson, *The Hearsts*, 100.

17. George Hearst Autobiography, 17.

18. *Carson Daily Appeal*, 4 November 1869.

19. There still isn't. Part of the stretch from Eureka to Pioche is on U.S. 50, a two-lane highway called "The Loneliest Road in America." Being on it is unsettling; you feel like you're driving through an endless, postapocalyptic hellscape inhabited by few, if any, tattered survivors.

20. Charles Sumner, "A Trip to Pioche," *Student's Journal* 21, no. 2 (February 1892): 20–24.

21. Sumner, "Trip to Pioche," 20–24. Stereotyping Chinese speech patterns was the pinnacle of humor in the nineteenth century.

22. Robinson, *The Hearsts*, 100; *San Francisco Chronicle*, 21 November 1880; *The Elite Directory for San Francisco and Oakland: A Residence Address, Visiting, Club, Theatre and Shopping Guide, Containing the Names of Over Six Thousand Society People.* San Francisco: Argonaut Publishing Company, 1879; *San Francisco Chronicle*, 28 April 1869.

23. *San Francisco Examiner*, 9 March 1869; Langley, *San Francisco Directory*, 315; *San Francisco Chronicle*, 19 March 1869; *San Francisco Chronicle*, 3 June 1869.

24. Cook, "Vestiges of Amador"; *San Francisco Chronicle*, 9 June 1869; *San Francisco Chronicle*, 16 June 1869.

25. *San Francisco Chronicle*, 18 June 1869; Bullough, *Blind Boss and His City*, 45.

26. George Hearst Autobiography, 17. Wall placard, Hearst Castle Museum, San Simeon, Calif.

27. Silver City Idaho missive to GH, 27 September, 1869, Hearst Papers.

28. *San Francisco Chronicle*, 18 November 1869; GH to PAH, 11 November 1869, Hearst Papers.
29. Nickliss, *Phoebe Apperson Hearst*, 57.
30. *San Francisco Examiner*, 17 February 1870, 26 August 1870.
31. Swanberg, *Citizen Hearst*, 10, 11.
32. Swanberg, *Citizen Hearst*, 11.
33. Coblentz, *William Randolph Hearst*, 14–15.
34. Swanberg, *Citizen Hearst*, 11; Coblentz, *William Randolph Hearst*, 10–12.
35. Marion Davies, *The Times We Had: Life with William Randolph Hearst*, edited by Pamela Peau and Kenneth S. Marx (New York: Ballantine, 1975), 319.
36. Coblentz, *William Randolph Hearst*, 13.
37. Older and Older, *George Hearst*, 179. Ella Sterling Mighels, *The Story of the Files* (San Francisco: Wakelee & Co., Druggists, 1893), 423; Coblentz, *William Randolph Hearst*, 3, 12.
38. Samuel McMaster to GH, September 10, 1870, Hearst Papers.
39. *San Francisco Examiner*, 27 May 1871.
40. *San Francisco Chronicle*, 20 May 1871.
41. George Hearst Autobiography, 17–18.
42. *San Francisco Chronicle*, 23 July 1871, 2 November 1871. Hearst was no more a colonel than Gashwiler was a general. During the Gilded Age it was common for men to give each other such military styling. Majors, colonels, and generals were a dime a dozen. Hearst's friends noted that he never adopted a military rank as a nickname. Of course, one is not always afforded the ability to choose one's nickname.
43. *San Francisco Chronicle*, 19 November 1871.
44. Lloyd Tevis to GH, September 26, 1871, Hearst Papers.
45. Robinson, *The Hearsts*, 107–8. Hearst ultimately did invest in the Montezuma District of Nye County. Hearst and Jeremiah Miller put out a prospectus on several mines in the area on March 3, 1875. They wrote that they "conditionally purchased the Montezuma Mill and some of the Mines near it, about three years ago. . . . We have taken a large amount of this Stock for ourselves and our personal friends, and would take it all if we were not so loaded down with other mining property." Cynical readers might conclude that Hearst and Miller were attempting to make money from the Montezuma mines through stock, being unable to make money off them by traditional means.
46. Samuel McMaster to GH, December 1871, Hearst Papers.
47. *San Francisco Chronicle*, 21 April 1872.
48. *Oakland Tribune*, 23 November 1889.
49. Bay, "A Brief Sketch," 9.
50. *Oakland Tribune*, 23 November 1889.

Chapter 7

1. John Koster, "The Great Diamond Hoax of 1872," *Wild West* 26, no. 3 (October 2013): 47–53.
2. Bank of California to GH, January 27, 1871, Hearst Papers.

3. Hearst and Dodge were acquainted, having established with Roberts, Gashwiler, and Lent the Minnesota Gold and Silver Mining Company on War Eagle Mountain in Idaho Territory in 1871.

4. Koster, "Great Diamond Hoax," 47–53.

5. Asbury Harpending, *The Great Diamond Hoax and Other Stirring Incidents in the Life of Asbury Harpending* (San Francisco: James H. Barry, 1913), 163–64.

6. Koster, "Great Diamond Hoax," 47–53.

7. *Salt Lake City Herald*, 31 August 1884.

8. Harpending, *Great Diamond Hoax*, 164; George Hearst Autobiography, 37.

9. *Cincinnati Enquirer*, 5 December 1872; *San Francisco Chronicle*, 4 December 1872.

10. William Randolph Hearst (WRH) to GH, 1885?, Hearst Papers. The details of Hearst's culinary pleasure are found in a letter sent from W. R. Hearst, probably in 1885. W. R. notes that while traveling he met "a porter who said he used to serve bacon and fried mush to you in Salt Lake, years ago, and on the strength of that acquaintance he became very familiar. Sang songs, stole our wine and enjoyed himself generally."

11. *San Francisco Chronicle*, 4 December 1872.

12. Henry Janin to GH, October 10–11, 1872, Hearst Papers.

13. Joe Clark to GH, October 15, 1872, Hearst Papers.

14. *Cincinnati Enquirer*, 5 December 1872.

15. Koster, "Great Diamond Hoax," 47–53.

16. J. B. Haggin to GH, November 12, 1872, Hearst Papers.

17. Robinson, *The Hearsts*, 104.

18. *San Francisco Chronicle*, 23 November 1872.

Chapter 8

1. George Hearst Autobiography, 22; *St. Joseph Herald*, 12 May 1895.

2. Lester Hood Woolsey, *Geology and Ore Deposits of the Park City District, Utah*, Professional Papers 77 (Washington, D.C.: Government Printing Office, 1912), 136; *Anaconda Standard*, 18 November 1923; *Nevada State Journal*, 15 February 1906; George Hearst Autobiography, 22.

3. George Hearst Autobiography, 18–19; George A. Thompson and Frasier Buck, *Treasure Mountain Home: Park City Revisited* (Salt Lake City: Dream Garden Press, 1968), 5.

4. George Hearst Autobiography, 22.

5. Thompson and Buck, *Treasure Mountain Home*, 5; George Hearst Autobiography, 19.

6. George Hearst Autobiography, 18–19.

7. George Hearst Autobiography, 19. Thomas Edwin Farish, *The Gold Hunters of California* (Chicago: M. A. Donohue, 1904), 215.

8. James G. Fair to GH, September 27, 1872, Hearst Papers.

9. *San Francisco Examiner*, 28 January 1873.

10. *San Francisco Chronicle*, 2 March 1873; Bonfils, *Life and Personality of Phoebe Apperson Hearst*, 30.

11. Bonfils, *Life and Personality of Phoebe Apperson Hearst*, 34; Robinson, *The Hearsts*, 117; Langley, *San Francisco Directory*, 317.

12. PAH to Eliza Pike, March 17, 1873, Hearst Papers; Nickliss, *Phoebe Apperson Hearst*, 69.

13. Kastner, *Hearst Ranch*, 44.

14. Paul W. Reeve, *Making Space on the Western Frontier: Mormons, Miners, and Southern Paiutes* (Chicago: University of Illinois Press, 2006), 31–32; George Hearst Autobiography, 18; *San Francisco Chronicle*, 22 August 1873.

15. Robinson, *The Hearsts*, 121.

16. Older and Older, *George Hearst*, 138; Robinson, *The Hearsts*, 127.

17. Edward William Tullidge, *Tullidge's Histories*, vol. 2 (Salt Lake City: Juvenile Instructor, 1889), 511; George Hearst Autobiography, 19.

18. Bullough, *Blind Boss and His City*, 52.

19. GH to PAH, June 30, 1873, Hearst Papers.

20. PAH to GH, November 11, 1873, Hearst Papers.

21. PAH to GH, December 3, 1873, Hearst Papers.

22. George Hearst Autobiography, 10.

23. *St. Louis Dispatch*, 16 April 1874; PAH to GH, April 20, 1874, Hearst Papers.

24. Kastner, *Hearst Ranch*, 40.

25. Annie L. Morrison and John H. Haydon, *Pioneers of San Luis Obispo County and Environs* (Los Angeles: Historic Record, 1917), 355.

26. *San Francisco Examiner*, 9 February 1874; *Salt Lake Tribune*, 26 April 1874; *Pioche Record*, 2 June 1874; *Pioche Record*, 6 September 1874.

27. George Hearst Autobiography, 19.

28. *Annual Mining Review and Stock Ledger* (San Francisco: Verdenal, Harrison, Murphy, 1876), 3.

Chapter 9

1. *Salt Lake Tribune*, 10 February 1875; Remi Nadeau, *The Silver Seekers* (Santa Barbara: Crest Publishers, 1999).

2. *San Francisco Examiner*, 9 May 1875; Hubert Howe Bancroft, *The Works*, vol. 24, *History of California*, vol. 7: *1860–1890* (San Francisco: History Company, 1890), 669–70.

3. *Yerington Times*, 6 June 1875.

4. *Pioche Record*, 31 July 1875; Nadeau, *Silver Seekers*, 170.

5. Nadeau, *Silver Seekers*, 177–78; J. J. Crawford, *California Journals of Mines and Geology*, Vols. 12–13 (Sacramento: A. J. Johnston, Supt. State Printing, 1894); *San Francisco Examiner*, 13 August 1875; Richard E. Lingenfelter, *Death Valley and the Amargosa: A Land of Illusion* (Berkeley: University of California Press, 1986), 137.

6. *Pioche Record*, 19 August 1875.

7. George Hearst Autobiography, 20.

8. *San Francisco Examiner*, 26 November 1875, 29 November 1875.

9. *San Francisco Chronicle*, 1 January 1876.

10. George Hearst Autobiography, 24.

11. *Coso Mining News*, 27 May 1876, Huntington Research Library.

12. *San Francisco Chronicle*, 3 May 1876; *Deseret News*, 17 July 1876; *Coso Mining News*, 27 May 1876, Huntington Research Library; *Salt Lake Tribune*, 23 July 1876.

13. George Hearst Autobiography, 20.

14. PAH to GH, September 30, 1876, Hearst Papers.

15. Paul Papers.

16. Paul Papers; J. C. Clark to GH, December 11, 1876, Hearst Papers.

17. W. W. Bishop and G. M. Sabin to GH, February 11, 1877, Hearst Papers.

18. PAH to Eliza Pike, December 13, 1876, Hearst Papers.

19. *Oakland Tribune*, 16 February 1877; *Weekly Nevada State Journal*, 24 February 1877.

20. *Yerington Times*, 7 March 1877; *San Francisco Chronicle*, 28 April 1877.

21. PAH to Eliza Pike, January 1, 1877, Hearst Papers; Robert P. Palazzo, *Ghost Towns of Death Valley* (Charleston, S.C.: Arcadia Publishing, 2014), 34; Lingenfelter, *Death Valley*, 126.

22. George Hearst Autobiography, 20; Steven T. Mitchell, *Nuggets to Neutrinos: The Homestake Story* (self-pub., Xlibris, 2009), 151; *San Francisco Examiner*, 1 September 1877; R. C. Chambers to GH, February 8, 1877, Hearst Papers.

23. Watson Parker, *Gold in the Black Hills* (Norman: University of Oklahoma Press, 1966), 196.

24. Mitchell, *Nuggets to Neutrinos*, 150.

25. George Hearst Autobiography, 21.

Chapter 10

1. *Black Hills Weekly Pioneer*, 11 December 1880.

2. Mitchell, *Nuggets to Neutrinos*, 151; *Bismarck Tribune*, 7 February 1878.

3. GH to James B. Haggin and Lloyd Tevis, November 1, 1877, Hearst Papers.

4. Parker, *Gold in the Black Hills*, 196; Mitchell, *Nuggets to Neutrinos*, 151.

5. GH to James B. Haggin and Lloyd Tevis, November 1, 1877, Hearst Papers.

6. Mitchell, *Nuggets to Neutrinos*, 151; GH to James B. Haggin, May 4, 1878; *San Francisco Examiner*, 7 December 1877.

7. *Bismarck Tribune*, 7 February 1878.

8. Mitchell, *Nuggets to Neutrinos*, 155, 156.

9. Mitchell, *Nuggets to Neutrinos*, 159.

10. WRH to GH, March 29, 1878, Hearst Papers.

11. GH to James B. Haggin, May 22, 1878, Hearst Papers; *State Journal* (Jefferson City, Mo.), 5 April 1878.

12. GH to James B. Haggin, May 4, 1878, Hearst Papers.

13. GH to James B. Haggin, May 19, 1878, Hearst Papers.

14. T. A. Rickard, "Arthur DeWint Foote, of Grass Valley," *Mining and Scientific Press* 121 (July 3, 1920): 174.

15. *Black Hills Daily Times*, 18 May 1877.

16. GH to James B. Haggin, May 22, 1878, Hearst Papers.

17. GH to James B. Haggin, May 23, 1878, Hearst Papers; Mitchell, *Nuggets to Neutrinos*, 161.

18. *State Journal* (Jefferson City, Mo.), 5 April 1878.

19. *Black Hills Daily Times*, 20 June 1878.

20. Rickard, "Arthur DeWint Foote," 174.

21. Mitchell, *Nuggets to Neutrinos*, 156.

22. *Black Hills Daily Times*, 7 August 1878.

23. RMS *Russia* passenger list, Hearst Papers; Kastner, *Hearst Ranch*, 44.

24. *Arizona Weekly Citizen*, 21 September 1878.

25. *Annual Report of the Secretary of the Interior on the Operation of the Department for the Year Ended June 30, 1879*, Vol. 1 (Washington, D.C.: Government Printing Office, 1879), 749.

Chapter 11

1. *Daily Deadwood Pioneer-Times*, 18 January 1879.

2. *Deadwood Pioneer-Times*, 17 May 1953.

3. *Daily Deadwood Pioneer-Times*, 18 January 1879.

4. *Daily Deadwood Pioneer-Times*, 24 January 1879.

5. Matthew Bernstein, "Murder in the Black Hills," *Wild West* 31, no. 4 (December 2018): 70–75.

6. PAH to GH, February 5, 1879, Hearst Papers.

7. GH to James B. Haggin, March 6, 1879, Hearst Papers.

8. *Black Hills Daily Times*, 27 March 1879.

9. GH to James B. Haggin, March 6, 1879, Hearst Papers.

10. GH to James B. Haggin, March 9, 1879, Hearst Papers.

11. *Black Hills Central*, 6 April 1879.

12. Jesse Brown and A. M. Willard, *The Black Hills Trails* (Rapid City: Rapid City Journal, 1924), 369.

13. GH to James B. Haggin, March 9, 1879, Hearst Papers.

14. GH to James B. Haggin, March 23, 1879, Hearst Papers.

15. *Oakland Tribune*. 15 April 1878.

16. George Hearst Autobiography, 32–33.

Chapter 12

1. *Black Hills Daily Times*, 25 January 1880.

2. Robinson, *The Hearsts*, 238.

3. *Arizona Daily Star*, 5 February 1880; *Black Hills Daily Times*, 30 May 1880; *Arizona Weekly Citizen*, 17 July 1880; William Ascarza, "Mine Tales: Trench Mine's History May Have Begun with Indian and Jesuit Miners," *Arizona Daily Star*, 12 February 2017.

4. Robert Weissler, "Executive Director's Report," Friends of the San Pedro River Roundup, Summer 2013, http://www.sanpedroriver.org/RiverRoundup_Summer_2013.pdf 13.

5. GH to James B. Haggin, July 18, 1880, Hearst Papers.

6. *Black Hills Weekly Pioneer*, 17 July 1880; Richard E. Sloan, *Memories of an Arizona Judge* (Stanford: Stanford University Press, 1933), 1.

7. *Bismarck Tribune*, 26 March 1880; Bonfils, *Life and Personality of Phoebe Apperson Hearst*, 53; *San Francisco Chronicle*, 21 November 1880; *Elite Directory for San Francisco and Oakland*.

8. George Hearst Autobiography, 34.

9. B. E. Lloyd, *Lights and Shades in San Francisco* (San Francisco: A. L. Bancroft, 1876).

10. Gordon Morris Bakken, *Practicing Law in Frontier California* (Lincoln: University of Nebraska Press, 1991), 12; George Hearst Autobiography, 35.

11. *San Francisco Examiner*, 24 October 1880.

12. *San Francisco Examiner*, 30 October 1880.

13. *San Francisco Examiner*, 20 January 1881, 23 January 1881, 27 February 1881, 10 April 1881, 19 April 1881, 1 May 1881, 8 May 1881, 22 May 1881.

14. *Idaho Statesman*, 26 May 1881, 16 June 1881; Wells, *Gold Camps and Silver Cities*, 103; William B. Shillingburg, *Tombstone, AT: A History of Early Mining, Milling, and Mayhem* (Norman: University of Oklahoma Press, 1999), 46.

15. *San Francisco Examiner*, 26 May 1882.

16. Bullough, *Blind Boss and His City*, 1, 5, 17; Carlson and Bates, *Lord of San Simeon*, 24.

17. *San Francisco Chronicle*, 1 July 1881.

18. *San Francisco Examiner*, 19 July 1881, 19 May 1882.

19. *San Francisco Examiner*, 28 August 1881, 15 September 1881; *Ogden Standard*, 29 August 1881; *Independent Record* (Helena, Montana), 3 September 1881; Mighels, *Story of the Files*, 421–22.

20. *Black Hills Weekly Pioneer*, 24 September 1881; *San Francisco Examiner*, 17 October 1881; *Black Hills Daily Times*, 8 December 1881.

21. *Los Angeles Times*, 23 December 1881; *Los Angeles Herald*, 27 December 1881; George W. Parsons, *The Private Diary of George Whitwell Parsons* (Phoenix: Arizona Statewide Archival and Records Project, 1939), 284.

22. Parsons, *Private Diary*, 285.

23. *Tucson Citizen*, 15 January 1882.

24. *Tombstone Weekly Epitaph*, 23 January 1882, 24 April 1882; *Los Angeles Herald*, 18 April 1882; *Arizona Daily Star*, 21 February 1882; *Los Angeles Herald*, 2 March 1882.

25. Bullough, *Blind Boss and His City*, 89.

26. *Los Angeles Herald*, 21 April 1882.

27. Jonathan S. Adams, *The Future of the Wild: Radical Conservation for a Crowded World* (Boston: Beacon Press, 2006), 127; Joseph P. Sanchez, Robert L. Sprude, and Art Gomez, *New Mexico: A History* (Norman: University of Oklahoma Press, 2013), 157.

28. *Tombstone Weekly Epitaph*, 24 April 1882; *Arizona Daily Star*, 25 April 1882.

29. *San Francisco Examiner*, 17 May 1882.

30. *Oakland Tribune*, 18 May 1882; *San Francisco Examiner*, 29 May 1882, 31 May 1882.

31. Carlson and Bates, *Lord of San Simeon*, 29.

32. Older and Older, *George Hearst*, 188.

33. *Los Angeles Herald*, 23 June 1882.

34. Older and Older, *George Hearst*, 190.

35. *Los Angeles Herald*, 23 June 1882.

36. Older and Older, *George Hearst*, 192–93.

37. *Sacramento Record-Union*, 24 June 1882; Older and Older, *George Hearst*, 191, 193.

38. Ben Fuller Fordney, *George Stoneman: A Biography of the Union General* (Jefferson, N.C.: McFarland and Company, 2008), 163.

39. *San Francisco Examiner*, 24 June 1882.

40. WRH to PAH, date unknown, Hearst papers.

41. Older and Older, *George Hearst*, 193.

Chapter 13

1. *Arizona Daily Star*, 9 December 1882; *Arizona Weekly Citizen*, 7 January 1883; *Arizona Daily Star*, 1 February 1883.

2. Whyte, *Uncrowned King*, 22.

3. WRH to GH, December 30, 1880, Hearst Papers.

4. *Arizona Weekly Citizen*, 31 December 1882.

5. *Arizona Daily Star*, 3 January 1883.

6. *Arizona Weekly Citizen*, 21 January 1883.

7. *Arizona Daily Star*, 23 January 1883; *Arizona Weekly Citizen*, 10 December 1882, 4 February 1883, 11 February 1883; *Arizona Weekly Republican*, 19 January 1883; *Arizona Daily Star*, 16 December 1882.

8. George Hearst Autobiography, 24; *Black Hills Daily Times*, 21 December 1883.

9. WRH to GH, 1885, date unknown, Hearst Papers; *San Francisco Examiner*, 11 December 1883.

10. WRH to GH, April 19, 1883, Hearst Papers. W. R. also described life in poetic terms, demonstrating the benefits of his Harvard education and his linguistic gifts: "The road of life may be a path of flowers through pleasant woods where glimpses of his destination through clefts between the trees urge the travelers on and encourage him; or it may be a toilsome march through a trackless desert where deluding mirages mock the wanderer with vain hopes of rest only to melt into empty air as he draws near."

11. *San Francisco Examiner*, 3 May 1883; *San Francisco Chronicle*, 24 May 1883; *Butte Weekly Miner*, 13 June 1883.

12. Chuck Lyons, "Copper—The Kingmaker," *Wild West* 30, no. 4 (December 2017): 24–25; *Butte Miner*, 14 June 1883.

13. *Butte Miner*, 14 February 1886.

14. *Wood River Times*, 13 July 1883, 2 July 1883, 3 August 1883.

15. J. G. Follansbee to PAH, January 4, 1884, Hearst Papers; Swanberg, *Citizen Hearst*, 32; *Las Cruces Sun-News*, 17 November 1883; *San Francisco Examiner*, 5 August 1883.

16. *Oakland Tribune*, 1 September 1883; *Fresno Republican*, 8 September 1883; *Nevada State Journal*, 13 September 1884.

17. *San Francisco Examiner*, 11 December 1883, 16 June 1884.

18. *San Francisco Examiner*, 22 December 1883, 24 December 1883.

19. J. G. Follansbee to PAH, January 14, 1884, Hearst Papers; J. G. Follansbee to PAH, January 18, 1884, Hearst Papers.

20. *Black Hills Times*, 3 August 1884; *Arizona Daily Star*, 6 April 1884; *Black Hills Weekly*, 23 February 1884.

21. *Record-Union* (Sacramento), 3 March 1884; *Arizona Daily Star*, 28 March 1884.

22. *San Francisco Examiner*, 20 April 1884; *Record-Union* (Sacramento), 24 April 1884, 29 April 1884.

23. *Fresno Bee*, 26 April 1884.

24. *San Francisco Chronicle*, 21 May 1884.

25. George Hearst Autobiography, 6; Robinson, *The Hearsts*, 25.

26. *Arizona Daily Star*, 19 June 1884; *San Antonio Light*, 10 July 1884.

27. *Record-Union* (Sacramento), 28 July 1884; *San Francisco Examiner*, 29 July 1884; *Oakland Tribune*, 11 October 1884; *Record-Union* (Sacramento), 18 October 1884.

28. Kastner, *Hearst Ranch*, 52–53. Thirty-five years later, in 1919, William Randolph Hearst began construction of just such a place.

29. *San Francisco Examiner*, 22 October 1884.

30. *Oakland Tribune*, 6 November 1884.

31. *San Francisco Examiner*, 7 November 1884.

32. *Critic* (Washington, D.C.), 30 November 1885.

33. GH to PAH, December 21, 1884, Hearst Papers.

34. *Black Hills Weekly Journal*, 2 January 1885; Mitchell, *Nuggets to Neutrinos*, 164.

35. *San Francisco Examiner*, 8 January 1885; *San Francisco Chronicle*, 10 January 1885.

36. *Record-Union* (Sacramento), 22 January 1885; *San Francisco Examiner*, 23 January 1885.

37. *Los Angeles Times*, 29 January 1885.

38. *San Francisco Examiner*, 21 March 1885, 4 April 1885. *Record-Union* (Sacramento), 16 April 1885.

39. Swanberg, *Citizen Hearst*, 26–27.

40. Swanberg, *Citizen Hearst*, 29–31.

41. *Oakland Tribune*, 30 June 1885; *Black Hills Weekly Times*, 8 August 1885; *San Francisco Examiner*, 26 June 1885.

42. *Evening Review* (East Liverpool, Ohio), 29 October 1885.

43. Whyte, *Uncrowned King*, 230–31.

44. Evan Thomas, *The War Lovers: Roosevelt, Lodge, Hearst, and the Rush to Empire, 1898* (New York: Back Bay Books, 2010), 92; David Nasaw, *The Chief: The Life of William Randolph Hearst* (New York: Houghton Mifflin, 2000), 68.

45. Ben Procter, *William Randolph Hearst: The Early Years, 1863–1910* (New York: Oxford University Press, 1998), 32; Davies, *Times We Had*, 319.

46. Whyte, *Uncrowned King*, 19–20; Thomas, *War Lovers*, 93–94; Procter, *William Randolph Hearst*, 32.

47. Coblentz, *William Randolph Hearst*, 22–23.

48. *Black Hills Daily Times*, 2 August 1885.

49. Thomas J. Grier to GH, May 25, 1888, Hearst Papers; *Black Hills Daily Times*, 21 December 1883.

50. *Black Hills Daily Times*, 7 August 1885, 14 August 1885; *Daily Deadwood-Pioneer Times*, 14 August 1885; *Black Hills Daily Times*, 22 August 1885; *Daily Deadwood-Pioneer Times*, 25 August 1885; *San Francisco Examiner*, 22 September 1885; Robinson, *The Hearsts*, 184.

51. PAH to GH, October 22, 1885, Hearst Papers.

52. PAH to GH, November 19, 1885, Hearst Papers.

53. *New York Times,* 10 March 1886; Nasaw, *Chief,* 56; Swanberg, *Citizen Hearst,* 31; *National Tribune,* 22 April 1886.

54. *Los Angeles Herald,* 7 January 1886; *San Francisco Examiner,* 11 January 1886; *Critic* (Washington, D.C.), 30 November 1885.

55. *Oakland Tribune,* 14 July 1882; Bullough, *Blind Boss and His City,* 184; Nasaw, *Chief,* 56; George Hearst Autobiography, 25.

Chapter 14

1. *Wilmington Morning Star,* 10 April 1886.

2. *Topeka Daily Capital,* 9 June 1890.

3. *Santa Cruz Sentinel,* 17 April 1886.

4. *Oakland Tribune,* 15 August 1890; Ambrose Bierce, *A Sole Survivor: Bits of Autobiography,* edited by S. T. Josshi and David E. Schultz (Knoxville: University of Tennessee Press, 1998), 194; *San Francisco Examiner,* 26 January 1896.

5. *Arthur McEwen's Letter,* 6 April 1895.

6. *Oakland Tribune,* 17 April 1886, 20 March 1887.

7. *Stanford Daily,* 11 February 1926; *Oakland Tribune,* 23 April 1892; Older and Older, *George Hearst,* 205–6; *Daily Republican* (Washington, D.C.), 29 November 1884.

8. Older and Older, *George Hearst,* 205–6; *Evening Star* (Washington, D.C.), 20 April 1886; *Critic* (Washington, D.C.), 28 April 1886.

9. Nasaw, *Chief,* 57; Roy Morris, *Ambrose Bierce: Alone in Bad Company* (New York: Oxford University Press, 1995), 195; Coblentz, *William Randolph Hearst,* 22; Thomas, *War Lovers,* 94.

10. Whyte, *Uncrowned King,* 21.

11. Whyte, *Uncrowned King,* 29; Coblentz, *William Randolph Hearst,* 30.

12. *South Bend Tribune,* 2 June 1886; *Pittsburg Daily Post,* 28 May 1886; *Rural Vermonter,* 4 June 1886; *Oakland Tribune,* 12 June 1886; *Salt Lake Herald,* 1 June 1886.

13. *New York Times,* 25 June 1886.

14. Bullough, *Blind Boss and His City,* 176; *San Francisco Chronicle,* 4 December 1887. Although Hearst adopted an anti-Chinese platform, he condemned the massacre of twenty-eight Chinese miners butchered by white miners in Rock Springs, Wyoming Territory. He voted on June 4, 1886 to have the United States pay reparations to the families of the murdered men.

15. *Sacramento Record-Union,* 24 May 1886.

16. *Sacramento Record-Union,* 15 July 1886.

17. *Frederick News,* 6 August 1886; *Quad-City Times,* 3 August 1886; *Arizona Daily Star,* 29 July 1886.

Chapter 15

1. *San Francisco Examiner,* 5 August 1886.

2. Matthew Bernstein, "The Playwright Who Captured Geronimo," *Wild West* 32, no. 4 (December 2019): 50–55. On January 29, 1885, Phoebe wrote her husband from Boston, recalling how much she enjoyed Thayer's *Joan of Arc*: "Sixty or more of the college

fellows came down and about forty of them took part in the Hasty Pudding Club theatricals that were given last Monday and Tuesday evenings at the University Club Theatre. The play was a burlesque & quite good."

3. Kastner, *Hearst Ranch*, 59.

4. *Record-Union* (Sacramento), 27 October 1886; *Oakland Tribune*, 2 November 1886.

5. *Oakland Tribune*, 11 October 1886; *Record-Union* (Sacramento), 9 October 1886.

6. *Oakland Tribune*, 8 October 1886; *Record-Union* (Sacramento), 23 October 1886; *Los Angeles Times*, 2 November 1886; *Record-Union* (Sacramento), 25 October 1886.

7. *Santa Cruz Sentinel*, 16 October 1886.

8. *Record-Union* (Sacramento), 19 October 1886; *San Francisco Examiner*, 21 October 1886; *San Francisco Chronicle*, 2 November 1886.

9. *San Francisco Chronicle*, 9 November 1886, 10 November 1886.

10. *San Francisco Examiner*, 14 November 1886.

11. *San Francisco Chronicle*, 17 October 1886.

12. *San Francisco Examiner*, 17 November 1886.

13. *Folsom Telegraph*, 20 November 1886; *Los Angeles Herald*, 26 November 1886; *Fresno Republican*, 10 December 1886; *Los Angeles Times*, 23 December 1886; *Petaluma Courier*, 15 December 1886.

14. *Los Angeles Times*, 27 November 1886; *San Francisco Chronicle*, 28 November 1886, 30 November 1886.

15. *Record-Union* (Sacramento), 19 February 1887; Nasaw, *Chief*, 56, 61.

16. Nasaw, *Chief*, 56, 60; W. F. Taylor to WRH, July 19, 1895, Hearst Papers.

17. Nasaw, *Chief*, 60.

18. *Oakland Tribune*, 8 December 1886; *San Francisco Chronicle*, 15 December 1886; *Record-Union* (Sacramento), 15 December 1886; *San Francisco Examiner*, 12 December 1886, 16 December 1886.

19. *Record-Union* (Sacramento), 18 December 1886; *San Francisco Chronicle*, 27 December 1886; *San Francisco Examiner*, 30 December 1886; *Los Angeles Times*, 30 December 1886; *San Francisco Chronicle*, 4 January 1887.

20. *Wasp*, 1 January 1887.

21. *San Francisco Chronicle*, 3 January 1887; *San Francisco Examiner*, 6 January 1887, 7 January 1887.

22. *Oakland Tribune*, 10 January 1887; *San Francisco Chronicle*, 11 January 1887.

23. *San Francisco Examiner*, 15 January 1887.

24. *San Francisco Examiner*, 20 January 1887.

25. *New York Times*, 19 January 1887.

26. Bullough, *Blind Boss and His City*, 183. Ambrose Bierce prattled a caustic poem linking Buckley and Geronimo in the *Wasp*:

When Boss Geronimo, fatigued of strife,
Renounced the carking cares of public life
Boss Buckley cried: "A vacancy at last!"
I'll fill it up before an hour is past."

Chapter 16

1. *Augusta Journal*, 6 October 1887; *Camden Daily Telegraph*, 2 March 1889.

2. *San Francisco Chronicle*, 4 February 1887; *Los Angeles Times*, 5 February 1887; *Sacramento Bee*, 5 February 1887.

3. Nasaw, *Chief*, 62.

4. Nasaw, *Chief*, 63.

5. Bakken, *Practicing Law in Frontier California*, 14.

6. *American Magazine*, November 1906. 10–11.

7. Nasaw, *Chief*, 68.

8. *Daily Alta California*, 5 March 1887.

9. *Oakland Tribune*, 16 March 1887.

10. *Weekly Nevada State Journal*, 16 April 1887; *San Francisco Chronicle*, 21 March 1887, 20 March 1887; *Los Angeles Herald*, 25 April 1887.

11. *New York Tribune*, 10 April 1887; Carlson and Bates, *Lord of San Simeon*, 33; *Record-Union* (Sacramento), 14 April 1887. During April 1887, a popular story was disseminated from California to New York:

> The story told of Senator Hearst . . . is that two Californians engaged in a dispute one day over the proper method of speaking. They agreed to leave it to the next man they saw, who happened to be George Hearst. He was seated on the stoop of a hotel with his feet on the railing. One of the gentlemen stepped up to him and said: "Sir, my friend and I have been having a dispute about a matter of speech. We have agreed to leave it to the next man we meet. Are you a grammarian?" "A what?" asked Senator Hearst. "A grammarian?" was the repeated inquiry. "No, sir. Not by a long sight," was the emphatic response; "I am a Missourian."

12. *York Daily*, 14 April 1887.

13. Nasaw, *Chief*, 79; Swanberg, *Citizen Hearst*, 56; Whyte, *Uncrowned King*, 145.

14. *San Francisco Examiner*, 31 March 1887.

15. Whyte, *Uncrowned King*, 32; *San Francisco Examiner*, 16 March 1887.

16. Morris, *Ambrose Bierce*, 197; *New York Times*, 25 June 1969.

17. *Times Picayune* (New Orleans), 27 April 1887; *San Francisco Examiner*, 30 April 1887, 2 May 1887; *Los Angeles Herald*, 2 May 1887.

18. *Arthur McEwen's Letter*, 6 April 1895, 10 November 1894.

19. *Buffalo Commercial*, 23 May 1887.

20. Kastner, *Hearst Ranch*, 107; *San Francisco Examiner*, 5 September 1888.

21. *Record-Union* (Sacramento), 11 July 1887; *San Francisco Examiner*, 23 July 1887.

22. *Park Record*, 6 August 1887; *Black Hills Daily Times*, 14 August 1887; *Great Falls Weekly Tribune*, 20 August 1887; *Butte Weekly Miner*, 27 August 1887; *Butte Daily Post*, 20 August 1887.

23. *Butte Weekly Miner*, 31 August 1887; *Weekly Nevada State Journal*, 10 September 1887; *San Francisco Chronicle*, 26 September 1887; *Record-Union* (Sacramento), 27 September 1887; *San Francisco Examiner*, 30 September 1887; *Mail* (Stockton), 30 September 1887.

24. *Daily Arkansas Gazette*, 15 October 1887; *Fort Worth Daily Gazette*, 25 November 1887; George Hearst Autobiography, 24; *Wood River Times*, 10 December 1887; *San Francisco Examiner*, 5 December 1887.

25. *Chicago Tribune*, 1 January 1888, 6 January 1888; *San Francisco Examiner*, 7 January 1888; *Critic* (Washington, D.C.), 18 January 1888.

26. *Herald and Review*, 10 February 1888.

27. *St. Louis Globe-Democrat*, 6 January 1888; *New York Tribune*, 10 January 1888; *Critic* (Washington, D.C.), 19 March 1888.

28. *Mail* (Stockton), 11 February 1887; *Journal Times*, 11 April 1888.

29. *Chicago Tribune*, 25 March 1887; John DeFerrari, *Historic Restaurants of Washington D.C.: Capital Eats* (Charleston, S.C.: American Palate, 2013).

30. *Chicago Tribune*, 18 March 1888; *Pittsburgh Daily Post*, 24 March 1888; *San Francisco Examiner*, 27 March 1888; *Record-Union* (Sacramento), 12 April 1888. W. R. Hearst later suggested that Sam Clemens and his father may have indulged in bourbon while swapping old stories at his parents' Dupont Circle mansion and that Clemens could not resist playfully needling Phoebe as he departed. Despite the festive atmosphere, Clemens said with a solemn face, "I am sorry, my dear lady, but I am never coming to your house again."

"Why, Mr. Clemens," replied Phoebe. "I am terribly grieved. Did anything happen to displease you?"

"Yes'm, it did—something very serious, too. You gave George spareribs and lye hominy, and all you gave me was terrapin and canvasback duck—so I'm never coming to your house again."

Phoebe took the hint. The next time Sam came to visit, he and Hearst sat together, feasting on spareribs and lye hominy.

31. *Herald and Review*, 30 May 1888.

32. *Pittsburgh Press*, 25 April 1888; *San Francisco Examiner*, 8 May 1888; *Critic* (Washington, D.C.), 27 June 1888.

33. *Congressional Record: The Proceedings and Debates of the Fiftieth Congress, First Session* (Washington, D.C.: Government Printing Office, 1888), 6461–62.

34. Older and Older, *George Hearst*, 221–23; Wells, *Gold Camps and Silver Cities*, 102. Idaho gained statehood on July 3, 1890.

35. PAH to GH, August 11, 1888, Hearst Papers.

36. *New York Times*, 15 August 1888; *Cincinnati Enquirer*, 29 August 1888.

37. *San Francisco Examiner*, 5 September 1888.

38. Nickliss, *Phoebe Apperson Hearst*, 143.

39. *San Francisco Examiner*, 6 October 1888; *Mail* (Stockton), 22 October 1888; *St. Louis Globe*, 5 March 1890.

40. *San Francisco Examiner*, 31 October 1888.

41. Bullough, *Blind Boss and His City*, 205; Charles W. Calhoun, *Minority Victory: Gilded Age Politics and Front Porch Campaign of 1888* (Topeka: University of Kansas Press, 2008), 23.

42. Nickliss, *Phoebe Apperson Hearst*, 146–48.

43. *San Francisco Examiner*, 22 November 1888; *Evening Star* (Washington, D.C.), 6 December 1888.

44. *New York Times*, 31 December 1888. Sherry Monahan, *California Vines, Wines, and Pioneers* (Charleston, S.C.: American Palate, 2013); *New York Tribune*, 30 December 1888; *San Francisco Call*, 2 December 1888; Richard P. Vine, Ellen M. Harkness, Theresa Browning, and Cheri Wagner, *Winemaking: From Grape Growing to Marketplace* (New York: International Thomson Publishing, 1997), 13; "Wine: Sonoma's Old Vineyards in Danger of Disappearing," *Mercury News*, 14 January 2013. To work the new Madrone vineyard, Hearst broke with the policy he'd previously supported and hired cheap Chinese labor.

Chapter 17

1. *Los Angeles Herald*, 8 February 1889; *Los Angeles Times*, 8 February 1889; *Los Angeles Herald*, 11 February 1889; *Albuquerque Morning Democrat*, 13 February 1889; *Oakland Tribune*, 16 February 1889.

2. *Chicago Tribune*, 24 February 1889; *Critic* (Washington, D.C.), 21 February 1889; *Monroeville Breeze*, 28 March 1889.

3. *Chicago Tribune*, 27 February 1889; *Courier-Journal*, 5 March 1889; *Norfolk Virginian*, 7 March 1889.

4. PAH to GH, March 15, 1889, Hearst Papers; *Record-Union* (Sacramento), 11 March 1889; *Evening Star* (Washington, D.C.), 19 March 1889; *Oakland Tribune*, 26 March 1889.

5. *San Francisco Examiner*, 27 May 1889.

6. *San Francisco Examiner*, 5 June 1889.

7. Robert McCaa, "Women's Position, Family and Fertility Decline in Parral (Mexico) 1777–1930," in *Annales de Démographie Historique* (Paris: Société de Démographie Historique, 1989), 235; H. Willis Baxley, *What I Saw on the West Coast of South and North America and at the Hawaiian Islands* (New York: D. Appleton, 1865), 302.

8. The revolutionary Pancho Villa, ten years old in 1889 and living two hundred miles south of Parral in Durango, would be assassinated in Parral as well.

9. *San Francisco Examiner*, 25 June 1889.

10. *Los Angeles Herald*, 3 July 1889; GH to H. B. Parsons, July 2, 1889, Hearst Letters.

11. *Los Angeles Herald*, 19 July 1889; *Evening Star* (Washington, D.C.), 20 July 1889; *San Francisco Chronicle*, 21 July 1889; *Ness City Times*, 12 September 1889; PAH to GH, August 1889, Hearst Papers.

12. *Oakland Tribune*, 21 September 1889.

13. PAH 1400 New Hampshire Avenue letterhead, Hearst Papers.

14. *Pittsburgh Daily Post*, 4 August 1889; *Butte Miner*, 6 October 1889.

15. *Los Angeles Herald*, 26 October 1889.

16. *San Francisco Examiner*, 9 November 1889; *Sacramento Bee*, 12 November 1889; *Record-Union* (Sacramento), 16 November 1889.

17. *San Francisco Examiner*, 2 December 1889, 3 December 1889; *San Francisco Chronicle*, 13 December 1889; *Los Angeles Herald*, 14 December 1889.

18. *Santa Cruz Sentinel*, 18 December 1889; *San Francisco Chronicle*, 18 December 1889.

19. *St. Paul Globe*, 23 February 1890.

20. *San Francisco Chronicle*, 19 January 1890; *Evening Star* (Washington, D.C.), 29 January 1890.

21. *Salt Lake Herald*, 14 February 1890.

22. *Record-Union* (Sacramento), 4 March 1890.

23. *Evening Star* (Washington, D.C.), 17 February 1890; Whyte, *Uncrowned King*, 15–16; *Decatur Daily Republican*, 18 February 1888; *San Francisco Chronicle*, 9 March 1890.

24. *Los Angeles Herald*, 23 March 1890; *Critic* (Washington, D.C.), 22 March 1890.

25. Irwin Stump to GH, March 20, 1890, Hearst Papers.

26. George Hearst Autobiography, 24.

27. *San Francisco Examiner*, 1 March 1891.

28. Robert Underwood Johnson, "Why Not More Forest Preserves?" *Review of Reviews: An International Magazine* 10 (July–December 1894), 651.

29. *San Francisco Call*, 7 June 1890.

30. *Salt Lake Tribune*, 13 June 1890.

31. *Daily Courier* (San Bernardino), 11 June 1890; *Los Angeles Herald*, 25 June 1890; *New York Times*, 3 July 1890; *San Francisco Chronicle*, 6 July 1890; *San Francisco Call*, 20 July 1890; *San Francisco Examiner*, 22 July 1890, 9 September 1890; *Fremont Tribune*, 13 September 1890.

32. *New York World*, 3 October 1890; *San Francisco Examiner*, 6 April 1890; *Lexington Intelligencer*, 11 October 1890.

33. George Hearst Autobiography, 37.

34. *Evening Star* (Washington, D.C.), 15 December 1890.

35. *Indianapolis Journal*, 29 December 1890.

36. Peck Papers; *Daily-Union*, 26 December 1890; *San Francisco Examiner*, 1 March 1891, 1 January 1891.

37. *San Francisco Examiner*, 12 January 1891.

38. *San Francisco Examiner*, 23 January 1891; *Record-Union* (Sacramento), 24 January 1891; *San Francisco Examiner*, 25 January 1891.

39. *Los Angeles Times*, 12 January 1891; Clara Anthony to Helen Peck, January 26, 1891, Peck Papers.

40. *San Francisco Examiner*, 1 March 1891.

Epilogue

1. *San Francisco Examiner*, 2 March 1891; A. E. Head to PAH, March 2, 1891, Hearst Papers.

2. *San Francisco Examiner*, 6 March 1891.

3. *San Francisco Chronicle*, 16 March 1891; Whyte, *Uncrowned King*, 12.

4. Older and Older, *George Hearst*, 158.

5. *Santa Cruz Surf*, 9 May 1896; *San Francisco Call*, 16 May 1897. In 1919 Phoebe joined her husband in the Cypress Lawn mausoleum, a casualty of the Spanish flu. William Randolph Hearst's bones were interred between them in 1951.

6. *New York Times*, December 25, 1898.

BIBLIOGRAPHY

Unpublished Sources and Manuscript Collections

Bancroft Library, University of California–Berkeley
 Bay, W. V. N. "A Brief Sketch of the Life of the Hon. George Hearst."
 George Hearst Autobiography, 1877–1890
 George and Phoebe Hearst Papers
 Scrapbooks of Ambrose Bierce Works, Vol. 1, clipped chiefly from the *Examiner*
 William Randolph Hearst Papers, 1863–1951
Huntington Research Library, San Marino, California
 Carleton E. Watkins Photographs
 Dwight Bartlett Letters
 George Hearst Letters
 Peck Family Papers
 Sierra Nevada Silver Mining Company Papers

Published Works on and by the Hearsts

Bonfils, Winifred Black. *The Life and Personality of Phoebe Apperson Hearst.* San Francisco: John Henry Nash, 1928.

Carlson, Oliver, and Ernest Sutherland Bates. *Lord of San Simeon.* New York: Viking Press, 1936.

Coblentz, Edmond D., ed. *William Randolph Hearst: A Portrait in His Own Words.* New York: Simon and Shuster, 1952.

Davies, Marion. *The Times We Had: Life with William Randolph Hearst.* Edited by Pamela Peau and Kenneth S. Marx. New York: Ballantine, 1975.

Hearst, Austine McDonnell. *The Horses of San Simeon.* San Simeon: San Simeon Press, 1985.

Kastner, Victoria. *Hearst Ranch: Family, Life, and Legacy.* New York: Abrams, 2013.

Nasaw, David. *The Chief: The Life of William Randolph Hearst.* New York: Houghton Mifflin, 2000.

Nickliss, Alexandra M. *Phoebe Apperson Hearst: A Life of Power and Politics.* Lincoln: University of Nebraska Press, 2018.

Older, Fremont, and Cora Older. *George Hearst: California Pioneer.* Los Angeles: Westernlore, 1966.

Procter, Ben. *William Randolph Hearst: The Early Years, 1863–1910.* Vol. 1. New York: Oxford University Press, 1998.

Robinson, Judith. *The Hearsts: An American Dynasty.* San Francisco: Telegraph Hill Press, 1991.

Stewart, William M. "Address of Mr. Stewart, of Nevada." In *Memorial Addresses on the Life and Character of George Hearst,* edited by United States Congress, 26–27. Washington, D.C.: Government Printing Office, 1894.

Swanberg, W. A. *Citizen Hearst.* New York: Scriber, 1961.

Whyte, Kenneth. *The Uncrowned King: The Sensational Rise of William Randolph Hearst.* Berkeley: Counterpoint, 2009.

Other Materials

Abbott, Willis J. *Watching the World Go By.* London: John Lane, The Bodley Head, 1933.

Abramson, Phyllis Leslie. *Sob Sister Journalism.* New York: Greenwood Press, 1990.

Adams, Jonathan S. *The Future of the Wild: Radical Conservation for a Crowded World.* Boston: Beacon Press, 2006.

Annual Mining Review and Stock Ledger. San Francisco: Verdenal, Harrison, Murphy, 1876.

Annual Report of the Secretary of the Interior on the Operation of the Department for the Year Ended June 30, 1879. Vol. 1. Washington, D.C.: Government Printing Office, 1879.

Appleton's Annual Cyclopedia and Register of Important Events of the Year 1899. New York: D. Appleton, 1900.

Ascarza, William. "Mine Tales: Trench Mine's History May Have Begun with Indian and Jesuit Miners." *Arizona Daily Star,* February 12, 2017.

Bakken, Gordon Morris. *Practicing Law in Frontier California.* Lincoln: University of Nebraska Press, 1991.

Bakken, Gordon Morris, and Alexandra Kindrell, eds. *Encyclopedia of Migration and Immigration in the American West.* Thousand Oaks, Calif. Sage Publication, 2006.

Bancroft, Hubert Howe. *History of the Life of Leland Stanford Senior.* Oakland, Calif: Biobooks, 1952.

———. *The Works.* Vol. 24, *History of California, Vol. 7: 1860–1890.* San Francisco: History Company, 1890.

Bean, Edwin F. *Bean's History and Directory of Nevada County.* Nevada City: Daily Gazette Book and Job Office, 1867.

"Benjamin Rowe of Ontario," American Colonial Origins, 2005–2015, http://www.amcolan .info/rowe/index.

Bernstein, Matthew. "Murder in the Black Hills." *Wild West* 31, no. 4 (December 2018): 70–75.

———. "The Playwright Who Captured Geronimo." *Wild West* 32, no. 4 (December 2019): 50–55.

Bierce, Ambrose. *A Sole Survivor: Bits of Autobiography.* Edited by S. T. Josshi and David E. Schultz. Knoxville: University of Tennessee Press, 1998.

Brown, Jesse, and A. M. Willard. *The Black Hills Trails.* Rapid City: Rapid City Journal, 1924.

Bullough, William A. *The Blind Boss and His City: Christopher Augustine Buckley and Nineteenth-Century San Francisco.* Berkeley: University of California Press, 1979.

Calhoun, Charles W. *Minority Victory: Gilded Age Politics and the Front Porch Campaign of 1888.* Topeka: University of Kansas Press, 2008.

Church of Jesus Christ of Latter-Day Saints. *Deseret Weekly: Pioneer Publication of the Rocky Mountain Region.* Vol. 46. Salt Lake City: Deseret News, 1893.

Congressional Record: The Proceedings and Debates of the Fiftieth Congress, First Session. Washington, D.C.: Government Printing Office, 1888.

Cook, Deborah Coleen. "Vestiges of Amador—A Hearst in Drytown? A California Icon and Amador Mines." *Ledger and Dispatch: Amador & Calaveras Objective Regional News,* January 28, 2018.

Crawford, J. J. *California Journals of Mines and Geology.* Vols. 12–13. Sacramento: A. J. Johnston, Supt. State Printing, 1894.

Crouch, Gregory. *The Bonanza King: John Mackay and the Battle over the Greatest Riches in the American West.* New York: Scribner, 2018.

DeFerrari, John. *Historic Restaurants of Washington, D.C.: Capital Eats.* Charleston, S.C.: American Palate, 2013.

De Quille, Dan. *The Big Bonanza.* New York: Alfred A. Knopf, 1967.

The Elite Directory for San Francisco and Oakland: A Residence Address, Visiting, Club, Theatre and Shopping Guide, Containing the Names of Over Six Thousand Society People. San Francisco: Argonaut Publishing Company, 1879.

Ericson, Duane. *Silver City Narrow Gauge.* Washingtonville, Ohio: M2FQ Publications, 2007.

Erwin, James W. *The Homefront in Civil War Missouri.* Charleston, S.C.: History Press, 2014.

Farish, Thomas Edwin. *The Gold Hunters of California.* Chicago: M. A. Donahue, 1904.

Fordney, Ben Fuller. *George Stoneman: A Biography of the Union General.* Jefferson, N.C.: McFarland, 2008.

Goodwin, Doris Kearns. *The Bully Pulpit: Theodore Roosevelt, William Howard Taft, and the Golden Age of Journalism.* New York: Simon and Shuster, 2013.

Gorenfeld, John, and Will Gorenfeld. "Dishonorably Discharged." *Wild West* 31, no. 1 (June 2018): 60–61.

Harpending, Asbury. *The Great Diamond Hoax and Other Stirring Incidents in the Life of Asbury Harpending.* San Francisco: James H. Barry, 1913.

Hatfield, Mark O. *Vice Presidents of the United States, 1798–1993.* Washington, D.C.: U.S. Government Printing Office, 1993.

Hazard, Wendy. "Thomas Brackett Reed, Civil Rights, and the Fight for Fair Elections." *Maine History* 42, no. 1 (March 2004).

History of Franklin, Jefferson, Washington, Crawford and Gasconade. Part 2. Chicago: Goodspeed, 1888.

Hittell, Theodore Henry. *History of California*. Vol. 3. San Francisco: N. J. Stone, 1898.

Hofstader, Richard. *The American Political Tradition: And the Men Who Made It*. New York: Alfred Knopf, 1948.

Holliday, J. S. *The World Rushed In: The California Gold Rush Experience*. New York: Touchtone, 1981.

Holzer, Harold. "Stop the Presses." *Civil War Times* 53, no. 3 (December 2014): 33.

Hornung, Chuck. *Wyatt Earp's Cowboy Campaign: The Bloody Restoration of Law and Order along the Mexican Border, 1882*. Jefferson, N.C.: McFarland, 2016.

Johnson, Joe. "Flash-in-the-Pan Creede." *Wild West* 30, no. 6 (April 2018).

Johnson, Robert Underwood. "Why Not More Forest Preserves?" *Review of Reviews: An International Magazine* 10 (July–December 1894): 651.

Johnson, Susan Lee. *Roaring Camp: The Social World of the California Gold Rush*. New York: W. W. Norton, 2000.

Keyssar, Alexander. *The Right to Vote: The Contested History of Democracy in the United States*. New York: Perseus Books, 2000.

Knudtsen, Molly Flagg. *Under the Mountain*. Reno: University of Nevada Press, 1982.

Koster, John. "The Great Diamond Hoax of 1872." *Wild West* 26, no. 3 (October 2013): 47–53.

Langley, Henry G. *The San Francisco Directory for the Year 1864*. San Francisco: Commercial Steam Press, 1864.

Lecci, Stephanie. "Paw Paw French: Two 20-Somethings Bet St. Louis Can Save a Vanishing Dialect." St. Louis Public Radio, July 13, 2015.

Lingenfelter, Richard E. *Death Valley and the Amargosa: A Land of Illusion*. Berkeley: University of California Press, 1986.

Lingley, Charles Ramsdell. *Since the Civil War*. New York: Century, 1920.

Lloyd, B. E. *Lights and Shades in San Francisco*. San Francisco: A. L. Bancroft, 1876.

Lord, Eliot. *Comstock Mining and Miners 1883*. San Diego: Howell-North Books, 1980.

Lyman, George D. *The Saga of the Comstock Lode*. New York: Charles Scribner's Sons, 1934.

Lyons, Chuck. "Copper—The Kingmaker." *Wild West* 30, no. 4 (December 2017): 24–25.

———. "The Great Western Flood." *Wild West* 28, no. 6 (April 2016): 36–41.

Masich, Andrew E. "Desert Warriors." *America's Civil War* 30, no. 3 (July 2017): 46.

McCaa, Robert. "Women's Position, Family and Fertility Decline in Parral (Mexico) 1777–1930." In *Annales de Démographie Historique*. Paris: Société de Démographie Historique, 1989.

McLachlan, Sean. "Grudge Match at the O.K. Corral." *America's Civil War* 29, no. 1 (March 2014): 49–50.

McPherson, James M. *Battle Cry of Freedom*. New York: Ballantine Books, 1988.

Michelson, Charles. *The Ghost Talks*. New York: G. P. Putnam's Sons, 1944.

Mighels, Ella Sterling. *The Story of the Files*. San Francisco: Wakelee & Co., Druggists, 1893.

Miller, Linda Karen. *Images of Early Las Vegas*. Charleston, S.C.: Arcadia Publishing. 2013.

Mitchell, Steven T. *Nuggets to Neutrinos: The Homestake Story*. Self-published, Xlibris, 2009.

Monahan, Sherry. *California Vines, Wines, and Pioneers*. Charleston, S.C.: American Palate, 2013.

Morris, Roy. *Ambrose Bierce: Alone in Bad Company*. New York: Oxford University Press, 1995.

Morrison, Annie L., and John H. Haydon. *Pioneers of San Luis Obispo County and Environs*. Los Angeles: Historic Record, 1917.

Moskowitz, Sam. *Science Fiction in Old San Francisco: History of the Movement from 1854–1890*. West Kingston, R.I.: Donald M. Grant, 1980.

Nadeau, Remi. *The Silver Seekers*. Santa Barbara: Crest Publishers, 1999.

Notables of the West: Being the Portraits and Biographies of the Progressive Men of the West. Vol. 2. New York: International News Service, 1915.

Palazzo, Robert P. *Ghost Towns of Death Valley*. Charleston, S.C.: Arcadia Publishing, 2014.

Parker, Watson. *Gold in the Black Hills*. Norman: University of Oklahoma Press, 1966.

Parsons, George W. *The Private Diary of George Whitwell Parsons*. Phoenix: Arizona Statewide Archival and Records Project, 1939.

Paul, Rodman Wilson. *Mining Frontiers of the Far West: 1848–1860*. Albuquerque: University of New Mexico Press, 1974.

Pomeroy, Earl. *The Pacific Slope: A History of California, Oregon, Washington, Idaho, Utah, and Nevada*. Seattle: University of Washington Press, 1965.

Powers, Ron. *Mark Twain: A Life*. New York: Free Press, 2005.

Rable, George C. "Damn Yankees." *Civil War Monitor* 6, no. 1 (July 2016): 39.

Reeve, W. Paul. *Making Space on the Western Frontier: Mormons, Miners, and Southern Paiutes*. Chicago: University of Illinois Press, 2006.

Rickard, T. A. "Arthur DeWint Foote, of Grass Valley." *Mining and Scientific Press* 121 (July 3, 1920): 174.

Sanchez, Joseph P., Robert L. Sprude, and Art Gomez. *New Mexico: A History*. Norman: University of Oklahoma Press, 2013.

Sears, Stephen W. "Badly Whipped He Will Be." *America's Civil War* 30, no. 4 (September 2017): 20.

"Senator George Hearst," *Wasp*, April 10, 1886.

Spencer, David R. *The Yellow Journalism: The Press and America's Emergence as a World Power*. Evanston, Ill.: Northwestern University Press, 2007.

Sloan, Richard E. *Memories of an Arizona Judge*. Stanford: Stanford University Press, 1932.

Stewart, William M. *Reminiscences of William M. Stewart of Nevada*. Edited by George Rothwell Brown. New York: Neale, 1908.

Sumner, Charles A. "A Trip to Pioche." *Student's Journal* 21, no. 2 (February 1892): 20–24.

Thomas, Evan. *The War Lovers: Roosevelt, Lodge, Hearst, and the Rush to Empire, 1898*. New York: Back Bay Books, 2010.

Thompson, George A., and Frasier Buck. *Treasure Mountain Home: Park City Revisited*. Salt Lake City: Dream Garden Press, 1968.

"Tin Cup Colorado Cemetery Burials." Eleanor Perry Harrington and June Shaputis, 1992, http://nebula.wsimg.com/64632476555aadf32417fe1cf6a8569f?AccessKeyId=08 93FF1714079A557EC1&disposition=0&alloworigin=1.

Townsend, Edward W. *Chimmie Fadden, Major Max, and Other Stories.* New York: Lovell, Coryell, 1895.

Tullidge, Edward William. *Tullidge's Histories.* Vol. 2. Salt Lake City: Juvenile Instructor, 1889.

Twain, Mark. *The Authorized Autobiography of Mark Twain.* Vol. 1. Berkeley: University of California Press, 2010.

Vine, Richard P., Ellen M. Harkness, Theresa Browning, and Cheri Wagner. *Winemaking: From Grape Growing to Marketplace.* New York: International Thomson Publishing, 1997.

Wait, Frona Eunice. *Wines and Vines of California: A Treatise on the Ethics of Wine-Drinking.* San Francisco: Bancroft, 1889.

Weissler, Robert. "Executive Director's Report." Friends of the San Pedro River Roundup, Summer 2013, http://www.sanpedroriver.org/RiverRoundup_Summer_2013.pdf.

Wells, Merle W. *Gold Camps and Silver Cities: Nineteenth Century Mining in Central and Southern Idaho.* Moscow: Idaho State Historical Society, 1983.

Winn, Melissa A. "I Thought I Had Received My Death Stroke." *Civil War Times* 57, no. 6 (December 2018): 58.

Winnerman, Jim. "Missouri French Still Spoken Here." *Wild West* 29, no. 3 (October 2016): 20–21.

Woolsey, Lester Hood. *Geology and Ore Deposits of the Park City District, Utah.* Professional Papers 77. Washington, D.C.: Government Printing Office, 1912.

Newspapers

Albuquerque Morning Democrat
Anaconda Standard
Arizona Daily Star
Arizona Miner
Arizona Republic
Arizona Weekly Citizen
Arthur McEwen's Letter
Augusta Journal
Bismarck Tribune
Black Hills Central
Black Hills Daily Times
Black Hills Weekly
Boston Evening Transcript
Boston Weekly Globe
Brooklyn Daily Eagle
Buffalo Commercial

Buffalo Daily Courier
Butte Miner
Butte Weekly Post
Camden Daily Telegraph
Chicago Tribune
Cincinnati Enquirer
Chicago Daily Tribune
Coso Mining News
Critic (Washington, D.C.)
Daily Courier (San Bernardino)
Daily Deadwood Pioneer-Times
Daily Republican (Washington, D.C.)
Deadwood Pioneer-Times
De Kalb Chronicle
Decatur Daily Republican
Democratic Banner
Deseret News
Evening Review (East Liverpool, Ohio)
Evening Star (Washington, D.C.)
Folsom Telegraph
Franklin County Tribune
Frederick News
Fremont Tribune
Fresno Republican
Galveston Daily News
Great Falls Weekly
Harrisburg Evening News
Herald and Torch Light
Hornellsville Weekly Tribune
Independent Record (Helena, Mont.)
Indianapolis Journal
Knoxville Journal
Ledger and Dispatch: Amador & Calaveras Objective Regional News
Lexington Intelligencer
Los Angeles Herald
Los Angeles Times
Mail (Stockton, Calif.)
Mercury News
National Review
Ness City Times
Nevada City Herald
Nevada State Journal

New York Sun
New York Times
New York Tribune
New York World
Oakland Tribune
Palmyra Weekly Whig
Park Record
Petaluma Courier
Philadelphia Inquirer
Pioche Record
Pittsburgh Daily Post
Pittsburgh Press
Quad-City Times
Record-Union (Sacramento)
Reno Gazette-Journal
Rolla Herald
Rural Vermonter
Sacramento Bee
Sacramento Daily-Union
San Francisco Call
San Francisco Chronicle
San Francisco Examiner
San Francisco Evening Examiner
Santa Cruz Sentinel
Santa Cruz Surf
Santa Cruz Weekly
Salt Lake City Herald
Salt Lake Herald
Salt Lake Tribune
South Bend Tribune
Stanford Daily
State Journal (Jefferson City, Mo.)
St. Clair Chronicle
St. Joseph Herald
St. Paul Globe
St. Louis Dispatch
Sullivan Tri-County News
Times Picayune (New Orleans)
Tombstone Weekly Epitaph
Topeka Daily Capital
Topeka State Journalxx
Tucson Citizen
Weekly Nevada State Journal

Washington Critic
Weekly Oregon Statesmen
Wilkesboro Chronicle
Wilmington Morning Star
Woodland Daily Democrat
Wood River Times
Yerington Times
York Daily

INDEX

Page numbers in *italic* type indicate illustrative matter.

Made in the USA
Las Vegas, NV
18 December 2021